House – The Wounded Heal(Television

GW00985316

House MD is a globally successful and long-running medical drama. *House: the Wounded Healer on Television* employs a Jungian perspective to examine the psychological construction of the series and its namesake, Dr Gregory House.

The book also investigates the extent to which the continued popularity of *House MD* has to do with its representation of deeply embedded cultural concerns. It is divided into three parts – Diagnosing House, Consulting House and Dissecting House – and topics of discussion include:

- specific details, themes, motifs and tropes throughout the series
- narrative, character and visual structure
- the combination of performative effects, text and images of the doctor and his team
- the activities of the hero, the wounded healer and the *puer aeternus*.

Offering an entirely fresh perspective on *House MD*, with contributions from medical professionals, academics and therapists, this book is essential reading for students and scholars of Jungian psychology. The inclusion of a glossary of Jungian terms means that this book can also be enjoyed by fans of *House MD* who have been seeking a more in-depth analysis of the series.

Luke Hockley, PhD, is Professor of Media Analysis in the Research Institute for Media, Art and Design (RIMAD) at the University of Bedfordshire, UK. Luke is co-editor of the *International Journal of Jungian Studies* (IJJS) and *Jung and Film Two: The Return* due to be published in 2011 by Routledge. Luke is also a psychotherapist in private practice in London and Bedfordshire.

Leslie Gardner, PhD, studied at the University of Essex Centre for Psychoanalytic Studies in the rhetoric of Jung, considering Vico as a precursor. She is on the Executive Committee of the International Association of Jungian Studies, a web-based organisation. She is presently running an international literary agency in London and is an occasional lecturer on writing at Manchester Metropolitan University.

House – The Wounded Healer on Television

Jungian and Post-Jungian Reflections

Edited by Luke Hockley and
Leslie Gardner

Routledge
Taylor & Francis Group

LONDON AND NEW YORK

First published 2011 by Routledge
27 Church Road, Hove, East Sussex BN3 2FA

Simultaneously published in the USA and Canada
by Routledge
270 Madison Avenue, New York, NY 10016

Routledge is an imprint of the Taylor & Francis Group, an Informa business

© 2011 Selection and editorial matter, Luke Hockley and Leslie Gardner;
individual chapters, the contributors.

Typeset in Times by Garfield Morgan, Swansea, West Glamorgan
Printed and bound in Great Britain by TJ International Ltd, Padstow,
Cornwall
Paperback cover design by Andrew Ward

All rights reserved. No part of this book may be reprinted or reproduced or
utilised in any form or by any electronic, mechanical, or other means, now
known or hereafter invented, including photocopying and recording, or in
any information storage or retrieval system, without permission in writing
from the publishers.

This publication has been produced with paper manufactured to strict
environmental standards and with pulp derived from sustainable forests.

British Library Cataloguing in Publication Data
A catalogue record for this book is available from the British Library

Library of Congress Cataloging-in-Publication Data
House : the wounded healer on television : Jungian and post-Jungian
reflections / edited by Luke Hockley and Leslie Gardner.
        p. cm.
    Includes index.
    ISBN 978-0-415-47912-7 (hardback) – ISBN 978-0-415-47913-4 (pbk.) 1.
House, M. D. (Television program) I. Hockley, Luke. II. Gardner, Leslie,
1949-
    PN1992.77.H63H653 2010
    791.45'75–dc22

                                                          2010017593

ISBN: 978-0-415-47912-7 (hbk)
ISBN: 978-0-415-47913-4 (pbk)

Contents

List of contributors: House guests   vii

Acknowledgments   x

Introduction   1

PART I
Diagnosing House   9

1   Doctoring individuation: Gregory House: Physician, detective
    or shaman?   11
    LUKE HOCKLEY

2   The physician's melancholia   27
    JOHN IZOD

3   Playing House: Convincing them of what you know simply
    by who you are   43
    CHRISTOPHER HAUKE

PART II
Consulting House   57

4   House's caduceus crutch   59
    TERRIE WADDELL

5   Anatomy of genius: Inspiration through banality and
    boring people   75
    LUCY HUSKINSON

6   Limping the way to wholeness: Wounded feeling and feeling
    wounded   101
    ANGELA COTTER

7   Our inner puer and its playmates, the shadow and
    the trickster   116
    SALLY PORTERFIELD

PART III
Dissecting House   131

8   House not Ho(l)mes   133
    SUSAN ROWLAND

9   Gestures of excess: An exploratory analysis of melodrama
    as a collective archetype   152
    LESLIE GARDNER

10 Not as a stranger   169
    JOHN BEEBE

11 'I feel like a failure' – in-House feminism   188
    CATRIONA MILLER

    Glossary   204
    Index   207

House guests

John Beebe was born in 1939 and graduated from Harvard University and the University of Chicago Medical School. He trained in psychiatry at Stanford University Medical Center and in Jungian analysis at the C. G. Jung Institute of San Francisco. The founding editor of the *San Francisco Jung Institute Library Journal* (now published by the University of California Press as *Jung Journal: Culture and Psyche*), he was also the first American co-editor of the London-based *Journal of Analytical Psychology*. In his writings and lectures throughout the world, he has offered additions and extensions to Jung's theories of archetypes, psychological types, dreams, conscience and moral character, and sexuality and gender. He has also pioneered the Jungian understanding of film as a psychological art. He is the editor of C. G. Jung's *Aspects of the Masculine* (1989), the author of *Integrity in Depth* (1992), and the co-author (with Virginia Apperson) of *The Presence of the Feminine in Film* (2008). He has also co-authored *Psychiatric Treatment: Crisis, Clinic and Consultation* (1975) and edited *Money, Food, Drink, Fashion, and Analytic Training* (1983) and *Terror, Violence and the Impulse to Destroy* (2002). He is in private practice of psychotherapy in San Francisco (johnbeebe@msn.com).

Angela Cotter is a Jungian analytical psychotherapist. Previously trained as a nurse, she has worked in a range of settings with different client groups including people experiencing bereavement, people with dementia, people who are dying, homeless people, older people and younger adults. She has had different roles in these settings, as practitioner, researcher, supervisor, educator and manager. For years she was Programme Director for the PhD in psychotherapeutic studies at Regents College, London. Presently she is Director of Training at the Minster Centre, London. She combines this with her private clinical practice.

Leslie Gardner, PhD, co-editor, studied at the University of Essex Centre for Psychoanalytic Studies in the rhetoric of Jung, considering Vico as a precursor. She has published a chapter in *Psyche and the Arts*, edited by

Susan Rowland (Routledge 2001), and an article on *Pathos* for the *International Journal of Jungian Studies* (2008). She is presently finalizing her book on Jung and Vico while running an international literary agency in London and is an occasional lecturer on writing at Manchester Metropolitan University.

Christopher Hauke is a Jungian analyst in London, and also a writer, film-maker, and Senior Lecturer at Goldsmiths, University of London. He is the author of *Human Being Human: Culture and the Soul* (2005) and *Jung and the Postmodern: The Interpretation of Realities* (2000), and co-editor of *Jung and Film: Post-Jungian Takes on the Moving Image* (2001) and *Contemporary Jungian Analysis: Post-Jungian Perspectives from the Society of Analytical Psychology* (1998). With Luke Hockley, he is editing the new collection of Jungian film writing: *Jung and Film Two: The Return* (2011). His films include the documentaries *One Colour Red* and *Green Ray*. A new short film, *Again*, is to be premiered in Montreal in 2010 (www.christopherhauke.com).

Luke Hockley, PhD, co-editor, is Professor of Media Analysis in the Research Institute for Media, Art and Design (RIMAD) at the University of Bedfordshire, UK. He is author of *Cinematic Projections* (2001) and *Frames of Mind* (2008). Luke is co-editor of the *International Journal of Jungian Studies* (IJJS) and *Jung and Film Two: The Return*, due to be published in 2011 by Routledge. Luke is also an integrative psychotherapist in private practice in London and Bedfordshire (www.lukehockley.com).

Lucy Huskinson, PhD, is a lecturer at the School of Theology and Religious Studies at Bangor University, UK. She is Associate Editor of the *International Journal of Jungian Studies* and author and editor of various books. These include *Nietzsche and Jung* (2004), *Dreaming the Myth Onwards: New Directions of Jungian Therapy and Thought* (2008) and *Introduction to Nietzsche: His Religious Thought* (2009). Lucy is a die-hard fan of Hugh Laurie alongside Stephen Fry, and she dreams of the day that Dr House lies on Dr Gordon Wyatt's couch.

John Izod, PhD, is Professor of Screen Analysis in Film, Media and Journalism at the University of Stirling, where he has taught since 1978. He has been Head of Department and Dean of the Faculty of Arts. A Fellow of the Royal Society for Arts, he is also a Founding Fellow of the Institute of Contemporary Scotland. As principal investigator funded by an Arts and Humanities Research Council grant, he leads a three-year project on the cinema authorship of Lindsay Anderson. He has published several books: *Reading the Screen* (1984); *Hollywood and the Box Office, 1895–1986* (1988); *The Films of Nicolas Roeg* (1992); *An Introduction to Television Documentary* (with Richard Kilborn) (1997); *Myth,*

Mind and the Screen: Understanding the Heroes of our Time (2001); and *Screen, Culture, Psyche: A Post-Jungian Approach to Working with the Audience* (2006).

Catriona Miller, PhD, has an MA in history from Glasgow University; a Postgraduate MA from the Northern Film School in Leeds, specialising in Art Direction; and a PhD from Stirling University: *Bloodspirits: a Jungian Approach to the Vampire Myth*. She is the author of *Angels, Aliens and Amazons: Cult TV Heroines* (2008); and co-edited *Encyclopaedia of Science Fiction Film Adaptation* with John Cook, Peter Wright and Sue Short (2008). Other publications include Dracula was a Woman in *Halloween* (2007); I Just Want to be Normal Again in *Investigating Charmed* (2007); and Apocalypse Now, Or Then? in *British Science Fiction Television* (2005).

Sally Porterfield, PhD, received her MA at Trinity College in Hartford, Connecticut, and her PhD at the University of Massachusetts Amherst. She is retired as Director of The Drama Program and University Players at the University of Hartford and past president of The Jungian Society for Scholarly Studies. She is author of *Jung's Advice to the Players: A Jungian Reading of Shakespeare's Problem Plays* (1994), co-editor of *Perpetual Adolescence: Jungian Analysis of American Media, Literature and Pop Culture* (2009), and author of the chapter Drs Jung and Chekhov, Physicians of the Soul in *Post-Jungian Criticism, Theory and Practice* (2004).

Susan Rowland, PhD, is Professor of English and Jungian Studies at the University of Greenwich, UK and author of books and articles on literature and myth, gender, Jung and literary theory. *C.G. Jung and the Humanties* was published in 2010 and her new project, *The Ecocritical Psyche*, is due for publication in 2011.

Terrie Waddell, PhD, is a senior lecturer in Media and Cinema Studies at La Trobe University, Australia. She has taught and written widely on contemporary media, gender and Jungian approaches to screen texts. Previous publications include *Wild/lives: Trickster, Place and Liminality on Screen* (2010); *Mis/takes: Archetype, Myth and Identity in Screen Fiction* (2006); *Lounge Critic: The Couch Theorist's Companion* (co-editor, 2004), produced in conjunction with the Australian Centre for the Moving Image (ACMI) and the former Australian Film Commission; and *Cultural Expressions of Evil and Wickedness: Wrath, Sex, Crime* (editor, 2003).

Acknowledgements

I gratefully acknowledge the support of the Research Institute in Media, Art and Design (RIMAD) at the University of Bedfordshire. I also want to thank members of the International Association of Jungian Studies and the Jungian Society for Scholarly Studies for their comments after several conference papers. I must thank my wife Mary for her patience and understanding around our home as I commandeered the television to watch and re-watch numerous episodes of *House MD*. Her comments on the series were almost surgical in their precision and helped keep my writing to the point.

Luke Hockley

Many thanks to the Centre for Psychoanalytic Studies at the University of Essex for support and a lively research space like no other internationally. I am grateful to Susan Rowland and Paul Bishop who have pointed me in new directions. And my colleague Nicholas Stratton PhD, deserves much gratitude from me.

Leslie Gardner

We both thank Kate Hawes, publisher at Routledge for her support of Jungian studies, and the production team at Routledge for their skilful editing and collegiality.

Introduction

Luke Hockley and Leslie Gardner

House MD is a globally successful and long-running television series which is in its sixth season at the time of this writing. Despite its focus on US-related medical issues, practice and technology, its production company, Fox, has sold the series worldwide to more than sixty different countries. Wherever it is distributed, viewers, fans and the television industry alike normally refer to the program simply as *House* and this book has also adopted that practice.

As the title of the series implies, *House* revolves around the preoccupations of its protagonist, Gregory House MD. A brilliant diagnostician, he takes over where other doctors have failed. House sees only the most baffling of cases and he engages in the most unorthodox of medical practices. Drilling into brains, risky chemical interventions and even stopping the life functions of patients (temporarily killing them) are all part of his investigative repertoire. His behavior with his team members and his boss is no less outrageous. House speaks his mind, partly to let other people know what he is thinking but mainly to watch how others react. He treats every conversation as an experiment and his co-workers as subjects to be examined verbally and dissected.

House is part of a long tradition of medical television dramas that have been a staple part of the television schedule since the 1950s. In his article in *The Television Genre Book* (Creeber 2001), Jason Jacobs tracks the shifting patterns of concern and modes of representation adopted by television's medical dramas. He notes how series such as *Medic* (US, 1954–5) and *Emergency Ward 10* (UK, 1957–67) followed a format that continues in *House* of weekly episodes, each with self-contained plot lines populated by familiar characters. Jacobs goes on to note the emergence of the medical team in the 1960s. These programs were often headed by a patrician figure such as the Senior Doctor as in *Marcus Welby MD* (US, 1967–75). In its own way, this show played with generic expectations as it portrayed Dr Welby (Robert Young) as a more unorthodox and radical family practitioner than his younger partner, Dr Kiley (James Brolin). The subversion of this particular generic trope is one familiar to viewers of *House*, whose central character has a bedside manner that is somewhat different to that of the kindly Dr Welby.

Jacobs notes how social concerns emerge in the genre in the 1970s and 1980s with programs such as *Casualty* (UK, 1986–present) and to an extent in *St Elsewhere* (US, 1982–7). Another important element in the make-up of medical dramas is comedy, as exemplified by series such as *M*A*S*H* (US, 1973–82) and *Scrubs* (US, 2001–present). The 1990s and the turn of the century saw the development of hospital-based medical dramas which had something of the quality of a soap opera. While episodes might be self-contained, plots could also run across programs and the personal lives of the characters were of as much interest as the medical procedures and diagnoses. Such series include *Chicago Hope* (US, 1994–2000), *ER* (US, 1994–2009), *Grey's Anatomy* (US, 2005–present). The BBC's *Angels* (UK, 1975–1983), along with the long-running *Casualty* (UK, 1986–present) and its spin-off set in the same hospital *Holby City* (UK, 1999–present), share some of these qualities. There are plenty of other series that could be mentioned: *No Angels*, *Quincy*, *Private Practice*, *The Royal* and so forth.

What is clear is that medical dramas make for popular television and have done so for a considerable time. *House* manages to combine aspects from its predecessors. In part it is a comedy but the show also contains elements of soap opera and, as Gardner suggests in Chapter 9, of melodrama. In this way *House* plays with genre boundaries and while subverting aspects of the medical drama it also incorporates elements which it has appropriated from the detective and police genres.

However, despite their prevalence and longevity, television medical dramas have gone somewhat unexamined by media academics. Of course there are exceptions, notably Anne Karpf's *Doctoring the Media* (1988), as well as John Turow's work, *Playing Doctor* (1989), and in addition to the previously mentioned article there is Jason Jacobs' *Body Trauma: New television medical dramas* (2001). More recently, Martin King and Katherine Watson have co-edited *Representing Health* (2005), whose concerns are focused on representations of specific aspects of healthcare, among other more technical works.

Approaching the television medical drama from a slightly different angle it is interesting to reflect on how Jason Bainbridge's (2009) comments on the popularity of many American legal televisions series might also apply to the medical series in general, and *House* in particular. He explores how the construct of 'texts, images, talk, codes of behavior, and narrative structures organizing these effects, seem to have impact well beyond their dramatic diegeses' (Bainbridge 2009). He points out that these shows do not participate in some kind of American hegemonic monoculture. Rather it is that the texts blend into a variety of cultures. In support of this claim he cites Scott Robert Olson who argues that producers of American media texts create

[a] narrative transparency . . . any textual apparatus that allows audiences to project indigenous values, beliefs, rites and rituals into imported media or the use of those devices. This transparency effect means that American cultural exports manifest narrative structures that easily blend into other cultures.

(Olson, 1999: 114, in Bainbridge, 2009: 298)

Using Olson's terminology for our own purposes, it is possible to view the American medical series as providing an archetypal representation of the doctor. In this way, 'the American media do not so much encode media as become (or function as) myths themselves, reducing myths to recombinant elements, or "mythotypes"' (ibid.). Seen from this perspective, medical dramas on television are a collection of cultural myths about doctors and the processes of doctoring; about health and illness; about life and death. From a Jungian perspective, we might say such series have an unconscious and archetypal aspect.

Of particular interest is the combination of performative effects, text and images of the doctor and his team which assist in the construction and drive of the narrative. Related to this are the deeper patterns of the activities of the hero, the wounded healer and the *puer aeternus*, which, as the contributors to this book consider, reach across cultures, decades and the specificity of individual cultural narratives. It is these collective and mostly unconscious patterns which drive the medical series and which inhabit its characters and reflect cultural attitudes to many issues including those of health and illness.

The collection of articles in this book explores the internal psychological construction of *House* and its namesake, Dr Gregory House. They show how narrative, character, and visual structure can all be examined through Jungian psychological introspection. The cumulative effect is to establish a matrix of meaning which reveals how the series deals with profoundly psychological material. While the international success of *House* has much to do with the central character, this volume also explores the extent to which the longevity of the series, and its continued popularity, has to do with its representation of deeply embedded cultural concerns; it shows how these can be articulated by deploying the precepts of Jung's psychological theories.

This work has been made possible because of two intersecting and superficially quite unrelated elements – one human, the other technological. To take the technological aspect first: the emergence of the DVD box set phenomenon has been instrumental in allowing the detailed analysis of material over the output of complete television series. Before such box sets appeared, collecting this amount of research data would required a substantial research grant. And the human element? The contributors to this volume have been able to watch at least five seasons of *House* and some have been able to include Season Six, available on air in the USA only at the time of this writing. The sheer volume of material has required a sustained process of critical engagement, the aim of which has been to provide a detailed psychological assessment of what has been one of Fox's most successful and acclaimed series.

The resulting analyses contained in this volume take place from a dedicated theoretical viewpoint, albeit one which allows for a considerable degree of variation, namely that of Jungian psychology. In so doing the intention is not to suggest that *House* is a particularly Jungian series, however. Rather, if Jungian theory has utility in aiding our understanding of both television programs and their associated media (websites, fan culture and the like), it lies in the way that it can be deployed in a range of contexts and situations. It is through this that its value as an analytical tool will become apparent. The reader who is unfamiliar with Jungian terminology may be reassured that most terms are explained as the need arises and may also be referred to in the glossary at the back of the book. More importantly, our contributors have not used the terms of technical Jungian analysis. Instead, *House* is brought into focus with the aid of a Jungian lens; sometimes this enables a wide-angle view of the series and at other times it allows the analysis to zoom in on specific details, themes, motifs and tropes.

To organize the different angles the book takes on the series, it has been divided into three sections: *Diagnosing House*, *Consulting House* and *Dissecting House*.

In *Diagnosing House* we turn to examine the eponymous diagnostician himself. What is it that drives House? Luke Hockley begins the book with an essay questioning our ideas about what wholeness of personality means. Does the process of individuation lead to a pleasant, socially adept personality? Indeed, should it? Gregory House is a perfect character for examination in this instance and it is here that House's shamanic qualities are first raised. Hockley asks us to consider the extent to which House might be an integrated personality, in command of his self-confidence, his persona and his darker side. While it is almost impossible for the people around him to deal with his acerbic qualities Hockley notes that there is no necessity that an individuated person would be pleasant to be around. In raising these issues Hockley questions what individuation might mean in a social context.

John Izod's piece weighs up the possibilities of archetypal analysis in the context of House in his confrontations with junior doctors, patients, hospital administrators, and his own drives as a healer. He postulates that House is not truly a wounded healer or truly a shaman, possessed of mystical and empathetic powers to heal – he is a full-bodied trickster. He teaches his staff and others by confronting them with their shadows, their weaknesses and fears. Given the long span of the series, characters have a chance to develop: Chase changes from a *puer* who weakly seeks his father's approval into a doctor able to make his own decisions; Cameron from an overly sensitive doctor to one who can stand up for herself. Izod suggests that it was House's confrontations with their demons that enabled this process. Seeking deeper into the interweave of inference of plot lines, Izod claims and includes commentary from fan websites which critique the medical diagnoses on the show, as he digs into the personal, social and dramatic depths of the figure of the doctor.

In Christopher Hauke's diagnosis of House, he explores the significance of Hugh Laurie's career as an actor and its relevance to the personality and character of House. In so doing he shows how Laurie, whose upper-middle-class authoritative repertoire of activity and personality stems from days at Eton and Cambridge, also has a repressed side to his nature in which his intellect and his eschewal of the rewards of seeking approval feed the underlying actor playing the role. Hauke recalls that in his teaming with Stephen Fry and Rowan Atkinson, Laurie was always the straight man and the sidekick. By contrast, now he is in the driver's seat and uses some of those attitudes and postures to assert himself against different kinds of authority in the hospital.

The second section, *Consulting House*, includes a series of pieces that seek out the kinds of healing and medical techniques House uses in deploying his diagnostic skills; a consultation with the process of healing. Terrie Waddell explores the significance of the walking stick House uses, and its history as a staff or wand of healing. She traces the history of the caduceus (the familiar image of the staff with a snake wrapped round it that can be seen in many medical contexts) and explores its implications for the posture and shamanic powers the doctor has. She reveals how it represents a fusion of Hermes, the trickster, and Asclepius, the wounded healer. From contemplation of the body-image of the man connected by touch to a cane, and his dependency on it, to the aspect of the walking stick as also a weapon, Waddell probes the mythic and physiological associations of House.

Lucy Huskinson explores the cognitive interweave with the temperament of House. She argues that his low threshold of boredom and exasperation with his patients' illnesses, not to speak of their personalities, are actually devices that edge him toward his brilliant deductions. She demonstrates in detail the ways in which connections suddenly coalesce into moments of insight for House.

This leads onto Angela Cotter's considerations of what the effects are of the heavy privilege House gives to his left-side brain processing. As she explores the embodied qualities of House the wounded healer, she assesses the way his kind of doctoring reflects the current trend in medical care in the West. Leaning too much on scientific and objective technique, House gets into trouble with his patients and colleagues for his insensitivity. Cotter sees this reflected in diminishing nursing care in UK health services.

Sally Porterfield tracks House's *puer* attributes, finding his adolescent attitude to patients and colleagues deeply reflecting the archetypal patterns fusing with the trickster to engender confrontations with the shadow element in those patients and colleagues. Feelings of unfounded superiority in all areas of life, deep resentments of authority and low self-esteem, are only a few of the elements of this posture she touches on.

In the final section, *Dissecting House*, contributors focus on pulling the doctor and his ambient apart to investigate what is unseen. Susan Rowland plays on the comparisons between House's techniques and those of Sherlock Holmes, which are endemic to the series. They are both drug users, and they both favor left-brain scientific, rationalist thinking. However, the reductionist and alienated Holmes, who is closely implicated with the crimes he investigates, is outflanked by the deeply immersed holistic House whose final passionate diagnoses are often desperate leaps into the unknown. Rowland concludes that the differences are greater than the similarities. Rowland establishes precepts of the crime story ethos that interweave with *House* to broaden its implications.

Leslie Gardner continues some of these themes, dismantling the genre-based scaffolding of the series by proposing that the melodramatic elements of the series go toward explaining the ubiquitous appeal of House. However, she is also suggesting that House is an emblematic figure, the hero in a larger mythic quest story to find and conquer disease. Disease is a metaphor of our course through the world. The source of melodrama is the same narrative source for House's actions as hero.

John Beebe's piece locates the archetypal dimension to Gregory House and his dissection of the psychological characteristics of his team and illuminates how personalities evolve in the process of individuation. He uses Jung's theory of personality types to understand the complexity of the interactions of the group of people, set against a series of deep-rooted archetypal concerns. In so doing he explores issues of sexuality, gender and the erotica of healing.

And finally, Catriona Miller's piece dovetails considerations of House's brilliance with the problem of Dr Cuddy (Lisa Edelstein), his boss – is all as it seems, Miller wonders? She develops her argument by examining what the nature of the feminine archetypal figure in authority is. She questions whether it has become distorted and explores the impact of this particular powerful and sexy person on the narrative, and on the character of House. She concludes that the trajectory of Cuddy's career is not all it seems to be.

If we are to summarize our views of what unfolds in the following pages, it is that the products of popular culture can profitably be understood as complicated and multifaceted sources of psychological insight. In understanding this, Jungian ideas are particularly useful. *House* provides a source of entertainment which spans the globe and we suggest that viewers are drawn to this series because they find something appealing in it, something which appeals to a need in them. Spread over the course of six seasons and still going strong, *House* allows its viewers the opportunity to live with its characters, to be drawn into their world and to reflect at leisure on what this experience might mean. Therapists and psychologically minded commentators on media know that such a strongly affective response is a clue that something profound is happening. The longstanding and global appeal of this series is one such response and the contributors to this volume variously diagnose, consult and dissect this phenomenon. In so doing *House* the series has become our patient and with great care it has been possible to understand some of the qualities which give the program its psychological richness.

It is tempting to see in the series what Jungians would identify as an event that is part of an *enantiodromic* movement. This is a movement where opposites run into each other in the world of the unconscious. Remarkably, a series with a difficult and cantankerous character, concerned with the investigation of life-threatening illness, turns out to offer an opportunity for insight into our cultural anxieties and concerns. However, the series is not so easily circumscribed. The contradictions, ambiguities and paradoxes of this show cannot be readily explained away and it is for that reason that we are left with a sense of joy in the richness of the psychological life of the television series that is *House*.

Luke Hockley, Leslie Gardner (2010)

References

Bainbridge, J. (2009) The bodies of law: Performing truth and the mythology of lawyering in American law shows. *European Journal of Cultural Studies, 12*, 395–413.

Creeber, G. (ed.) (2001) *The Television Genre Book*. London: BFI.

Jacobs, J. (2001) *Body Trauma: New Television Medical Dramas*. London: BFI.

Karpf, A. (1988) *Doctoring the Media*. London: Routledge.

King, M. and Watson, K. (eds) (2005) *Representing Health: Discourses of Health and Illness in the Media*. Basingstoke: Macmillan.

Olson, S.R. (1999) *Hollywood Planet: Global Media and the Competitive Advantage of Narrative Transparency*. London: Routledge.

Turow, J. (1989) *Playing Doctor: Television Storytelling and Medical Power*. Oxford: Oxford University Press.

Part I

Diagnosing House

Doctoring individuation

Gregory House: Physician, detective or shaman?

Luke Hockley

Introduction

Gregory House (Hugh Laurie) is both a gifted diagnostician and an unpleasant human being. He is also curiously likeable. Indeed Hugh Laurie (despite the change in accent and the newly acquired walking stick) is now seemingly inseparable from his character in *House*. He has become a somewhat improbable heartthrob, at least so far as UK viewers are concerned, where he is better known as a comic actor from television series such as *Jeeves and Wooster* (1990) and *Blackadder* (1982/3).

Nonetheless, in 2005 the US publication *TV Guide* labelled him one of 'TV's Sexiest Men' (5 June 2005) and in 2008 he came second on the list of sexiest television doctors ever, just behind ER's Doug Ross (George Clooney). But not everyone is a fan of Gregory House, perhaps because he embodies contradictions. As this volume shows it is almost as though his internal divisions manifest themselves in the opinions of viewers and theorists alike.

This tension is encapsulated rather neatly in another headline from *TV Guide*: 'House, the man you love to hate' (17 April 2004). In the Jungian world opposites run into each other and unconscious projections run rife. House is a figure who embodies both the best and the worst aspects of being a doctor. Sometimes he saves lives, and at other times he is almost complicit in his patient's death. He is what is sometimes called a 'wounded healer' both literally and metaphorically. Indeed this chapter is going to suggest that to understand the complicated appeal of House we need to see him as a complicated character rooted in a range of different literary, filmic and anthropological traditions. As a doctor he is part detective and part shaman and it is this proximity to the shadow and the unconscious which is both appealing and frightening.

However, little is served by trying to come up with a 'balanced' view of Dr House. That enterprise would be thwarted by his contradictory nature and end up being merely an attempt to allay our own fears that something unconscious is at play. Instead I want to suggest that it is not that we are seeking to come to a reasoned interpretation of who this Dr House is, but that Dr House can more fully be understood as someone who experiences life as an individuated person. Not perfect, but whole. Not pleasant, but the person he is. As the subject of analysis, he does not need to be reined in or pinned down with the appropriate archetypal tag, such as 'wounded healer'. It is precisely because there are unpalatable forces at work that temptation to neuter the unconscious with neat archetypal terms should be resisted. Instead we, along with the 16 million American viewers that this show attracts each week, are better off savouring the contradictions.

What is individuation?

One of the many distinctive contributions to the psychology of the individual made by Jung is the idea of 'individuation'. Jung positions himself quite differently to Freud who came to the view that psychological disturbances in adult life were always the result of unresolved difficulties from childhood. Jung thought this was at best partial and at worst inaccurate. Instead, Jung wanted to re-orientate the psyche and rather than constantly looking back to childhood he thought it was important to examine the current situation. Why look into the past when there is every possibility that the current situation will contain enough material to tell the therapist what is happening for the client? Jung thought that there was no need to overly complicate the matter.

Along with this emphasis on the present moment, Jung's view was that the psyche was teleological, which is to say that it has a goal. He suggests that the aim of every human is to live to their fullest potential and to become completely the person they are. This is not an easy undertaking as family, friends and society all have views about how we should behave. So at its simplest, individuation involves just aging and letting the body grow old and eventually die. However, the complexity arrives when we try to understand what it means for us to live in a personal and unique manner within this context, since it makes the contradictions between our individual psychology and collective expectations explicit.

Individuation is also a psychosomatic concept, linking the unconscious with the body. This link is important since it is a theme that we are going to return to as we consider both *House*, the television series, and Gregory House, the man. Jung puts it as follows:

> In so far as this process [individuation], as a rule, runs its course unconsciously as it has from time immemorial, it means no more than that the acorn becomes and oak, the calf a cow, and the child an adult. But if the individuation process is made conscious, consciousness must confront the unconscious and a balance between the opposites must be

found. As this is not possible through logic, one is dependent on *symbols* which make the irrational union of opposites possible.

(Jung 1952: para. 755, emphasis as original)

As a diagnostician Gregory House is concerned with the health of the body and in making sure that it can run its course. His medical interventions are designed to restore the body to a state of health and as such we conceive of him as someone who supports and assists in the biological aspects of individuation. However, as we will see, House's evolving personal psychology, or his process of individuation, gets mixed up with the treatment of his patients – indeed this unconscious aspect of his psyche is crucial in coming to a view about why he treats patients as he does, and how he interacts with both his immediate team and the hospital in general.

The interweaving of the personal and the social is significant for while individuation is a personal matter it also has broader collective and cultural aspects. Jung suggested that to undertake the work of individuation was to place the need for personal authenticity over and above cultural norms and expectations. There is a catch here. Jung seems to be suggesting that the only way to be fully the person you are is to reject the social conventions and etiquette of the day. Yet this interpretation of matters is only partly true. What Jung is really driving at is that individuation requires that we are conscious in broader contexts about the choices that we make. In making these choices we are inclined to privilege our inner preferences, even if they fly in the face of what society regards as 'normal' or acceptable behaviour. In so doing we opt for authenticity over social or cultural expectation and personal need over social conventions. The downside to this is that the comfort of the collective, the easy life of fitting in and going with the flow, is abandoned in favour of the personal struggle to be fully ourselves. For Jung, this call to individuation is a vocation. Indeed, Jung thought that when the individuation process was made conscious it took the form of quests, heroic tasks, labyrinths and other maze-like forms. He comments:

The words, 'many are called, but few are chosen' are singularly appropriate here, for the development of personality from the germ-state to full consciousness is at once a charisma and a curse, because its first fruit is the conscious and unavoidable segregation of the single individual from the undifferentiated and unconscious herd. This means isolation, and there is no more comforting word for it. Neither family nor society nor position can save him from this fate, nor yet the most successful adaptation to his environment, however smoothly he fits in. The development of the personality is a favour that must be paid for dearly.

(Jung 1934: para. 294)

Clearly Gregory House is not overly concerned with the niceties of everyday social interaction. His numerous 'House-isms' encapsulate his frustration with the demands of patients and colleagues alike to moderate his behaviour to a social norm: 'Everybody lies,' House opines (*Pilot*, 1: 1), and again, 'Normal's not normal' (*Autopsy*, 2: 2), and 'Guilt is irrelevant' (*House Training*, 3: 20) and 'Lies are like children: they're hard work, but it's worth it because the future depends on them' (*It's a Wonderful Lie*, 4: 10), to cite only a few examples.

The point is that individuation does not offer a model of personal perfection, rather it is more usefully thought of as an ongoing life process in which the challenge is to make conscious the unconscious as a particular individual is driven to do. Jung stressed that individuation was not about losing our imperfections, rather he thought it was about 'wholeness' which for him involved not eradication of imperfection but rather its acceptance. We can go further. Individuation does not offer a paradigm for psychological health, it is not about being free from complexes or fantasies. Rather it offers a way of being in the world, a way which others might find threatening, distasteful or bizarre. Put another way, the challenge of individuation is to find a personal myth, a way of understanding how we want to live in the world. Like it or not, it seems clear that Gregory House has found his personal myth.

The body – the unconscious and disease

Jung's model of the psyche is a psychosomatic one, making it a good fit for my proposal about House, i.e. that it is a drama about the interplay between medicine and personal psychology. Of course there are other narrative tropes and inflections at play. *House* is also partly about the institutional politics of a large hospital. It explores the role and power of individuations in such an organisation, from the Executive Board down. But sitting underneath all this, or we might say at the centre of all this, is Gregory House – it is his psyche, his way of thinking and behaving, which permeates the series.

As mentioned, individuation is the lifelong process of bringing unconscious contents closer to consciousness with a view to living a more authentic and fulfilling life. Jung hypothesised that underlying this process there were a series of psychological structures which regulated how individuation would unfold, and he called these 'archetypes'. Archetypes can roughly be thought of as analogous to psychological genes. They are partly inherited and partly arise from the circumstances of our upbringing. Another way of thinking about them is to regard archetypes as a predisposition to behave and to conceptualise the world in certain ways.

Archetypes influence all aspects or our lives. For example, they impact on how we present ourselves and how we try to fit into society, what Jung called the 'persona' – the archetype of social adaptation. Similarly our gender identity arises from the interplay of the 'contrasexual archetypes'. In essence this is the idea that our biological sex should not limit our access to ways of being which tend to be culturally prescribed in terms of femininity and masculinity. Contrasexuality suggests that everyone has access to a much fuller range of human gendered sexuality than culture generally allows. Jung outlines numerous other archetypal patterns, noting that often archetypes appear in clusters or groups with one prefiguring the other. This notion of underlying patterns is a useful consideration as it moves us away from thinking about individuation as a linear process predicated on a series of steps. Instead it is more productive to see individuation as something 'messy' with different archetypes and aggregates of archetypes coming into consciousness at different times over the course of an individual's life. The question of what might be going on 'archetypally' in *House* is something we will get to in a moment.

But first the perennial question about archetypes: if archetypes such as the contrasexual archetypes are invisible then how can their presence be deduced? Jung had two related answers to this problem. The first is that archetypal patterns manifest themselves in images. While the pattern may be fixed, the images that give expression to that pattern come from the interaction of the archetype with its social setting. For example the underdeveloped part of the psyche is what Jung termed the 'shadow'. We are both attracted to and afraid of this part of ourselves, especially when it is not well understood, or to use a more psychological language, integrated into consciousness. The exact form the shadow takes will vary from person to person but typically it will induce a certain attraction combined with a sense of fear or unease. The vampire and the criminal are common images of this archetype. We are unaccountably fearful or drawn to these figures. As we shall see, in *House* disease expresses both House's fascination with his shadow and his frustration and anxiety when it eludes his conscious grasp – something that he is at different times more and less relaxed about.

Jung goes still further in suggesting that it is the interplay of archetypes and society which gives rise to the fundamental ideas on which cultures are founded. There is a sense in which again this can be thought of as the interplay between pattern and image, only this time the interaction is occurring in society as a whole rather than in the life of a particular individual.

> The unconscious . . . is the source of the instinctual forces of the psyche and of the forms or categories that regulate them, namely the archetypes. All the most powerful ideas in history go back to archetypes. This is particularly true of religious ideas, but the central concepts of science, philosophy, and ethics are no exception to this rule. In their present form they are variants of archetypal ideas, created by

consciously applying and adapting these ideas to reality. For it is the function of consciousness not only to recognise and assimilate the external world through the gateway of the sense, but to translate into visible reality the world within us.

(Jung 1931: para. 342)

It is easy to develop this point to realise that there is an archetypal component to our conception of what constitutes 'health'. This is to see illness in psychosomatic terms. Jungian authors such as Maguire (2004) and Ramos (2004) have in their different ways explored this territory. Their approach is to see illness as a disruption of the body's healthy and balanced system of self-regulation. It follows that one way of conceptualising disease is that it is an image of disruption to the archetypal substrata of the psyche. While Ramos explores how the body may symbolise and express such disruption, Maguire concentrates on the archetypal dimension of skin, as the semi-permeable barrier between the inner self and the outer world that is breached by illness. It is also to conceptualise health in holistic terms which sees humans as body and psyche immersed in a social environment. (Lipowski 1984). This is also how House thinks. As he succinctly puts it, 'Your mind controls your body. If it thinks you're sick it makes you sick.' (*Airborne*, 3: 18).

This consideration of what constitutes health takes us to another under-standing of how 'health' is considered. What 'health' is varies from person to person and changes over time. In Jungian terms, the archetypal view of health is that it is a state of being in which the body's energy is balanced and flowing freely. Jung calls this type of energy 'libido' and it is both activated and channelled via the archetypes. Importantly, to have a mind and body that are in balance with each other does not require adaptation to the social setting – indeed the social setting may be contributing to the imbalance in the first place. Again this corresponds to Gregory House's view of matters and is what underlies his constant berating of the manage-ment of Princeton-Plainsboro Teaching Hospital. House's work is largely mental, he works on solving why patients react in the way they do. His request to the management is not ever for more resources (House uses those available to him with abandon and as he sees fit) but rather for less interference to enable him to deduce why a given disease is taking the particular course it is. The problem with his actions is that they often involve complicated and sometimes life-threatening interventions.

The disease detective

This raises the question: why is House driven to such ends? Part of the answer to this lies in the association that the screenwriters have created between House and the filmic and literary genres of detective fiction. While House is a physician and a medical diagnostician, the way he approaches his job, and indeed the way that he opts to live his life, is more like that of his legal counterpart, the detective. Throughout the series the parallels between House and Conan Doyle's Sherlock Holmes are made clear and deliberate. (They are explored thoroughly elsewhere in this volume by Susan Rowland in her chapter *House Not Ho(l)mes*.) For our purposes it is enough to note the similarity in their names: House and Holmes. Both House and Holmes have close male colleagues: Holmes has Dr J Watson as his *fidus Achates* (faithful friend) and House has Dr J Wilson. Both House and Holmes are musical: Holmes played the violin and House's instruments of choice include the electric guitar, piano and harmonica. While Holmes used cocaine recreationally, House takes large amounts of Vicodin to relieve the pain of an infarction in his leg muscles (which also provides the narrative justification for House's cane). Finally, House lives at 221B (*Hunting*, 2: 07) and Holmes famously lived at the fictional address of 221B Baker Street, London. (This list is not definitive . . .)

Detectives on the screen come in different guises of which Holmes as an intellectual gentleman detective is one variant. Another type is from the hard-boiled detective of 1940s *film noir*. Films such as *The Big Sleep* (1946), *The Maltese Falcon* (1941) and *Laura* (1944) typify the genre. Normally those detectives are loners, seemingly incapable of forming steady relationships and often with an addiction (often to alcohol). These detectives are tortured souls. Pictorially the screen suggests this through the use of dark shadows, canted camera angles and rain-soaked city streets which in combination express the detective's sense of isolation and inner turmoil.

Gregory House succeeds in combining elements from both traditions. Swapping a trench coat and trilby for jeans and trainers (sneakers) he nevertheless adopts some of the traditional elements of the hard-boiled detective's persona. For example he sets about the process of diagnosis in an intellectual mode, i.e. a puzzle to be solved. What Holmes shares with the hard-boiled detective is their mutual reliance on leaps of intuition and insight while apparently using logic and deduction. For these detectives the world of ratiocination is not enough, they need proximity to the non-logical world of the unconscious to solve the crime. So too does House.

House parts company with these traditions, however, when it comes to relationships with women. The *femme fatale* of *film noir* is all but missing from the series. Indeed Gregory House often sees women as sexual objects to be either manipulated at work or used for his gratification, not as alluring women whose dangerous charms cannot be ignored. Instead he makes numerous sexual references to his boss, Lisa Cuddy (Lisa Edelstein), and in one episode goes so far as to fantasise about her pole-dancing in a schoolgirl's uniform. (this is a hallucination which arises from an injury to the head [*House's Head*, 4: 15]). Another important part of this episode concerns a mystery woman (Ivana Milicevic) who House sees while he is hypnotised. Returning in a dream which House has at the end of the episode she provides him with clues which help him solve the episode's core problem. In some ways she represents House's normally hidden feminine side – what analytical psychology might refer to as his *anima*, a representation of his contrasexual archetype. The episode is clear about this and the audio commentary makes it explicit, noting that her character's script title is The Women in Black – the title of a ghost story by Susan Hill (1983). Further, she has two forms, the woman on the bus and Wilson's girlfriend Amber. Interestingly, when Amber makes her first appearance in the episode (while Chase hypnotises House) she is shot at 40 frames per second to make her appear 'ethereal' (Audio Commentary, *House's Head*, 4: 15) and this serves to further enhance her supernatural qualities. Giving added weight to this interpretation, the producers comment that their reason for casting Ivana Milicevic was that there was something 'completely otherworldly and hard to place about her' (ibid.).

Exploring a similar theme, the episode *It's a Wonderful Lie* (4: 10) plays with House's view of women as either pure or (and) available to him sexually. This cine-literate reference in the title suggests the setting of this episode at Christmas. House decides that one of his outpatients, Melanie (Jennifer Hall), is a prostitute – largely because she is wearing a medal of St Nicolas who as well as being Father Christmas, is also patron saint of children and prostitutes. When she returns with a rash House diagnoses contagious ecthyma as a result of contact with donkeys which he assumes are used in a sex show. Melanie does nothing to dispel his belief and gives him a flyer for a show she is in. Of course, she turns out to be playing the Virgin Mary in a church nativity in which she rides a donkey.

What this suggests about *House* is that in some ways it subverts audience expectations about the detective genre, while relying at the same time on these tropes to provide an element of narrative engagement. Psychologically, it shows that House is both highly manipulative but also retains a secure sense of self which can withstand the personal criticism that is bound to come his way as a result of his behaviour. So Gregory House contains a duality. Sometimes he uses women for his own ends, as recipients of sexual commentary (particularly to Lisa Cuddy). The character of Allison Cameron (Jennifer Morrison) poses more challenges for House as she is in love with him. In the episode *Role Model* (1: 17) Cameron resigns her post agreeing to come back only if House will go on a date with her. This happens in *Love Hurts* (1: 20) although House comments that he will not do it again; Cameron is more ambivalent. House seems both attracted to the caring and compassionate side of Cameron but perhaps also keen to keep his feelings at a distance.

Visually *House* owes little to the style of *film noir*. What the series does share with feature film production more generally is the use of single-camera shooting. This production technique is in contrast to the multi-camera set-ups that are more commonly used for soap operas. *House* is not unique in this respect. Television series including *Star Trek: The Next Generation*, *Desperate Housewives*, *The OC* and *The Sopranos* are all shot using single-camera. However, the effects of this are different in each of the series, although in each case the camera becomes a sort of character in the scene. In *House*, the result on-screen is lots of steadicam shots of House striding down long hospital corridors, moving from room to room. This would not be possible if *House* had been shot on a series of three-wall sets using multi-camera techniques. The effect is to suggest the hospital belongs to House – he can be where he wants, when he wants. Not that the camera is always with him. We often see the team without him, tending patients and carrying out various medical tests and procedures – as such, the viewer becomes House's proxy, viewing his team at something of a distance.

Single-camera work also means that the common set-up of shot-reverse-shot, where the camera moves between two talking heads with one nodding while the other speaks, is a rarity. Instead, the viewer is offered an insight, a close-up if you will, into the disdain House feels for those round him. The result is subtle but over the course of the multiple series of *House*, where there is the time and scale to be subtle, what happens is that gradually viewers get to find out more about the inner workings of House and his relationship with those around him. This is not a plot-driven series as essentially the plot is the same each week. *House* is character-driven television, and this gives it an inherently psychological feel that is enhanced through its references to the world of the detective and the act of detection. Such psychological territory is well served by the use of single-camera technique.

If Gregory House is a detective this raises the interesting issue of what crime has been committed and who is the criminal? In *film noir* the crime is nearly always murder but in *House* there aren't criminals and murders *per se* but there are viruses, infections and pathologies all of which attempt to rob the patient of life. The result is that in the narrative of *House* the crime is the corruption of the body while the disease becomes the criminal. This casts House in the role of the detective but unlike his punning namesake Sherlock Holmes, House is at least nominally part of a team – not a lone detective, working outside the institutional structures of the police and the judiciary. Of course House does his utmost not to fit into Princeton-Plainsboro Teaching Hospital. In part this outsider stance is what viewers expect of the generic detective, but it is also important for House that he exists on the edge. He needs a liminal space in which he can move between the world of rational thought and the brilliance of intuitive insight. Put another way, he needs to stay close to the material world of consciousness while also being able to descend into the underworld of infection and disease.

Being in a hospital also gives House access to complicated medical machinery and extensive diagnostic testing. The medical science in the series remains inaccessible to the viewer. We are not supposed to understand the body, its distress and disease. After all, this is not a documentary nor is it educational television. (c.f. the chapters by John Izod and John Beebe in this volume.) The machines, the diagnostic procedures, all remain the stuff of medical magic yet House is able to move between these two seemingly incompatible worlds and as an insider can reveal its secrets. Levi-Strauss describes such individuals as anomalous characters – 'anomalous' because they exist neither in the world of good nor in a world of bad. Instead they straddle this type of binary divide and are able to contain the competing tensions of X and X. What engages us, therefore, is House's fluidity and familiarity with these two realms as he moves between intellect and insight. As a blog post on the website *Polite Dissent* put it:

> There seemed to be no logic behind his [House's] deductions, he just seized on some minuscule fact and used it to concoct some untenable theory. That he turned out to be right in the end seemed more luck than skill.
>
> ('Scott' 2004)

Following a hunch, and making leaps of logic and insight are what all detectives do when they solve a crime. They can do this because they are close to the criminal and inhabit the same psychological space of the criminal underworld. Alternatively, as we might put it, they live close to the unconscious. We have already seen that individuation requires that the unconscious becomes conscious and that unconscious contents express themselves as images which can be projected onto those round about us. It follows that the shadow side of the detective is the criminal and that in many ways the detective and the criminal are different sides of the same coin – opposites that run into each other, a psychological principle that Jung termed *enantiodromia* (a description he took from Heraclitus). In fiction, at least, the reason detectives can catch criminals is that they understand the psychology of the underworld, for this is their milieu too. It is no accident that House has a dead leg muscle – he carries the pathology with him – he is the stuff of shadow. Put another way, the detective needs to get close to the criminal, right alongside him, shoulder to shoulder.

House – doctor or shaman?

The everyday language for the insights that House has is, as the quote above puts it, more luck than skill. Those versed in the discourse of analytical psychology or of the mythological world might put it differently. House behaves in an intuitive and apperceptive manner; he relates to the physical world partly as an actual corporeal reality and partly as a source of inspiration and insight. In this respect House has something of the persona of the magician, the shaman or healer. Jung's umbrella term for this type of psychological presentation is 'mana personality'. Now this might seem at odds with House's disdain for anything other than medicine routed in a strictly hi-tech bi-medial model. However, it is worth reflecting that this type of medicine fails House and his team on a regular episode-by-episode basis. Indeed, the dramatic tension of most episodes relies on the differential diagnosis proving inadequate. Partly this is the result of the narrative requirements of an episodic series in which narrative expectation and familiar characters with which to populate the show week in week out are demanding. But it is also the case that House is schooled in a particular type of medicine which he cannot eschew, yet at the same time he cannot work within the strictures that this type of ideological and institutional confinement confer.

This dysfunction hints at a certain *puer*-like (or childlike) quality in House. As the producers comment, 'He's at his best when he's speaking from his inner child . . . or outer child' (*House's Head*, 4: 15). The audience imagines what it would feel like to be unfettered (like House): if only the management did not insist on such and such, we tell ourselves; if only we could be allowed to get on and do our jobs . . . then finally the bosses would realise my full potential and I could 're-think' this business. House acts out that fantasy for us. And because it is a childlike fantasy that is not based in the reality of the world but on acting out a fantasy streaming from an arrested part of the self, it carries with it a powerful, archaic and archetypal appeal.

This, then, is part of the function of the mana personality. Jung borrowed the term from anthropology to explain the specific power that some people appear to have in influencing the behaviour of others. This is seen most clearly in the characters in fairy stories, myths or indeed dreams who seem to have a mystical insight into what is happening. As a result, they are often able to direct the hero forward, or at least put him back on the right track. The reason for this capacity is that they have a proximity to the unconscious and are essentially archetypal figures who are able to use their intuition to tap into the energy of the unconscious. Samuels *et al* (1986: 89) put it as follows:

> Mana is a word derived from anthropology, being Melanesian in origin; it pertains to the extraordinary and compelling supernatural power which emanates from certain individuals, subjects, actions and events as well as from inhabitants of the spirit world. The modern equivalent is 'charisma'. Mana suggests the presence of an all-pervading vital force,

a primal source of growth or magical healing that can be likened to a primitive concept of psychic energy.

So there is a sense in which modern media stars, including actors and actresses, have something of a mana personality. House has the two aspects. One derives from his work as a healer, the other stems from the inter-fictional carryover of Hugh Laurie, who is an unusual figure as a British actor in an American series, playing an American. As noted in the introduction, Laurie is well known to UK audiences for playing comedic roles, and his appearance as an American diagnostician contributes to a certain strangeness to his casting as Gregory House, at least for that section of the viewing audience who are familiar with his previous work (c.f. Dyer 1979: 121 on audience foreknowledge).

But of more immediate concern here are the quasi-shamanistic practices which form part of House's persona. These are sometimes subtle, sometimes less so. Like some shamans House relies on drugs in order to work effectively. Sometimes he also feels the need to isolate himself in order to gain an insight into a given situation. For example in *It's a Wonderful Lie* (4: 10) House immerses himself in cold water in an effort to clear his mind, and to bring some clarity to what are partial memories. Of course, immersing yourself in cold water is not in and of itself a shamanic practice. Where the shamanistic aspect manifests itself is in House's ritualistic need to mark his position as someone outside the norms of society in order to effect healing within the same society. The shamanic part of this is that House is both part of the institutionalised practice of medicine and yet he also needs to be outside this frame. His immersion in cold water encapsulates this inside and outside-ness and is redolent with suggestions of birth, of someone who exists in a liminal and transitory space.

The dialogue in *House* also seems to suggest that House's proximity with disease is closer to that of a shaman than a western doctor. It is almost as though House summons up disease, as though it is House's own wounded nature, both physical and psychological, which brings the disease into being. Almost every episode starts with an apparently healthy person suddenly falling ill. Once he or she encounters House they invariably get worse. But sometimes the opposite is true, as the character Thirteen comments, 'House has gone and so have her symptoms' (*Not Cancer*, 5: 2). The idea that an inner psychological condition is activated as part of a process of healing is an idea that will be familiar to psychotherapists. It is not that the therapist causes illness, rather it is the clinician's own wounded nature that partly facilitates the process of identification and healing; it allows for empathy and a sense of recognition. In the case of *House* there is a rather literal representation of this process translated into the medical realm. *House* amplifies qualities which can be thought of as being present in many types of healing. I have in mind here the dual need to believe in the expert nature of someone who knows more about ourselves and our health than we do, and also in the effectiveness of the medicines and treatments we are given. In the case of the character of Gregory House, both have a dark side. House deals with extreme cases and his treatments are also extreme as his patients are often close to death.

Interestingly the use of special effects sequences in *House* also promotes the proximity of Gregory House to both shamanistic practice and the shadow side of his psyche. From the first episode of the first series *Pilot* (1: 01) most of the programmes feature a sequence in which the camera seemingly enters the body of the patient and follows the course of the disease as it tracks its progress either through various organs or sometimes at the molecular level. This is visually spectacular and in terms of the series the device has several narrative effects. First it suggests to the viewer that House is engaged in medical science that is serious and yet also magical – the ability of the viewer to transcend the limitations of physical space and to see inside the patient's body as a magnified image reflects what is happening in House's mind – is this what he sees, or at least imagines is happening inside his patient? In this way, these images reflecting the 'insights' of House become a channel for the viewer into the mysteries of the human body. As the producer of *House* remarks on one of the audio commentaries, 'So much of what we do takes place in House's head, usually metaphorically' (*House's Head*, 4: 15).

Second, these incursions into the body reinforce the view of House as a detective, who uses his intuition to get close to the criminal – in this case, the disease. My suggestion is that to do so House needs to get close to his own shadow. Interestingly special effect sequences normally start as House gives a diagnosis for a patient and they continue in voice-over as House continues his narration. It is almost as though he is conjuring up the disease, as though he is bringing it into being for the purposes of healing, bringing it to life for viewers and characters alike who cannot see and cannot understand without his intervention thereby initiating the process of healing. This raises the interesting possibility that it is House's shadow, his dark, painful and shamanistic side which is needed to invoke the disease and somehow pull it into consciousness where it can be understood and treated. Citing Eliade, Jung notes, 'Dismemberment is a practically universal motif of primitive shamanistic psychology. It forms the main experience in the initiation of a shaman' (Jung 1938/1954: para. 91*n*.). Perhaps there is a sense in which House's invasive exploration of the patient's body serves as an initiatory rite for both himself and for his team. House's team frequently get caught up in this shadow play, as when he requires them to break into patient's homes, or when he pits one against the other and when he toys with the affection they feel for each other and the wariness with which they treat him. House disturbs and provokes his team, yet he cannot work without them. Even the differential diagnosis scenes, which feature in most of the episodes, are combative and challenging in tone and nature. In short, House needs a home for his shadow and he finds that home in the interactions with his team and his patients.

Conclusion

What arises from this set of relationships between Jungian psychology and *House*? I want to suggest that *House* provides us with a particularly clear example that Jungian individuation is not about psychological health. Indeed, and perhaps somewhat ironically for a medical series, it would clearly be perverse to claim that *House* offers models for psychological health. Instead, we need to see *House* from quite another angle. Instead of framing the series as providing examples of psychological qualities and attributes, it is more helpful to start with the psychological theory. From this perspective the idea of individuation offers an explanation as to why a manipulative, cantankerous and drug addicted character can be voted as one of the sexiest doctors on television. It also provides a new take on the popularity of the series. There is something deeply appealing and basic in people being themselves. This comment should not be taken lightly as it goes to the very root of what individuation is about. One of the distinctive aspects of Jungian psychology is the challenge it offers to be truly oneself and it sees this as the core psychological undertaking of life.

The extent to which Gregory House can be considered a character who is actively engaged with the work of individuation is a moot point. He remains a character in a television series and not one who is prone to self-revelatory psychological speculation. However, we should not be deterred from the attempt to find something of psychological value in the series and its characters. As Jung remarked of the novel, 'In general, it is the non-psychological novel that offers the richest opportunities for psychological elucidation (Jung 1930/1950: para. 137). What we know about House is that it is his acknowledgement of his own addicted and manipulative nature which is central to his work as a diagnostician. He functions in a space that exists between the inner mysteries of the body and the rationality of the medical and clinical world. House needs to contain these quite separate demands. In so doing, he struggles to be the person he is, namely an imperfect container for the conflicts that exist between the body, the mind and how these enact themselves in everyday life.

The realisation of the interconnectedness of our being is part of what individuation demands of us. Jung does not often make his views about individuation quite so explicit but in the following extract from a letter to a German physician, referred to as Dr S, Jung makes his views on the psychosomatic nature of the psyche clear. There are several published letters between Jung and Dr S. In this letter he expresses his view that the biological concepts of the parasympathetic and the sympathetic nervous systems (which along with the enteric nervous system form the autonomic nervous system) are the physiological counterparts to the unconscious.

> If you do not go along with the unconscious properly, i.e. if it finds no expression through consciousness and conscious action, it piles up its libido in the body and this leads to physical innervations . . . The unconscious is largely identical with the sympathetic and parasympathetic systems, which are the physiological counterparts of the polarity of unconscious contents. You won't get out of the 'old house' until you have drained to the last drop what is going on there. Only then can the situation change.
>
> (in Adler and Jaffé 1973 (Letter of 20 October 1939): 278)

One suspects that Gregory House has little intention of getting out of the 'old house'. In part this is in the nature of long-running television series. If the persona of House changed radically it might well jeopardise what is a successful and enduring television series. But what it also shows is the psychological insight that the idea of a cure is misplaced. House cannot cure himself and he does not want to. If he did he would cease to *be* House – he needs his demons. The effect week after week of what is essentially the same plot is to foreground the inevitability that the body and the psyche are tied together in a struggle to cope with life's difficulties and to use these as a source of insight and understanding. As Jung comments:

> But it does contradict a certain misplaced enthusiasm on the art of the therapist as well as the view that analysis constitutes a unique 'cure'. In the last resort it is highly improbable that there could ever be a therapy that got rid of all difficulties. Man needs difficulties; they are necessary for health. What concerns us here is only an excessive amount of them.
>
> (Jung 1916/1958: para. 143)

My suggestion, then, is that individuation is not devoid of pathology nor is it a model of health. Rather, as Gregory House shows, it is a way of living in the world. This way of living, or we might say 'being', is one in which the biological and psychological are deeply entwined. It eschews the conventions of society when it comes to the norms of social behaviour and cultural expectation. In short, House not only needs life's difficulties but he also thrives on making life problematic for anyone he is close to.

References

Adler, G. and Jaffé, A. (eds) (1973) *C. G. Jung Letters Vol 1, 1905–1950*. London: Routledge & Kegan Paul.
Dyer, R. (1979) *Stars*. London: British Film Institute.

Hill, S. (1983) *Woman in Black*. London: Hamish Hamilton.

Jung, C. G. (1953–1979) *The Collected Works*, 20 Vols (Bollingen Series XX), Trans. R. F. F. Hull; H. Read, M. Fordham and G. Adler (eds). Princeton New Jersey: Princeton University Press.

Jung, C. G. (1916/1958) *The Transcendent Function, Collected Works 8*.

Jung, C. G. (1930/1950) *Psychology and Literature, Collected Works 15*.

Jung, C. G. (1931) *The Structure of the Psyche, Collected Works 8*.

Jung, C. G. (1934) *The Development of the Personality, Collected Works 17*.

Jung, C. G. (1938/1954) *The Visions of Zosimos, Collected Works 13*.

Jung, C. G. (1952) *Answer to Job, Collected Works 11*.

Lipowski, Z. J. (1984) What does the word 'psychosomatic' really mean? A historical and semantic inquiry. *Psychosomatic Medicine, 46*, 2: 153–171.

Maguire, A. (2004) *Skin Disease: A Message from the Soul*. London: Free Association Books.

Ramos, D. G. (2004) *The Psyche of the Body: A Jungian Approach to Psychosomatics*. London: Brunner-Routledge.

Samuels, A., Shorter, B. and Plaut, F. (1986) *A Critical Dictionary of Jungian Analysis*. London: Routlege & Kegan Paul.

'Scott' (pseudonym) (2004, November) House – Episode 1: 'Pilot' [Blog post]. Retrieved from http://www.politedissent.com/archives/388

Chapter 2

The physician's melancholia

John Izod

The dramatic arc of a feature film or a one-off television play is convenient for the scholar attempting archetypal readings. As found in mainstream productions, the form is dominated in most instances by the norm of an opening status quo that is disturbed, thereby obliging the main characters to act in order to resolve the resultant difficulties in order to reach closure in an altered status quo. In leading characters toward solving their problems, this structure maps readily onto their attainment of a new staging point on the route toward individuation. In contrast, an open-ended series, running over as many episodes and seasons as its commercial success warrants, may lack (or at the very least complicate) the definite resolutions that one-off dramas make possible. The open-ended series may seem more like life to the extent that the principal characters may not achieve lasting development. The psychological peaks and troughs that they touch as a result of the dramatic action in any one episode are seldom inhabited for long – with the effect that anxiety and uncertainty may be prolonged. It follows that the great catharses that spectators (and, alongside them, Jungian screen analysts) enjoy after sharing vicariously the movie hero's seemingly final triumph over adversity are less common in series television drama.

House displays elements of both the one-off and the series format. This becomes clear after every calamity, and nowhere more than in the break up of his original team, as we shall see.

Deep into the text

In almost every episode of *House*, a visual device first seen in the pilot plunges us into the heart of the matter. It recurs episode after episode in a succession of variants appropriate to the medical condition of whatever patient Gregory House's team of experts is diagnosing. Typically cued when the patient suffers a sudden reversal, these sequences comprise shots that penetrate the body, rushing into sites of crisis so deeply that physical form recognizable by lay members of the audience is all but lost to the eye.

Sometimes we can make out an organ, like the fatty pulp of a sickly beating heart; sometimes we encounter the cellular nature of the body, watching, for example, the swirl of red corpuscles in the bloodstream. However, there are occasions when we go so deep that to the untrained eye we seem to be engaging with the psychoid (the hypothetical quasi-mystical zone where physis and psyche blend – a zone the possible existence of which Dr House would deny to his last breath).

The use of medical imaging technology (with data screens visible on set) seems at first to guarantee the plausibility of these vivid invasions of the body. Dramatically insistent, these 'insights' grab our attention and (except for medical staff) stimulate the imagination of viewers. However, many such episodes are enhanced or entirely generated by computer, and some are endowed with elements of fantasy in the process. Even a layman cannot miss that the colour-saturated register is fantastic when, for example, platelets the size of green saucers pulse down the veins accompanied by sinister, quasi-musical electronic whooshes (of a kind the body does not produce). Repeated deployment of the device eventually distances interpretation from naturalism and any claim that we are watching nothing more than an accurate representation of bodily processes.

The complex armature around which House is wound

These sensuous, noisy dives into the interior call attention to themselves as one of the show's master metaphors – the bewildering search for health and clarity within. The dramatic shock they deliver can cause excitation in viewers when experienced in a complex and evolving narrative context that typically features first, the physical ailment of the patient; second, crises in the relationships among the principal members of House's team; and third, turmoil in the psyche that he so resolutely denies possessing. Broken strands of quick-fire dialogue triggered by those interlocking crises run across each other as team members argue concurrently about two topics (say a diagnostic problem and personal relationships between members of their group) with no apparent connection. The effect is augmented by crosscutting between scenes of action that carry the several arenas of narrative forward. Thus House might be holed up reluctantly in the walk-in clinic ridiculing a hyper-anxious parent by hinting that her infant has serious problems; in the lab two of his team discuss their boss's appetite for humiliating people while always being right in his diagnoses; House reveals that the infant has a common cold but at that moment the hospital manager, Cuddy, bursts in to rebuke him for his attitude to another case; meanwhile a critically ill patient suffers a seizure as a consequence of being mistakenly diagnosed; we zoom into the liver where something indistinct bubbles ominously. Sequences as intense as this present the viewer with a storytelling complexity that, not unlike the old poetic form, invites quasi-allegorical textual analyses through their invocation of a tightly interlocked weave of inferences.

Entertainment versus facts

At the viewer's point of entry, where storyline and character development register, the patients' sicknesses are signified. Since the first focus of the show *must* be to entertain (inevitable with a series that needs to satisfy Fox's ambitions to maximize ratings), events such as swift plunges into the body or fracturing relationships between the team of doctors are a convenient starting point from which to engage with crisis for patients, doctors and viewers.

Understandably, the diagnosis and treatment of patients at the fictional Princeton-Plainsboro Teaching Hospital (PPTH) is the somewhat obsessive focus of actual medics. On the website *Polite Dissent*, run by a family practitioner with the pseudonym 'Scott', much commentary dwells on the fictional team's accuracy in diagnoses and treatments. While on balance the series is quite well regarded for its drama, debates over the fictional doctors' practices go to and fro, sometimes for years.[1]

An early case arose when 'Scott' complained of the *Pilot* (1: 1) that the hospital seemed to have no technicians and, implausibly, the doctors have to run their own lab tests ('Scott', 2004a). He returned to the theme after episodes *Maternity* (1: 4) (2004b), *Fidelity* (1: 7) (2004c) and *Histories* (1: 10) (2005), and was by no means alone among those blogging. The contrary view was eventually expressed by 'Sara' (2007), who argued that the lab scenes are too important dramatically for bit-part players to take the technicians' roles: they provide the young doctors with an opportunity to debate their diagnoses and complain about their boss. Not drawn to arguments about dramatic necessity, however, 'Scott' revisited the fictional violation of medical practice three years after introducing the topic, citing regulations with confidence:

> There are strict Federal guidelines (CLIO) over who can run which tests, and the doctors wouldn't be qualified to run the tests, and the hospital labs could lose their credentials for letting them.
>
> ('Scott', 2008)

Although they are obsessed with creating intricate case histories for the patients that will be hard for House's team to diagnose, concern with medical accuracy has, however, never held more than a peripheral appeal for the show's producers. Indeed that appeal diminished as the seasons passed. Executive producer David Shore (who came up with the initial idea) recalled that originally the show did not focus on people:

> The series was sold to Fox without the House character as part of the initial sales pitch. The show was sold as a crime/police procedural, but instead of bad guys, the germs were the suspects.
>
> (in Frum, 2006)

Shore soon realised that this would become dull after a few episodes because, as he put it, germs don't have motives like humans – they just do what they do. He concluded that it would benefit the show if he left the medical puzzles to specialist writers while devoting his attention as a lay scriptwriter to character development and byplay:

> I am interested in the story turns that aren't really medically motivated. I am more interested when House does something outrageous – and everyone knows it's outrageous – than just discussing medicine in a way that only a doctor would find interesting.
>
> (in Frum, 2006)

The tension between character-based dramatic situations and mysteries generated by life-threatening conditions that challenge understanding contributes to the *noir* flavor of the series and hints that much lies hidden beneath the surface.

Whenever House thinks it might help trace the source of an infection, he dispatches members of his team to break into patients' abodes. In actuality hospital doctors never enter, let alone invade, patients' homes, a factor that caused one contributor to *Polite Dissent* to refer with irony to such an incident in *Histories* (1: 10):

> What I found interesting about this one is how the medical team that specialized in breaking into houses handled a homeless case: They found her tarp-covered box in an alleyway and poked through it, and then they found her former address and broke into that.
>
> ('Saint Nate', 2005)

Breaking in may violate medical practice but it adds dramatic tension (and reveals the divergent physical conditions of the hospital's New Jersey patients in the supposedly classless society of the USA). It is also a device that reveals how the series' seeming naturalism has a role in luring spectators and giving them the illusion of being in a 'real' world. But the main function of such incidents, like so many others in *House*, is to add entertaining suspense, as in playful *noir*. Are the doctors acting unlawfully? Will they be caught in the act? Are they in danger?

The fictional and fantasy elements incite us to pursue links into spheres of inquiry deeper than the show's enjoyable entertainment. The desire to find out something of which we are kept ignorant is a primary motivator in dramatic entertainment and (given the unpredictable outcome of the team's interim diagnoses) a constant structuring device in *House*.

The hospital micro-world

Scripts ingeniously juxtapose the micro-realm of the hospital with the larger world beyond. It's not just that there is inevitable interaction between doctors and patients. There are episodes in which the predicaments of a bed patient and another in the walk-in clinic each provide complementary angles on the other's problems. In addition, although they manifest differently, similar issues may face members of House's team. At first, because we are more puzzled than House's diagnostic team by incoming patients' conditions, lay viewers see the latter from an objective, rather than the subjectively engaged point of view with which we view the doctors. Because the personal histories of the team develop over many episodes, we tend to feel involved with them.

Fidelity (1: 7) provides a fine example. The hospital admits Elise, unable to get out of bed for several days, who seems to exhibit symptoms of depression. However, after extensive testing, during which time she almost dies, her illness turns out to be trypanosomiasis – African sleeping sickness. Since Elise has never travelled to Africa, the eventual diagnosis reveals that there must be an undisclosed personal issue within her marriage. House believes that her husband has had an affair and communicated the disease to her, but he denies it resolutely.

Meanwhile, a kindergarten teacher attends the walk-in clinic complaining of breathlessness: Mrs Campbell has had her breasts spectacularly augmented as a gift to her spouse, but tests have revealed no problems with the implants. Apprised of this, House does a Sherlock Holmes, deducing that her husband has high blood pressure and is secretly mixing his medication into her food in order to reduce her sex drive. As the suggestion that she should take a lover comes to his lips, House finds a tangential insight gripping his mind. He associates the idea of a lover with his other patient, Elise. When he confronts her with his realization that she must have had the affair, she has to admit the truth to save her lover from dying, and that destroys her marriage.

So much for the patients in this episode, but within the hospital's microsociety, House taunts his friend Dr Wilson for sporting an uncharacteristically smart outfit, charging him with trying to seduce a nurse. Although Wilson denies it, his infidelities to his wife are an open secret between the two men, so doubt hangs in the air. Meanwhile, the back history of junior doctor Allison Cameron has been emerging over a number of episodes with House trying to deter her from what he regards as a professionally unsafe tendency to become emotionally empathic with her patients. Under his probing, Cameron admits to having formerly been married to a man who contracted cancer. House calculates that she must have known it was terminal when she married him. In a later episode she will confess to having been attracted to a friend while her husband was dying – but not giving way to temptation. Thus this one episode contains all or segments of no less than four stories about married love, each placed to reflect varying lights on the others.

The centre ground of these interlocking stories is, as ever, for good as well as dubious ends, the eponymous hero. We move with him into the next sphere of our inquiry.

Dr Gregory House

House's colleagues rightly accuse him of being rude, defended and lonely. None of them misses his intellectual brilliance; but his energy is no less compelling. From the first, he perceives life through a darkened but sharply focused lens, a high-definition vision that colors the show's universe. His mantra is, 'Everybody lies!' Sure enough, events often prove him correct.

Thanks to sharp writing, repartee provides one of the show's dependable pleasures and House's mindset is initially accessed via a sardonic wit so perfectly targeted that a Metaphysical poet would enjoy its diamond edge. Endowed with a brilliant mind embellished by encyclopedic knowledge of the body and its ailments, he is formidably equipped as a diagnostician, relishing challenges from anyone bold enough to counter his opinions. Indeed, such is his delight in the thrust and parry of debate that he often turns on individuals who have agreed with him and unwisely let their guards drop. Having built near impenetrable defenses against his own chronic physical and mental pains, he ridicules, in order to toughen, those colleagues who lack equally strong barriers.

Like everyone else in his world he lies (sometimes drawing attention to it). So although he argues that he wants to keep his distance the better to diagnose people without being distracted by their deceptions and emotional entanglements, when the suffering of a patient does move him, his face reveals his failure to hide pain behind the mask of a rational man. This occurs, for example, when in *Autopsy* (2: 2) he is touched by the bravery of a nine-year-old cancer victim who insists on painfully extending her life because her mother needs her.

Fleeting glimpses of patients' bodily malfunctions complement (the instant before he denies them) occasional insights into House's psyche. Notwithstanding his emotions and plenty of evidence that contradicts him, he derides as New Age vacuity claims that the mind might have powers independent of the brain's rational or mechanical functions. For House, the unconscious does not exist, a resistance so monomaniacal that thoughts of repression inevitably loom.

House is best reckoned as a delicious monster, dedicated to accurately diagnosing his patients yet willing to inflict aggressive injury in doing so. His conflicted personality is high-wired across the juxtaposition of extreme oppositions that his character often generates: black comedy switches to pathos; humor fights despair; romance, cynicism and betrayal swirl around him. Nor can caustic wit conceal the disjunction between his Holmesian, rapier-sharp powers of deduction and (at its worst when driven by doubt and addiction) occasional dogmatic insistence on diagnoses that are wrong.

House's passion for his vocation has a quasi-mystical origin. In *Son Of A Coma Guy* (3: 7), Gabriel, a coma patient whom he has recalled from the sleeping dead, asks him why, when he obviously hates people, he chose to become a doctor instead of going into research. Forced to speak honestly by the other's refusal to accept smartass backchat, House recalls being in Japan when he was fourteen and taking a friend to hospital after an accident. His friend caught an infection and the medics did not know how to treat it. So they brought in the janitor, a Buraku (one of Japan's untouchables) for whom the medical staff had no time except when they needed him. Nor did this man bother to ingratiate himself with the doctors. However, when the latter could not resolve a case, they summoned the janitor because his medical opinion was always right. Through this man's example House had found his calling; he also adopted the stance of an outcast although, unlike the Buraku, not one by birth.

Though yearning for love and human warmth, House has become an outsider to defend himself against physical and emotional hurt. Pain makes it easier to snarl at people than to treat them tenderly. As the series develops, evidence of his past accrues. He is not the unchanging rock he pretends, but has been altered by suffering. *Three Stories* (1: 21) and *Honeymoon* (1: 22) reveal this when Stacy, the only woman he once loved, asks his help on behalf of her husband. Mark's changed behavior tells her that he is sick, but other doctors have failed to diagnose him. House, still anguished that she left him and married the other man, refuses, confessing to Wilson that that part of him wants Mark to die – so that either he can be with Stacy again or she should suffer.

Immediately after Stacy's visit, House lectures on diagnostics, and sets the students a test. Three people present with leg pains. One will be near to death in two hours and one will be discharged for faking. They have to diagnose which is which. The filmmakers and House develop his *Three Stories* (1: 21) in a scintillating play with mock scenarios which shimmer with ever changing dimensions, puzzling both his students and the viewers. House deploys the same Socratic Method that he uses with his team, searching for the right diagnosis by examining wrong ones while deploying logical deduction and lateral thinking. Characters in the three stories switch roles illogically to fit the students' mistaken hypotheses – a male victim becomes female; students in the lecture theater disappear and reappear; and the more courageous among them advance wrong diagnoses that cause the death of one or other imaginary patient. As the plots thicken, House's colleagues join an increasingly rapt audience in the lecture hall, the mood intensifying as it becomes apparent that House himself is the subject of the final investigation, the patient whose leg pains brought him close to death.

In flashback we discover that House suffered a blood clot which was not diagnosed for four days. The consequent cell death in his muscles made amputation the only safe option, but House, in excruciating pain, refused to allow it although Stacy (then his devoted partner) tried to persuade him otherwise. But when House sought release from the terrible pain in a morphine-induced coma, she exercised her powers as his medical proxy to authorize the removal of dead tissue. Then, as he summarizes for the students, because of the extent of the muscle removed, the use of his leg was severely compromised and he continues to experience chronic pain. He forbears to mention that he and Stacy subsequently separated, but his colleagues know that chronic physical and emotional pain have ever since cut him deep. His addiction to Vicodin painkillers enables him to cope with physical pain; and he blanks what must be a vivid inner life as part of his defense against emotional suffering, allowing only his love of music, the most abstract of arts, to pierce his inner being.

Given House's vocation and the evidence of his physical and psycho-logical injuries, it is impossible to miss that he is a wounded healer. But how well does he fit the archetypal figure modeled on the doctor of Ancient Greek mythology, Asklepios? This offspring of the sun god Apollo and the mortal Coronis was an outsider from birth (like the Buraku). Snatched from the womb when his mother was put to death for infidelity to Apollo, Asklepios's liminal position was doubled by his having been educated in medicine by the centaur Chiron, half-man, half-horse. Thus his genealogy centered him midway between the spiritual and animal elements of the human condition.

Although House's behavior and isolation define him as an outsider, there are obvious differences between the Asklepian tradition and House's practice. The former was concerned for the well-being of the whole person, seeing the injuries of body and mind as interdependent so that effecting a cure demanded simultaneous attention to both (Hillman, 1988: 121–2). House is notoriously reluctant even to see his patients. Because of his own past suffering, Asklepios responded empathically to his patients' psycho-logical needs, but House battles against any such intimacy. When one of his team argues in the *Pilot* (1: 1) that they came into medicine to treat patients, House snaps back: 'Treating *illnesses* is why we became doctors. Treating patients is what makes most physicians miserable.'

It is not that he lacks intuition. The stolidly grounded 'Scott' admitted that he had problems with the way House arrived at his conclusions in the *Pilot*. In the passage Luke Hockley cited in Chapter 1, 'Scott' made this plain: 'There seemed to be no logic behind his deductions, he just seized on some minuscule fact and used it to concoct some untenable theory. That he turned out to be right in the end seemed more luck than skill' (2004a). But 'John' called him on this, arguing that some brilliant people reach insights by a quantum leap when they are doing something seemingly unrelated that takes their minds off the subject entirely: 'House does this many times in the upcoming series and it [is] part of the brilliance of his character' (2007).

John Beebe has noted that there is frequently a tension between those who combine intuition with thinking and those who combine it with feeling.

> It has to do with the way rigor is routinely expected by the one with thinking and not attended to nearly so meticulously by the intuitive who combines with feeling. The one with thinking doesn't make the same intuitive leaps, because for him or her the steps have to all be established, as in geometry proofs . . . And it can shock the intuitive thinker as to what the intuitive feeler is willing to assert without proof.
>
> (Beebe, 2009)

Beebe argues that intuitive thinking can seem tedious and limiting to the intuitive feeler who has a powerful need to get a novel weighting of key ideas across and feels a need to put their worth ahead of logic in so doing (ibid.). House leaps to diagnostic conclusions employing the swift mental processes of an intuitive feeler.

Because his diagnoses are often extraordinarily astute, House's powerful intuition can seem magical. Taken in the context of his self-appointed status as an outcast and his erratic behavior, it hints at shamanic inflation. Shamans often make a mental journey into a patient's body to confront the spirit that is making the individual sick. House does not confront the spirit, but he does visualize the imagined symptoms within patients' bodies – and of course we take those swift journeys (comparable to the shaman's out-of-body experiences) with him.

As Dean Edwards notes, shamans may use drugs to help free the mind to roam beyond the bounds of consciousness (1995: 2). House's increasing consumption of Vicodin causes him to behave so erratically that it becomes the ostensible focus of a hostile police investigation and court case (episodes 3: 5 to 3: 11). In common with some shamans, he manifests unpredictable behavior: sudden, unexpected moves (both physical and tactical), mocking humor, and a disposition to alternate between threats and gentleness, and unremitting rudeness that is painful for those who are its object. Nor are his assaults exclusively psychological. For example, in *Meaning* (3: 1), he terrifies a patient before stabbing her with a syringe. The procedure saves her life but is needlessly brutal.

House's ungoverned behavior is never more evident than when, under the relentless pressure of the police investigation and crazed by his colleagues' refusal to let him have painkillers, he makes a wrong diagnosis in a particularly difficult case. It is no small matter because he sends his patient for an immediate double amputation. When Chase makes the correct diagnosis, and tries to prevent House performing unnecessary surgery, his boss punches him for intervening (*Finding Judas*, 3: 9).[2]

Shamanism is focused on the transpersonal movement of the shaman's consciousness into higher or lower realms of consciousness and existence (Edwards, 1995: 7). When House visits the dark realms of disease in his imagination, it seems that he journeys not unlike the shaman into the lower world. There he exposes himself to the risk of spiritual contamination to which, in refusing to accept that psyche has an independent existence, he lays himself open. This is ironic because, just as shamans balance knowledge of the lower with experience of the upper world via ecstatic trances which extend rather than eradicate consciousness, House's ecstasy in listening to and playing music seems to gain him entry into the higher world, negating his assertion that emotion is pointless.

Since the core shamanic function is to make a bridge between the worlds (Edwards, 1995: 4), the notion of secular shamanism is by definition unsustainable. House is stuck. He cannot dwell in an exclusively rational world, as his pain-ridden, unstable thrashing around shows. The alternative would be to recognize the psyche's powers, but that, too, he refuses. Nowhere is his enduring predicament clearer than in *Top Secret* (3: 16) when, asleep in his office, he dreams he is a Marine who loses a leg during combat in Iraq. Cuddy awakens him with the file of Sergeant John Kelley, a Gulf War veteran whom she has just admitted to hospital. In the dream, this very soldier has just saved House's life. Badly shocked, House (insistent rationalist to the last) devotes far less energy to the Marine's case than to proving that he himself had not dreamt a premonition. His alarm reaches such levels that he sends his team out under the pretence of researching Kelley's medical history but actually to relieve his intense anxiety by proving he has seen the soldier before. When it eventually comes, that 'proof' is that they must have been in the same room for ten minutes two years previously – on the occasion when Kelley had a one-off date with Cuddy. This satisfies House's panicky need for a rational explanation by demonstrating his supposed residual jealousy – as if jealousy lives with a rational state of mind. However, the 'proof' does not account for the nightmare's drama, intensity and timing. The Marine, having saved House in his sleep, needs life-saving help from him, but the fearful doctor fails to act with the soldier's heroism, facing neither the other man's nor his own needs.

Despite House's insistence that the unconscious does not exist, in the course of four seasons, he lives through several incidents that urge the contrary. In *Three Stories* (1: 21) he reported near-death visions but, asked whether he thought they were real, replied that he believed they were 'just chemical reactions that take place while the brain shuts down.' In *No*

Reason (2: 24) almost the entire episode consists in House's hallucinations after a would-be assassin shoots him. And in the linked episodes that conclude the fourth season, *House's Head* and *Wilson's Heart* (4: 15, 4: 16), the story is narrated in large part through House's mind. The plot, concerning the two friends and the crash that kills the woman both love, is recovered through hypnosis, overdoses of medical drugs, dreams, surgical probing and a coma as House desperately scans his subconscious to find out how Amber disappeared while in his company. She and the other crash victims resolve the mystery by presenting themselves to House in fantasy.

As a delicious monster, House is both beguiling and rebarbative. A diagnostic genius (as befits the heir to Sherlock Holmes) he shows himself to be a cantankerous dogmatist when mistaken. Simultaneously deeply cynical and secretly tender, he has the soul of an angel when given wings by music, yet, a self-denying outsider who manages only erratically to cope with the demands of friendship and love, wards off disappointment in human relationships. He is almost, but not quite the wounded healer, almost, but not quite the shaman. In sum, he is a typically mosaic incarnation of the trickster, who, Jung says, shares some of the characteristics of the medicine man (1956: para. 457). As such House flickers with the light of powerful archetypal borrowings that he never fully or enduringly inhabits while he bewilders everyone (possibly including himself) with his coruscating presence. His character holds a fascination which, as realized in Hugh Laurie's performance, has endured through the show's five seasons. A conundrum that viewers no less than the characters try to solve, House is animated by one of the trickster's archetypal functions: he teaches by confronting people with the shadow. As Terrie Waddell puts it,

> The ability to 'trip up' the psyche through wily behaviors, unconscious slips, lapses, moral ambiguity, or foolery enables trickster to alter perceptions and consequently initiate personal and collective change.
>
> (2006: 29)

House and his team

Writing 'A Review of the Complex Theory', Jung noted the paradox that, while in commonplace parlance people refer to having complexes, in a more important sense complexes can have us. This hypothesis, he added, threw serious doubt on the assumption that individuals have unity of consciousness and supremacy of will since at times the complex has greater energy than our conscious intentions. He said 'a "feeling-toned complex" . . . is the *image* of a certain psychic situation which is strongly accentuated emotionally and is, moreover, incompatible with the habitual attitude of consciousness' (1948: para. 201). A characteristic of complexes is that they may constellate, or bring into association, a number of fragments each of which possess a high degree of autonomy – rather as if the bearer of the complex had more than one mindset. 'These fragments subsist relatively independently of each other and can take one another's place at any time . . .' (ibid.: para. 202).

Jung's description invites the comparison of House's team to a constellation of autonomous fragments or sub-personalities who amplify elements of their leader's psyche. This is a viable proposition because the trickster can be seen as a leaky holding vessel, a form of the shadow that has a tendency to split. Trickster's sub-personalities do indeed fly apart, as when he takes off a bit of his body that may take on a semi-independent existence (see Jung, 1956: para. 472). This is analogous to the way House's team members break away from him at the end of Season 3.

In that season, House, as ever caustically urging his team to be more inventive in differential diagnoses, vindicates his trickster behavior thus: 'How are you going to learn to swim unless I take off your floaties and throw you into shark-infested waters?' (*Whac-A-Mole*, 3: 8). Albeit not a full account of his motivations (he enjoys bullying too), helping his junior colleagues gain medical knowledge and deeper insights into themselves should make them better doctors. It is his justification for treating them abrasively: the trickster as teacher. His quasi-parental impact shows when they start mirroring him. Later, not unlike growing teenagers, they contest his dominance.

Each junior takes on a different aspect of House's personality. Dr Robert Chase begins as a *puer*, the adult who has not grown out of boyhood. In this he echoes House's disastrous relationship with his own father, whom the world-famous physician believes he has disappointed (*Daddy's Boy*, 2: 5). Through the first two seasons Chase responds to the logos facet of House's personality. More a follower than a leader, he finds it hard to refuse even when House asks him to do something unethical ('Awi', 2006a). Paradoxically his dependency is underlined when Vogler, a wealthy businessman, takes over the hospital and sets about cost cutting – a program that House does his best to sabotage. Afraid for his job, Chase rats out House to Vogler in *Role Model* (1: 17). In effect he merely switches his affiliation temporarily to the more powerful man. That a recurrent pattern is in play becomes clear when Chase's father, a renowned auto-immunologist, arrives unannounced at the hospital (*Cursed*, 1: 13). The son has not forgiven his father for abandoning him aged fifteen to care for an alcoholic mother. Challenged by House, Chase lies that he doesn't hate his father, but (mirroring House's coping mechanism) just ignores his existence to suffer no more disappointments. Although they achieve a wary reconciliation at the visit's end, the old man conceals that he has cancer and dies a few weeks later never having shared that truth with Chase.

House has become a surrogate father, a distinguished medic replacing the other, always absent one. Despite his many failings, House does not abandon the young doctor, making a powerful, sometimes shocking impact on him. After Chase resists his boss's crazy order to perform a double amputation and House fells him, Chase whinges to Wilson, 'I got it right. And I told him. And it didn't matter' (*Finding Judas*, 3: 9). He stages a walk out but comes back without mentioning House's behaviour – confirmation of his *puer* nature.

It shows again when he accepts Cameron's proposal that they share uncomplicated sex until either of them falls in love with someone else (*Insensitive*, 3: 14). Yet notwithstanding his readiness to be led, he matures. He never betrays House again after the Vogler incident although the cop Tritter threatens to destroy Chase's career unless he testifies to House's drug abuse (*Finding Judas*, 3: 9). And as the relationship with Cameron continues, he falls in love with her, finding the courage to tell her and even remind her periodically in case she should develop similar feelings. Nevertheless he remains House's 'son'. When the team believe that House has inoperable brain cancer, Chase hugs him and weeps, sharing closeness his natural father denied him (*Half-Wit*, 3: 15).

Dr Allison Cameron starts her career with House as the soft member of the team. Since House lacks or represses access to the feminine, she seems to some viewers like a perfect fit for him, as the very image of Jung's gentle, submissive *anima*, a woman who is tender-hearted with suffering patients and yearning for House's love. Her history fits that archetypal role: before joining the team, she had compassionately married a man whom she knew was dying of cancer. This tendency to self-sacrifice continues in her new post: when the tyrannical Vogler orders House to fire one of his team, it is she who offers to resign (*Role Model*, 1: 17). Her motives reflect her dominant personality traits of that time: first, to save her colleagues and second, to protect herself because she can deal with her feelings for House in no other way.

As one blogger noted, 'Cameron is a better doctor than people give her credit for, often being the one to solve the problem, but doing so very quietly and being overlooked' ('Awi', 2006a). She lacks support because House scorns her softness in order to toughen her, and her colleagues do not come to her defense. Another blogger mentions that at this point Cameron is an adolescent of sorts, always amazed at the vicious things some patients do ('Advance', 2007).

However, Cameron grows too. Exploited by Foreman when he publishes without due credit her medical findings, she learns anger. She begins to lie like everyone else in the team, though not as successfully. More importantly, by Season 3 she has learned how to say no, refusing to give way to House when she knows she is right (*Meaning*, 3: 1). She also begins to ask for what she wants. As we saw, she coolly propositions Chase for sex (he being, she says, the last person she would fall in love with) (*Insensitive*, 3: 14), but this suggests her emotions are not fully matured. The point is accentuated when the team suspect House is dying. Chase is not the only one to kiss him. In a scene of passion *and* calculation, Cameron does so fervently, House responding before pulling from her housecoat the needle with which she meant to draw blood for testing. 'A little whorish,' he says, 'to kiss and stab!' Some weeks later Chase tells Cameron that he feels love for her. But she doesn't want that: 'It was fun – that's it. And now it's over' (*Airborne*, 3: 18).

Although Cameron once modeled the sweet anima, the *puella*, still a virgin in spirit, drawn Persephone-like into the underworld by her husband's dying, she is no longer that type. Nor would seeing her as Jung's anima-figure in its reversed, potentially destructive infamy be other than a travesty. Rather, her character represents the development of a young professional woman experiencing evolving archetypal energies. If formerly ruled by her Persephone nature, her premeditated seduction of Chase marks the arousal of her inner hunter, Artemis (see Bolen, 1985: 46–74, 197–223). She has by the start of Season 4 fulfilled three of the four tasks that Jean Shinoda Bolen ascribes to the myth of Psyche, learning (i) to sift what truly matters from the insignificant; (ii) to gain and use power without losing compassion; and (iii) to say no when necessary. Yet she longs for the relationship (that she cannot find with Chase) to summon her inner Aphrodite and complete her engagement with life (ibid.: 258–62).

The team's neurologist Dr Eric Foreman is not cast in the role of archetypal black shadow despite House's fondness for drawing attention with deliberate political incorrectness to his African-American race and juvenile criminal record. Rather, as the episodes pass we find a dangerously ambivalent feature of Foreman's personality growing more dominant. It derives from House: the doctor as all-powerful hero and omniscient demi-god ('Awi', 2006b). When Hermes the trickster rules House, his ungoverned 'heroism' urges him to act preposterously: for example, after diagnosing a patient with a tapeworm, he takes on the role of surgeon, opens her belly and extracts it (*Insensitive*, 3: 14). Foreman, however, appears not to have registered that House is a trickster, and as such not a true, dependable hero.

Foreman's governing deity was never Hermes but Hephaestus (the Roman Vulcan), evident in his resolute dedication to his craft (see Bolen, 1990: 219–50).

> A Hephaestus man is an intense, introverted person. It's difficult for others to know what is going on in his depths or for him to express his feelings directly. He can become an emotional cripple, a smouldering volcano, or a highly creative productive man.
>
> (Bolen, 1990: 228)

Foreman shares these characteristics. Perhaps the painful absence of his mother through her creeping dementia has deprived him of emotional succor.

When he breaks with his girlfriend on Valentine's Day (*Insensitive*, 3: 14), she describes him sadly as preferring a rational discussion to sharing emotions. He can be brutally self-interested, publishing without acknowledgement a paper based on Cameron's work, a betrayal he refuses to acknowledge for a long time. His focus, as an inventive medic whose life outside the hospital matters comparatively little to him, is always on his work.

Of all the juniors, Foreman makes the most decisive break from House, emphasizing that he does not want to turn into his former boss. However, his mentor's influence has tainted him: in his new post he defies hospital regulations while treating a patient, believing he knows best. As a result he loses the job and no hospital other than PPTH will employ him. In mythological terms, he has failed to become an Oedipal hero by slaying the dragon parent. So he finds himself trapped with his House whom he has failed to break free from (*97 Seconds*, 4: 3; *Guardian Angels*, 4: 4).

Although House's diagnostic team falls apart at the end of Season 3, Cameron and Chase do not try to leave PPTH but self-assuredly take new positions in the hospital. Nevertheless, in Season 4 everything has changed in that all three former juniors now have minimal commitment to House. Chase and Cameron have grown into their own orbits; Foreman's failure to break away leaves him resentful of his former boss and psychologically stuck.

House now sets about constructing a new team of doctors from forty hirelings in a knock-out process that hilariously parodies *The Apprentice* and displays his familiar erratic and autocratic mannerisms, intensified by messianic zeal. As one fan blogged, 'his teams are not based on who the best "diagnosticians" are, but which personalities provide the best sounding boards to *his* personality . . . House needs to hire people who complement his quirks' ('McDee', 2007). To judge from these developments, he is repeating his earlier behavior with the first team but ever more compulsively.

Jung noted in his work on the psychology of the trickster figure that 'the "making of a medicine-man" includes, in many parts of the world, so much agony of body and soul that permanent psychic injuries may result' (1956: para. 457). This is true of House. At the heart of our allegory lies the core of this physician's melancholy. Trapped by its relentless insistence on performance, trickstering denies him the progress toward individuation that two of his protégés have made. As trickster he oscillates endlessly between high peaks and deep troughs, like a shooting star out of control, but the benefit is others', not his. For House, the trickster complex obscures the self.

References

'Advance' (2007), Blog comment (6 April). Retrieved from http://politedissent.com/archives/1604

'Awi' (2006a) Blog comment (6 April). Retrieved from http://politedissent.com/archives/1184

—— (2006b) Blog comment (19 April). Retrieved from http://politedissent.com/archives/1193

Beebe, J. (2009) Contribution to The International Association of Jungian Studies Online Discussion Forum (18 April). Retrieved from iajsdiscussion@iajsdiscussionlist.org

Bolen, J. S. (1985) *Goddesses in Everywoman: A New Psychology of Women*. San Francisco, CA: Harper and Row.

Bolen, J. S. (1990) *Gods in Everyman: A New Psychology of Men's Lives and Loves*. New York, NY: Harper Perennial.

Edwards, D. (1995) *Shamanism General-Overview*. Retrieved from http://deoxy.org/shaover.htm

Frum, L. (2006) Q&A with 'House' creator David Shore. *Macleans* (14 March). Retrieved from http://www.macleans.ca/culture/entertainment/article.jsp?content=20060320_123370_123370

Hillman, J. (1988) *Suicide and the Soul*. Dallas, TX: Spring Publications.

'John' (2007) Blog comment (12 October). Retrieved from http://politedissent.com/archives/388

Jung, C. G. (1948) A Review of the Complex Theory. In *The Structure and Dynamics of the Psyche, Collected Works 8*. London: Routledge & Kegan Paul.

—— (1956) On the Psychology of the Trickster Figure. In *The Archetypes and the Collective Unconscious, Collected Works 9*. London: Routledge & Kegan Paul.

'McDee' (2007) Blog comment (24 October). Retrieved from http://www.polite-dissent.com/archives/1783#comment-189942

'Saint Nate' (2005) Blog comment (17 February) Retrieved from http://politedissent.com/archives/560#comment-3203

'Sara' (2007) Blog comment (16 July). Retrieved from http://politedissent.com/archives/469

'Scott' (2004a) *House MD*, Episode 1 'Pilot', *Polite Dissent* (19 November). Retrieved from http://politedissent.com/archives/388

—— (2004b) *House MD*, Episode 4 'Maternity', *Polite Dissent* (7 December). Retrieved from http://politedissent.com/archives/426

—— (2004c) *House MD*, Episode 7 'Fidelity', *Polite Dissent* (28 December). Retrieved from http://politedissent.com/archives/488

—— (2005) *House MD*, Episode 10 'Histories', *Polite Dissent* (8 February). Retrieved from http://politedissent.com/archives/560

—— (2008) Blog comment (4 January). Retrieved from http://politedissent.com/archives/396

Waddell, T. (2006) *Mis/takes: Archetype, Myth and Identity in Screen Fiction*. London: Routledge.

Notes

1 Occasionally patients who have suffered from a condition featured in an episode contribute to the *Polite Dissent* website with their opinions, drawing on their own experiences and understanding of relevant diagnostic methods and treatment.
2 These escapades fall so far outside the pale of behaviour acceptable in a medical practitioner that they remind viewers, since House is not struck off the register for misconduct, that this series' story world is not concerned with social realism.

Chapter 3

Playing House

Convincing them of what you know simply by who you are

Christopher Hauke

This chapter will look at the construction of expert authority and knowledge in the context of the television series *House* where the leading actor brings a backstory to the screen through his personal origins, British national persona and history of previous acting roles. Hugh Laurie's portrayal of Dr Greg House benefits from the authority that derives from these factors. Theoretical authority and practical authority are compared and, while the character of Greg House is written as if he were a maverick, it is concluded that the casting of Laurie reinforces an unexamined validation of (and a conservative trust in) expert authority, in general, and its 'right' to disobey protocol and convention especially in the field of medicine.

Casting: "You either are that guy or you aren't"

> Casting is destiny, particularly in movies, because casting *is* character – and character is plot. Casting really controls story. One guy would do a thing, another guy wouldn't. And if you're the guy in the close-up, character acting isn't going to help – you either are that guy, or you aren't.
>
> (Warren Beatty, quoted in Harris, 2008: 188–189)

When Bryan Singer, executive producer of *House MD* viewed Hugh Laurie's audition tape for the part of Dr Greg House, he commented, "Now *this* is the sort of strong American actor I'm looking for!" (Challen, 2007: 39). The writer and creator of *House*, David Shore, was a fan of Laurie's TV comedy work – upper-class English twits like Lieutenant George and the Prince Regent in *Blackadder* and Wodehouse's Bertie Wooster – "But", he says, "I honest-to-God never thought he'd be right for this role" (ibid.). And, knowing Laurie mainly from twenty years of British comedy shows, it took me quite a few episodes of *House* to get over the expectation that, any minute, Greg House would pull one of Lt George's faces with an "I say! D'you really think so Blackadder?"

By asking how Hugh Laurie got the part of Greg House and made it so hugely successful, this chapter will be exploring the effects of such unpredictable casting on the role and character of Dr Greg House and the TV series as a whole. As we unpack all the elements I will show how the themes of authority, expert authority (especially in medicine) and anti-authority are particularly well carried by the actor Hugh Laurie. This is partly due to his being British and upper-middle-class – a strange thing to say when this aspect is completely obscured Laurie's New Jersey-accented Dr House. I will also show how Laurie's biographical background, personality traits and previous roles offer clues to his casting and a route into the character of Dr Greg House. The unobvious and unpredictable in casting Laurie as House has lead indirectly to the show's greater success. This does not contradict Warren Beatty's (and much of Hollywood's) view of casting as character, but suggests how a more obvious, conventional choice of actor may have approached the House character more directly and consequently ended up way off target.

Radical casting is not something that the studios and networks are good at imagining. David Shore reports that selling the casting of Hugh Laurie (who was then forty-five) to the suits at Fox network was a challenge. Laurie had just been playing a middle-aged dad in *Fortysomething* on UK TV and the executives had to be persuaded along the lines of the depth and experience Laurie would bring to the role. Because he was certainly not what Fox might have had in mind for a male lead in "the increasingly youthful world of primetime show casting in the US" (Challen, 2007: 40). This was Hugh Laurie's assumption too; he reports that when he was sent the lines to record an audition tape for the part of Dr House he believed this curmudgeonly character was a supporting role not the lead, and merely for a pilot show at that.

The circumstances of this audition tape, the first sighting that Singer and Shore would have of Laurie "as" House are fascinating in hindsight. Laurie was on location in Namibia shooting a small part in the movie *The Flight of the Phoenix* (2004). At the end of a long location day and thinking of his next possible acting job, Laurie got a colleague to film him reciting the script excerpts by the light of a shaving mirror in a Namibian bathroom. With no conscious intention to offer ideas for House's "look", the few-days stubble Laurie needed for his movie character had to be retained, and he wore the character's costume as well – a dusty leather jacket (both of which he apologizes for on the tape). However, Laurie says he saw something in the role of Dr House that was special for him, "He was all there in those pages they faxed me, I could hear him in my head – the rhythm of his speech. What he was hiding behind the meanness and sarcasm. I could see him very clearly in my head from the start" (Challen, 2007: 38). It seems that Hugh Laurie knew he could be convincing as Greg House, while Singer and Shore intuited he could surpass all their expectations. Where might such convictions have come from?

Before *House*, Hugh Laurie had three excursions onto the US screen: as Jasper the henchman to Cruella De Vil (Glenn Close) in the rather poor 1996 remake of the animation *101 Dalmations*; as Vincente Minelli (father of Liza) in a 2001 TV biopic *Life with Judy Garland: Me and My Shadows*, which gave Laurie more of a chance; and in *Stuart Little* (1999) and *Stuart Little 2* (2002). It is in these last two, where he plays Frederick Little, head of a fairly affluent New York family consisting of his wife and their two young sons, one human and one who is a mouse (no mention is made of adoption). In this part we see for the first time how convincing Laurie is as an American with his East Coast accent. The upper-class Brit twang of Bertie Wooster and Lt George are nowhere to be found. What does remain, however, is the look of goggle-eyed surprise and the exaggerated down-turned gurning of the mouth and rapid shakes of the head in bafflement at the world as Mr Little sometimes finds it. Put these together with a bright and bushy disposition and smart, colorful costumes and Dr Greg House is as far away as Alaska. Or so you would think. An attentive viewing of *Stuart Little* shows some character traits that, together with the voice coaching, offer a bridge across the Atlantic to Laurie's eventual casting as Dr House. For example, as father of the Little household, Mr Little has authority. His sons and his wife, sometimes after a good-natured struggle, ultimately end up respecting the father's word. He is the Father of the house who will bring the authoritative "father" to the role of House. He also has a degree of the same skepticism and irony when talking to the family. When his wife is worried that Stuart the mouse-son might be trod underfoot on the soccer field by other boys who do not notice him, Fred Little pipes up cheerily with reassuring remarks suggesting boys have to find their own way through the rough and tumble for their growing-up. On one level his response is absurd (it ignores the fact that Stuart is a tiny mouse) but Laurie's delivery is all the more ironic because we know that he *knows* Stuart is a tiny mouse – and he *still* asserts his homilies. Essentially, much like House, Laurie delivers the line with authority, giving his wife no option but to agree.

Fred Little's wife plays the role of the sidekick in *Stuart Little* – a structurally similar role to Dr Wilson, the oncologist and House's "only friend" and sidekick in *House*. All of Laurie's major roles have seen him participating as one of a dynamically opposed pair – Jeeves and Wooster, Blackadder and George, Fry and Laurie. Each time Laurie has been coupled with another, it has produced a foil for the character of each. Out of such a syzygy has emerged sets of twinned qualities such as humanity and cynicism, arrogance and heart, stupidity and brilliance. The sidekick makes it easier for these qualities and conflicts to emerge without additional characters and complexity. While he still played Brits (the pre-American-accent years) Laurie was the sidekick. He was the fool to Blackadder's brilliance, the bumbling Bertie to Jeeves's insights. The sidekick, as one writer puts it, appears, "where a secondary character is entrusted with the job of reflecting the spotlight back onto the star – in the solar system of celebrity, the sidekick is the moon" (Millman, in Wilson, 2007: 186).

In writing the characters of Butch Cassidy (Paul Newman) and the Sundance Kid (Robert Redford), William Goldman managed to split certain character traits across two individuals and had them played out in that way. But pairs like Butch and Sundance are equally charismatic and so neither (or both) is the sidekick. This in contrast to *bona fide* functioning sidekicks – as is Robin to Batman – who are always in the shadow of the More Charismatic Friend (ibid.: 185). The sidekick in *House* functions to reinforce Greg House's authority. When it comes to playing Greg House, Laurie is no longer the Smithers to anyone's Mr Burns. He is now the main man and has his own sidekick in Wilson. Typical of the sidekick, Wilson takes an inordinate interest in House's love-life, his challenges to authority, his pill-popping and his diagnostic decisions. Sometimes Wilson acts as a Greek chorus, commenting on the actions of his hero. One writer – upon noticing Wilson seems to "appear" in the same place as House while others ignore him as if he were not there – reckons he is a figment of House's own psyche: Wilson as House's imaginary friend (Sinor, in Wilson, 2007). Sometimes Wilson defines and underlines House's character and actions by acting as an obstacle. When House refuses to employ another team of colleagues in Series Four, Wilson kidnaps House's beloved vintage Gibson Flying V (a guitar costing $12,000) to force him to begin interviewing.

The British, class and comedy

Tracking the role of the sidekick as a route to puzzling out Laurie's success as House reminds us how, in previous roles in Britain, Laurie himself has been the sidekick. Even as the upper-class Bertie Wooster he is sidekick to his manservant Jeeves (Stephen Fry) – it is Jeeves who knows stuff and Bertie who needs him to work things out (like when he makes the "mistake" of getting married to two women). So, in *House*, Laurie has not only switched accent but has also structurally switched his role – from the sidekick to the More Charismatic Friend. In doing so, he not only gains authority – the chance to have the last word – but also inherits qualities from the British comedy shows of his past that are of central importance to playing Greg House in the new show.

One writer reckons of his character, "Often the only factors that save the patient (and thus the hospital) are House's manipulative cunning and his willingness to hijack authority at every level" (Baker, in Wilson, 2007: 212–213). Where have we heard that phrase before – "manipulative cunning and willingness to hijack authority at every level"? This description of Greg House matches exactly that of the character Laurie paired up with for several years – Blackadder, played by Rowan Atkinson. In this and many other examples, what is curious about the roles and characters Laurie was once paired with is the way that he seems to have adopted their traits and subsequently incorporated them in his own roles. A general summary of the character of Dr Greg House would call him blunt, cynical, clever, witty, sarcastic, distrusting (especially of the authority of other medical colleagues and patients), disobedient (especially of the institution of the hospital) and full of his own authority and willingness to assert it. And while Laurie was playing Lt George (in *Blackadder Goes Forth*) and the Prince Regent *(Blackadder 3)* he witnessed Rowan Atkinson portraying Blackadder with these qualities identical to House. Blackadder speaks with total authority to his own sidekick, Lt George, to Captain Darling (the sidekick of Colonel Melchitt), and to his own servant (and quasi sidekick) Baldrick. He is witty and sarcastic to all and very clever. Similar to Greg House, Blackadder applies his brilliance in schemes to avoid work and attempts to get what he wants in the face of a highly resistant institution. For Blackadder this involves schemes to get away from the trenches to Paris or back home; for House it is avoiding Clinic duties or ensuring a good supply of Vicodin tablets. The desire of both characters, although tending toward the illicit, gains legitimacy for Blackadder and House in the context of an irrational situation not of their making – the trench warfare of the First World War for Blackadder, or the pain-ridden leg and cash-conscious hospital bureaucracy for House. Common for both characters is their battle with the *poor leadership and protocols of the organizations they each serve.*

Blackadder and House are also identical in the way they rarely show any empathy for others. But their self-seeking behavior masks a broader aim that calls on higher values which are potentially of benefit to all. As House says: "What would you prefer – a doctor who holds your hand while you die or one who ignores you while you get better?" (*Occam's Razor*, 1: 3).

Blackadder's schemes are all aimed at getting him out of an absurd, unwinnable war and free of its madness and dreadful leadership. Both characters have a serious point for general humanity at the heart of their individual game plan.

Hugh Laurie and Rowan Atkinson – along with Stephen Fry, Emma Thompson and, earlier, John Cleese and the Monty Python team – came from a particular niche in British comedy driven by the acting and writing talent that emerged from the Cambridge University Footlights revues. Peter Cook, Dudley Moore, and Alan Bates were comics and writer/artists of an earlier generation who stayed with a mocking of simple, working-class folk in their characters and sketches as had been common in British TV comedy such as *Steptoe and Son* for years. Cleese and chums, swiftly followed by the Fry–Laurie generation, were upper-middle-class, public school-educated[1] young men who happily targeted "their own". Their mocking of upper-class assumptions of superiority and entitlement, their pillorying of institutions such as the church, the monarchy, the military and government departments were brand new vehicles for comedy in the Britain of the Sixties and Seventies. Fry, Laurie and Atkinson continued this trend into the Eighties and Nineties, eventually delivering, with Richard Curtis as director and writer, the British films *Four Weddings and a Funeral* and *Notting Hill*, which took a sanitized version of Brit-on-Brit mockery across the Atlantic on a genre vehicle of Romantic Comedy.

There was an irony in such a comedic move. Only upper-class comedy actors and writers could attack their own class and its institutions without the laughs being spoiled by the taint of envy or political nuance that would have been unavoidable coming from any artist lower in the social hierarchy. Only these actors, barely out of their public schools (and, yes, Hugh Laurie went to Eton), had the *authority* to make us laugh at the establishment. Because it was their relatives and forebears who *were* the establishment – the ones who really had *authority* to say what goes in government, finance, science and medicine. The authority of Hugh Laurie's Greg House, although acted out in New Jersey, stems from the playing fields of Eton via the University of Cambridge. The wonderful thing is that despite this translation into such a different character, when he is not dazzling us with his brilliance, Laurie still makes us laugh.

Although *House* is not a comedy show, Laurie as House has many funny, witty lines still directed at the establishment. But now the establishment consists of the hospital system, medical knowledge, superstition and religion, and assumptions about what doctors "know" or "should care about" or are able to achieve. These are all fields in which House is a player as well as a commentator. Once again he assumes the authority to be an expert critic of his own field.

Authority

The move from sidekick to main man, the sense that Laurie has brought to his new role powerful character traits from others (roles where he was on the receiving end), and the significance of the British class system, begin to build a picture of *authority* itself – both as a character trait for an actor to use and as a vehicle of dramatic conflict in general.

Expert knowledge and expert authority go hand in hand. They may be derived from rational sources such as a long medical training that makes a medical doctor or consultant the "one who knows" and, therefore, the "one who should be obeyed". In the first episode of Series Four, House is without his team of Cameron, Foreman and Chase and, when faced with the demands of differential diagnosis, he has no one to bounce his ideas off. In a wry undermining of how we identify the "one who knows", House puts a white coat on a male janitor and runs through symptoms and ideas with him. Weirdly, the guy comes back with semi-apt lines that mimic what we have heard from the team in the past – "She's going to get better" (Cameron) and "I wouldn't break into a house for less than $50" (either Foreman or Chase, that one). Later in the series, House – who otherwise spurns such a signifier of medical authority – himself dons a white coat so he can sit in on an interview where Wilson has to tell a patient he does not have cancer after all. As House had predicted, the patient is not relieved but devastated. Being told he had cancer by the doctor was a fact of life to be accepted; knowing he had been told wrong by the expert leaves him more aghast than relieved. Expert knowledge gone wrong is worse than no knowledge at all, it seems.

Using the janitor may be a playful experiment with the idea that simply donning a white coat makes someone an authority, but expert authority has been rooted in even more irrational sources, such as the authority of the aristocracy and (often closely linked) the authority of the officer class in the armed forces. In *Blackadder Goes Forth* Colonel Melchitt (Stephen Fry) is the upper-class fool whose inexpert military decisions Blackadder and Lt George have no option but to obey. Modeled on the reputation of the British General Haig of the period, he is portrayed as the quintessence of an authority which is void of any expertise whatsoever.

In the case of institutional managers such as hospital administrators like Cuddy in *House* authority acts with partial expertise – usually only that derived from the balance sheet, insurance risks and *protocol*. This is where there arises a clash of expert knowledge – where the rationalities of medicine and profit collide. In the very first episode of *House*, Cuddy uses her authority to stop a treatment she judges as unjustified, saying, "It's my hospital." House challenges back with equal validity, "It's my patient" (*Pilot* 1: 1). Both have the authority to do so; both have the expert knowledge too. It's just that they are not the same. Expertise does not necessarily mean agreement. Especially in medical science – or in business, for that matter.

The paradigms of medical knowledge and expertise are derived from specializations. The holders of this range of specialized knowledge are known, in the British system, as "consultant", a title of seniority and expert qualification in their field. In medical training, expert knowledge is delivered to trainee doctors through a series of consultants who train them in teams (or "firms") where that consultant's knowledge, views, preferences and ways of doing things constitutes a paradigm that is *The Word* when it comes to that area of medicine. Then the young medics rotate on to a new consultant and the "facts" have to be learnt anew: the new consultant's "knowledge" has the same authority but with a new paradigm. In medicine itself, expert knowledge is not expert agreement. In medicine there is an assumption of collective knowledge going back to Hippocrates, a sort of collective unconscious which is ready to inform every case and condition. But by the time it meets the real world of a patient (who, according to Dr House, always lies), and symptoms (which also lie), a medical diagnostician, his colleagues and his institutional context, the expert "knowledge" may be fractured into many versions, each with its own claim to part of the truth.

In a way, it is *only the authority of those in charge which validates any knowledge at all*. This knowledge derives from different directions and different foci of attention. What you know depends on what you are looking at and on your priority of interests. Greg House and the whole show express what Nietzsche pointed out in his critique of scientific epistemology, "There is *only* a perspective seeing, *only* a perspective 'knowing'" (Nietzsche, 1887/ 1967, para. 12). There is no true objectivity, just a range of perspectives driven by the viewer's own (affective) interests. In *House* these interests may be governed by emotions generated by the cost of treatments, the patient's word, medical esotericism, what may be seen through a microscope, the interests of the hospital manager (Cuddy) or investor in the medical business (Vogler in Series One), humanist relational medicine (Cameron), the buzz of diagnostic expertise itself (House as Sherlock Holmes) or random information that arises by chance. With such a range of validations, knowledge itself can become neutralized. All that is left is the powerful clash of authoritative voices, as House himself asserts:

> I'm sure this goes against everything you've been taught, but right and wrong do exist. Just because you don't even know what the right answer is, maybe there's even no way you could know what the right answer is, doesn't make your answer right or even okay. It's much simpler than that. It's just plain wrong.
>
> (*Three Stories*, 1: 21)

House *is* the expert. Even when he is wrong, it is right. And so *he* is right. It is as if the postmodern scrutiny of the contextuality of "Truth(s)" had never happened. Especially when the doctor talks to his team: "You're right about me being wrong. You're wrong about you being right" (*Ugly*, 4: 7), and, also in Series Four:

THIRTEEN: There's exceptions to every rule.
HOUSE: No there isn't. That's kinda what makes it a rule.

(*Games*, 4: 9)

House uses his authority to push against "known" and "not known". He risks patients' lives in the midst of his compulsion (yes, we have to call it that) to discover what they have so that he may save them. In *Pilot* (1: 1) he thinks steroids might help the patient:

HOUSE: We treat, she gets better, we know we're right.
FOREMAN: And if we're wrong?
HOUSE: Then we learn something else.

As it happens, after initial "success" with the steroids, the patient temporarily loses her sight and then she suffers a stroke.

HOUSE: Steroids did something.
CHASE: We will watch how fast she dies to tell us what it is?
HOUSE: I got nothing else. What about you?

House is so full of his potential for eventually getting the right answer, his *virtual expertise* if you like, he can happily stay with ignorance. And he does this, even if it seems to risk the patient's life. In *Occam's Razor* (1: 3) he parades himself as fallible expert to the masses in the waiting room:

> For most of you, this job could be done by a monkey with a bottle of Motrin. Speaking of which, if you're particularly annoying you may see me reach for this. This is Vicodin. It's mine. You can't have any. And no, I do not have a pain management problem, I have a pain problem. But who knows? Maybe I'm wrong. Maybe I'm too stoned to tell.

The writers of *House* excluded any psychologist or psychiatrist from the cast. As a series, *House* refuses to push the idea of expert authority so far that we have to swallow psychological, let alone psychoanalytic, interpretations along with the medical. These "diagnoses" stay where they always should – at the status of hypotheses. Psychological reflections are allowed no more authority in the mouths of doctors who, not being specialists in psychology, may be regarded as unqualified, as a layman. Apart from Dr Cameron (who covers the more cuddly person-to-person stuff) psychological and psychoanalytic comments benefit from the authority conveyed by House's friend Dr Wilson, whose insights into mind, motivation and character compete with his own – and House's – expert medical knowledge and authority on many occasions. Dr Wilson is an oncologist, hence expert in acknowledging real physical pain, and yet he is the one who "constantly insists House's pain is psychogenic and that he has no need for Vicodin . . . he wants House to accept his pain and let it make him a better person" (Gilmer, in Wilson, 2007: 178).

However, in his attempts to be a caring friend and doctor, Wilson, the expert authority on pain management, bumps up against the diagnostic authority of Greg House. To avoid losing in this clash of titans, Wilson resorts to the shrink-bite of personality interpretation: "You don't like yourself. But you do admire yourself. It's all you've got so you cling to it . . . Being miserable doesn't make you better than anybody else . . . it just makes you miserable" (*Need To Know*, 2: 11). For House, "care" for the patient gets replaced by "expertise". As Wilson puts it: "You know how some doctors have the Messiah complex; they need to save the world? You've got the Rubik's complex; you need to solve the puzzle" (*DNR*, 1: 9). What Wilson fails to realize here is that with House *his expertise is the care*.

Many times, whether the knowledge of an expert authority is true or not, their authority may go unquestioned by others simply because such others *think* that they themselves do not know. But even those who are *qualified* to disagree (such as other doctors) are required to obey the knowledge emanating from a senior authority whether it is correct or not. The fact is, things go right – or wrong – despite medical knowledge, scientific truth and expert authority.

In addition to competing with rival medical opinions, adding a further layer of conflict in House's struggle with the patient's disease, is the struggle with his boss, Cuddy, and the Authority of the Hospital. House has to outwit them all. Not only in battle with bodies and symptoms that mislead and confuse, House is also up against the hospital establishment that provides the conditions under which he may exert his authority. As one writer puts it, *House* is where "administration as a fulcrum for conflict brilliantly underscores the places where medicine and profit collide" (Baker, in Wilson, 2007: 204). But in the end, "In House's world, deviousness trumps authority every time" (ibid.: 212). Sometimes, when confronted by Cuddy, House does not argue but just makes his point: "If you think I'm wrong tell me I'm wrong. Don't talk about protocol" (*Living the Dream*, 4: 14).

In the end there is far more mutuality between these two authorities than not. This must be partly due to the fact that, unlike in the British NHS hospital system, Cuddy is a manager who is also medically qualified in her own right. In one episode both House and Cuddy have the opportunity to say to each other: "I'm going to do you the biggest favor one doctor can do for another. I am going to stop you from killing your patient" (*Damned If You Do*. 1: 5). Neither authority is more expert, or has more right to authority than the other. Ultimately there is no resolvable opposition between House and Cuddy.

> He pushes the boundaries and finds the answers. She deflects, in fact she sometimes draws the line herself. He often goes round it. There is no *versus* here. There is only the spin of opposition, in the differences that reveal two sides of the same coin and, with it, a similar sort of honor.
>
> (Baker, in Wilson, 2007: 219)

Two kinds of authority

It was another woman's decision that ultimately brought about Greg House's crippling leg pain. In *Three Stories* (1: 21) we learn how his long-term girlfriend, Stacy, decided to have the dead muscle tissue from his leg excised – a compromise decision between the alternatives of amputation and possible death which saved his leg but left the nerves delivering permanent pain. While House was in an induced coma, Stacy used her legal authority to make the decision on his behalf to remove leg muscle and save his leg and his life – despite his previous request not to have this intervention. Although Stacy is using her *legal* authority as House's medical proxy, she is acting much like House himself does with his patients where, as a medical expert, he is entitled to go ahead with radical treatment in his search for diagnostic answers. When Foreman suggests a "risky and invasive" treatment for a patient in the episode *Half-Wit*, House responds with "That's why God invented the long consent form." This sort of authority based on knowledge and expertise philosophers call *theoretical* authority. It is reliant on the belief that those exerting the authority know better than us on some subject.

House's painful leg gives rise to his need for a powerful pain medication and he uses his own theoretical authority to assert his need for the drug Vicodin, saying "The pills don't make me high, they make me neutral" (*Detox*, 1: 11) and "I don't have a problem with addiction. I have a problem with pain." But his colleagues notice he is overdosing, which is proved when Cuddy's doling out the regular dosage has little effect on House's pain. As if to abolish all further doubt about his "addiction", House is found to have a stash of six hundred pills in his home.

This is revealed through a number of episodes involving Tritter, a man who comes to the clinic for treatment, gets humiliated by House, and wants to humiliate him in return. Until now, although they may have had the motivation, few people have had the ability or the persistence to bring House down. But Tritter is no ordinary, sucker patient. He is a plainclothes police detective. "Tritter as a cop who doesn't appear to have any special knowledge . . . represents a pure form of the other kind of authority, which philosophers call 'practical authority'" (Ehrenberg, 2009: 176). *Practical* authority may be exerted by someone entitled to control you – the type of authority a policeman has when he orders you to pull over in your car. Sometimes practical authority is backed up by a sanction such as arrest and imprisonment. The authority of a parent – who has a right to control a child for their well-being *and* has more expertise than the child – will be seen to demonstrate a combination of both these types of authority.

Although appearing to act with pure vindictiveness, Tritter accords with the suppositions that *practical* authority "supposedly works in the public good . . . sacrificing an individual's interests to that important good" (ibid.: 182). He justifies his pursuit of House with a *version* of theoretical authority derived from the medical profession itself. After all, if another doctor found out how addicted House was to Vicodin, how he would lie to get a prescription, that doctor would be justified in concluding that House's judgment may be in error and his patients in danger, Tritter reasons. What Tritter's analysis ignores is what the viewers can see:

> House's practically superhuman expertise, and perhaps the particularities of his field. People turn to House when they cannot get a proper diagnosis by other doctors. House's ability to diagnose difficult cases transcends his Vicodin addiction.
>
> (ibid.: 179–80)

However, in the conclusion to the episode, a judge rules in court that "Tritter's actions exceeded his mandate . . . [and his] authority is subservient to the judge's, who is arguably in a better position to decide what is really in the public interest" (ibid.: 182).

The clash between two kinds of authority in the Tritter episodes provides a third dimension to the weft and warp of authority depicted elsewhere in *House*. House's own authority derives partly from expertise gained through his medical training and experience, and partly from a grumpy arrogance in believing he is right. In the first case he may get into conflict with other theoretical authorities such as his medical colleagues. In the second case he can come into conflict with anyone. While his theoretical authority may benefit patients when he uses a medical justification to exert his will over theirs, this is often tangled up with his practical authority, which arises out of belief in his right to control the decisions of others. He also uses his theoretical authority to undermine medical authority when urging his young team to think outside the box. At his bullying worst, he uses his practical authority to push them out of the box.

The third kind: On personal authority

WILSON: That's why religious belief annoys you. Because if the Universe operates by abstract rules you can learn – then you can protect yourself. If a Supreme Being exists – he can squash you any time he wants.

HOUSE: He knows where I am.

(House versus God, 2: 19)

This chapter began with the idea that casting Hugh Laurie as Greg House – although an unlikely choice on the face of it – has its provenance in certain aspects of Laurie's previous roles, especially the characters he played opposite and the dynamic qualities expressed between them. Connected with this is his personal background as a Cambridge and Eton-educated upper-middle-class male who has, in the main, grown up alongside and worked with actors and writers of a similar class Southern British background. Much of this then helps account for his authority on the screen playing the brilliant, maverick diagnostician Gregory House at the Princeton-Plainsboro where the aristocracy of his medical expertise entitles him to ignore and rebuke the shabby restrictions of hospital management, patients' wishes and colleagues' opinions.

There is another side to House's character that Hugh Laurie brings, but through a different route. There is another subtle, quieter authority in Greg House which is facilitated by something different in Hugh Laurie. House's pain – permanent and crippling as his limping, his cane and his wincing show – is one part of House's personal *woundedness*. The other parts are his addiction to Vicodin and his solitary life, empty of intimate relationships. He is often seen alone playing his piano or guitar, or watching a TV soap opera. House riding his motorcycle suggests not only his physicality, but again a solo life where such excitements are experienced alone. House leaves the party when it is in full swing. Although he acts like saving patients' lives is his prime objective, he finds little to celebrate in his own life or in humanity in general.

The son of a Cambridge family doctor, Hugh Laurie went to the University of Cambridge to study anthropology but he admits this was simply to indulge in his primary love of rowing. He was at world-class level in his youth, and apart from when he was interrupted by glandular fever in 1979, Laurie rowed for Cambridge in the Boat Race (a long-standing annual event against Oxford University). Even that had its sourness, however, when Cambridge lost by five feet to Oxford in 1980. Says Laurie, "I really shouldn't say this, because I still to this day wouldn't want to give any pleasure or satisfaction to the opposing crew. But yes, it's true – it was a very bitter defeat" (Challen, 2007: 11). Laurie points out how he came from a family where the expression of emotions and celebrating achievement were not the done thing, and it was many years later that he found hidden in the attic a Gold Medal his father had won in the 1948 Olympic Games. Over all the years his father had never told Hugh that he, too, had been a champion rower. Apparently quite unlike Dr Greg House, and yet, I believe informing the vulnerable, wounded aspect that makes the character's arrogance work so well, Laurie's is a complex relationship with success. "Humility", says Laurie, "was a cult in my family" (Challen, 2007: 12).

Years later, with much comedy success behind him, Hugh was at a stock-car race meeting and, in the middle of what should have been so exciting, he realized he was totally bored; ambitions and desires meant nothing to him any more. He recognized he was deeply depressed and (largely to stop being a burden to his family and friends, he claims) took himself into psychotherapy. But even this he dismisses with an ironic, "I figured I might as well give someone a hundred bucks an hour to hear my woes. At least someone can make a living listening to my tedious problems" (Challen, 2007: 34).

Nowadays, unlike Dr House, the actor Hugh Laurie has a wife and teenage children and has recently taken up boxing. But in common with

House, Laurie has a passion for fast motorbikes, and playing guitar and piano. The authority Hugh Laurie brings to his portrayal of Greg House stems from several quarters – some are personal and predictable, while others are obtuse and, frankly, inverted, like his past career as a clowning Brit. Further authority comes from the way the public and hence TV audiences the world over trust doctors to know and make the right decisions and, even, act in the best interest of their patients. For Fox's series *House*, the casting of Hugh Laurie as Greg House was "destiny", because, in casting him, the producers ensured the authority of their main character, hence sealing the success of all the stories in *House M.D.*

References

Baker, V. (2007) House vs. Cuddy. In L. Wilson (ed.) *House Unauthorized: Vasculitis, Clinic Duty, and Bad Bedside Manner*. Dallas, TX: Benbella Books (pp. 203–220).

Challen, P. (2007) *The House That Hugh Laurie Built: An Unauthorized Biography and Episode Guide*. Toronto: ECW Press.

Ehrenberg, K. (2009) House vs. Tritter: On the clash of theoretical and practical authority. In H. Jacoby (ed.) *House and Philosophy: Everybody Lies*. Somerset, NJ: Wiley (pp. 174–185).

Gilmer, J. (2007) Does God Limp? In L. Wilson (ed.) (2007) *House Unauthorized: Vasculitis, Clinic Duty, and Bad Bedside Manner*. Dallas, TX: Benbella Books (pp. 171–184).

Harris, M. (2008) *Scenes From a Revolution: The Birth of the New Hollywood*. Edinburgh and London: Canongate.

Jacoby, H. (ed.) (2009) *House and Philosophy: Everybody Lies*. Somerset, NJ: Wiley.

Millman, J. (2007) The sidekick'. In L. Wilson (ed.) *House Unauthorized: Vasculitis, Clinic Duty, and Bad Bedside Manner*. Dallas, TX: Benbella Books (pp. 185–196).

Nietzsche, F. (1887/1967) *On The Genealogy of Morals*. (Trans., R. J. Hollingdale and W. Kaufmann). New York, NY: Random House.

Sinor, B. H. (2007) The little doctor who wasn't really there. In L. Wilson (ed.) *House Unauthorized: Vasculitis, Clinic Duty, and Bad Bedside Manner*. Dallas, TX: Benbella Books (pp. 197–202).

Wilson, L. (ed.) (2007) *House Unauthorized: Vasculitis, Clinic Duty, and Bad Bedside Manner*. Dallas, TX: Benbella Books.

Note

1 In Britain, for historical reasons, private, fee-paying schools such as Eton or Harrow, are known as *public* schools.

Part II

Consulting House

Chapter 4

House's caduceus crutch

Terrie Waddell

Fox's *House* substitutes the spectacle of *CSI*'s dissected cadavers for the not so forthcoming diseased but still pulsing body. This complex and highly volatile organism is no match for the morally earnest, law-bound characters that haunt prime-time procedurals. Such a body needs to be coaxed into revealing its secrets by a similarly wounded and duplicitous trickster. This explains why Dr Gregory House (Hugh Laurie), the misanthropic prodigy gifted with curing the incurable, overshadows each formulaic 42-minute episode. Left partially crippled and permanently in pain from a clotted aneurysm in his upper leg, House is a self-medicator who hoards the narcotic Vicodin with all the cunning of a junkie. As he limps through the Princeton-Plainsboro Teaching Hospital (PPTH), considering himself special and so above authority, the very colleagues he emotionally abuses glorify him as a latter-day Asclepius. There is not a great deal of 'meat' in this character-driven series without its drug-riddled heartbeat. Wresting him from the text (even abstractly) is a bit of a struggle, so this discussion of healing, trickster and the dis-ease of identifying with an inflexible persona, would not even attempt to shift the spotlight.

Unable to effect and accept personal change, House nevertheless fancies himself as the embodiment of trickster energy; a boundary transgressor compelled to inflict suffering in order to heal and provoke self-reflection in others. Just as he tries to emulate the free-spirited *enfant terrible* while constrained by rationality and the pitfalls of ego-inflation, the series, too, is crippled by its own predictable structure, plot clichés, and medical pretensions. Although it all ostensibly boils down to seizures, MRI scans followed by seizures, abnormal pre- or post-seizure bleeding, and, for variety, liver failure and suspected lupus, these mainstays are undermined by the in-your-face ailment that dominates each story – House's crippling *heart attack in the thigh muscle*, or for in-the-know fans, *quadricep infarction*.

It is not a great leap to think of our walking-stick-bound anti-hero as a fusion of the Greek gods Asclepius (the healer) and Hermes (the trickster). In this light, the ever present cane becomes a caduceus of sorts, suggesting medical acumen and guile. House wields it as a weapon, form of amour, and crutch against those who attempt to rupture his self-absorption by trying to elicit the kind of inner-reflection/change that might limit his freedom to misbehave. Yet there is something jarring in the way that he awkwardly clutches the cane. Weakness in the right leg would ordinarily require a walking aid to be placed in the left hand, but it is habitually hugged to the same (right) side as the injury. This might be passed off as yet another non-conformist affectation, but considering the shamelessly unethical ruses he pulls to ease any discomfort, it is a curious quirk. Surprisingly, the other main-cast medical characters ignore this behavior completely: his toadying research crew, Foreman (Omar Epps), Cameron (Jennifer Morrison), Chase (Jesse Spencer), Taub (Peter Jacobson), Hadley (Olivia Wilde) and Kutner (Kal Penn); loyal friend and colleague, Wilson (Robert Sean Leonard); and the much undermined and sexually harassed Dean of Medicine, Cuddy (Lisa Edelstein)[1]. This stick-misuse can be associated with a twisting of the medical caduceus/staff and the two demi-gods (or in a Jungian frame, unconscious energies) attached to the symbol.

It is therefore fitting that the Fox Network's viral 'snakes on a cane' marketing campaign, designed to launch season six, revolved around caduceus-tweaked iconography – the wand spine of the symbol having been replaced by House's cane. The glossy photographic image developed from this simple drawing has Laurie (as House) wrapped in a large snake with two angel-like wings sprouting from his back and a second snake curling over his left shoulder. Call it synchronicity, but a week after this chapter was initially submitted to the book's editors (August 2009), Fox released the first shots of a T-shirted House wearing the symbol across his chest; the arty still followed in September. Prior to this I was unaware of the campaign packaging *House*/House in this way. The coincidence was as unnerving as it was validating.

Asclepius, Hermes and the caduceus

Both the ancient physician Asclepius (later appropriated as a demi-god) and Hermes are suggested through the caduceus – American medical culture's most recognizable symbol. This double-snake-entwined herald's rod, as apposed to the Asclepian single-snake-coiled staff, is largely associated with Hermes. Its adoption by branches of the medical community and commercial interests related to medicine is, some have argued, a misreading of the Hermetic icon (Friedlander, 1992; Froman and Skandalakis, 2008; Wilcox and Whitlam, 2003). This collapse of two disparate mythic figures/energies has ironically come to serve as a comment on modern-day American medicine and pharmacology, inextricably fused as these industries are with commerce, profit and the practice of servicing those who pay above those who suffer.

For Jung, the gods of myth represent collectively unconscious energies: patterns of behavior, or archetypes (Jung, 1969: para. 457). James Hillman similarly argues that the

> Irreducible language of these archetypal patterns is the metaphorical discourse of myths. These can therefore be understood as the most fundamental patterns of human existence. To study human nature at its most basic level, one must turn to culture (mythology, religion, art, architecture, epic, drama, ritual) where these patterns are portrayed.
>
> (Hillman, 1983: 3)

As I have suggested elsewhere (Waddell, 2006, 2009), television has the potential to fall into categories of storytelling where mythic characters and narratives can be understood as re-imagined/reshaped unconscious energies able to illuminate the personal and collective psyche. Even contributing areas of production can create the illusion of archetypal forces driving the text. House is not your standard trickster incarnation, savior, or even wounded healer. Series creator David Shore, Laurie, and the various writing teams have given us a character that embraces and battles the dynamic of all three energies. He's a problematic cluster of psychological twists and knots that reflect the contaminated nature of archetypal motifs: fusing structures that complement and challenge each other. His walking cane-cum-caduceus-cum-Asclepian staff symbolizes these interlaced patterns.

Asclepius

The much modified *Hippocratic Oath* (c. 400 BCE), named after but not written by the Greek physician Hippocrates (460–375 BCE), begins by honoring Apollo, Asclepius, and his daughters, the goddesses Health (Hygieia) and Healing (Panacea). Although Hippocrates is loosely credited with ancestry dating back to Asclepius's mortal son Podalirius, the opening stanza of the original Oath recognizes all physicians as having a symbolic lineage to the four deities, evoked as the 'witnesses and progenitors of medicine' (Miles, 2004: 26). The Homeric hymn 'To Asclepius' credits him as the 'son of Apollo and healer of sickness. In the Dotian plain fair Coronis, daughter of King Phlegyas, bore him, a great joy to men, a soother of cruel pangs' (Hesiod, 1950: 441). The mortal Coronis, however, took Ischys as a lover while pregnant with Asclepius. Apollo was unaware of her condition when he arranged to have her murdered for infidelity. On learning of the pregnancy, he sent Hermes to rescue the fetus from Coronis's funeral pyre. Asclepius was then placed in the care of Chiron the centaur, who tended to his medical education. Asclepius's wife Epione bore five immortals: the four goddesses Hygieia, Panacea, Iaso (medicine) and Aceso (healing), and the god Telesphorous (convalescence) (Hart, 2000: 6–35). Their mortal children, the physician-warriors Podalirius and Machaon appear in Homer's Trojan war epic *The Iliad* (c.750 BCE) (1991).

According to the historian Pausanias, the sanctuary of Asclepius was founded in the ancient city of Messene in the fourth century BCE. From that period, Asclepian healing temples (Asclepieions) flourished throughout the ancient Mediterranean world, beginning in Athens and spreading to Crete, Smyrna, Cyrenaica, Kos, Trikka, and Pergamum and Epidavros (Habicht, 1985: 155). The poor and sick came to the oracles at these sanatoriums and, among other remedies, were treated through dream interpretation, sleep incubation and the curative powers of sacred snakes (Graves, 1960: 179; Froman and Skandalakis, 2008).

The myths based on Asclepius highlight his ability to raise the dead: the war heroes Capaneus and Lycurgus, Tyndareus (the Spartan king), Glaucus (king Minos of Crete's son), and Hippolytus (son of Hippolyte, queen of the Amazons). Hades took offence at all these stolen souls and appealed to Zeus for justice. Asclepius was subsequently killed via a thunderbolt for playing with immortality, considered the exclusive prerogative of the gods (Graves, 1960: 358). Bruno Currie also argues that this punishment 'could be seen as a means to heroization or apotheosis, signifying his [Asclepius's] incorporation among the gods or heroes' (2005: 354). One of the most popular stories explaining how Asclepius learnt the art of resurrection tells of how he killed a snake that crept up on him while he was nursing the dead Glaucus. Shortly after, he caught sight of the snake's partner healing its mate with herbs. He mimicked this practice to revive Glaucus, and in homage, his branch-like staff came to bear a singular sacred snake (Wilcox and Whitlam, 2003).

Hermes

The caduceus, a Latin term etymologically derived from the Greek *kerux*, meaning to herald, depicts two snakes coiled around a phallic wand in the geometric form of a double helix (now an allusion to DNA patterning). A pair of wings sprouting from the apex signifies the role of messenger. After placing the wand between two fighting snakes that then embraced it in an act of friendship, Hermes adopted the twin snake emblem as a sign of mediation (Wilcox and Whitlam, 2003; Froman and Skandalakis, 2008). Although the serpents can be interpreted as copulating (suggestive of renewal), their cordial relationship also implies balance and negotiation.

Incarnated at various mythological periods, Hermes had a complex history as the Egyptian *Thoth* (later Hermes *Trismegistus* or *three times great*), Homer's Greek trickster, and Rome's *Mercury*. Despite his ancestral credentials, Hermes is most commonly remembered as the messenger and *puer* (eternal boy) of the Hellenic pantheon. The Homeric hymn 'To Hermes' (510 BCE) describes this son of Zeus and the nymph Maia as a child 'of many shifts, blandly cunning, a robber, a cattle driver, a bringer of dreams, a watcher by night, a thief at the gates, one who was soon to show forth wonderful deeds among the deathless gods' (Hesiod, 1950: 365). Known as the fleet-footed courier of messages between the Olympians, the cunning half-brother of Apollo, con-artist, god of life's crossroads and commerce, transformer, psychopomp (death guide), shameless sycophant, and trickster, Hermes has come to personify an energy synonymous with the benefits and consequences of postmodernity, the media age, and globalization. In his paper *The Charm of Hermes: Hillman, Lyotard, and the Postmodern Condition*, Bernie Neville argues that

> the culture of late capitalism is in the grip of a Hermes inflation, revealed in the artifacts of popular culture, in the abstractions of the deconstructionists, in the practices of the postmodern organization, in the gelatinization of values, in the obsessions of the economic rationalists, in the commoditization of knowledge, the arts, education, health and therapy.
>
> (1992: 353)

Neville, though, avoids inflaming a sense of loss and despair at Western culture's reverence toward the kind of energy trickster gods encourage by also attributing our worship at the altar of Hermes-consciousness to a desire for honoring difference, multiple perspectives, polytheism and change.

Karl Kerényi understands Hermes to communicate the energy of childlike exploration and exploitation, able to take us beyond the mundanity of imposed cultural strictures and ideologies (Kerényi, in Radin, 1972: 190). As opposed to more demonic or duplicitous trickster figures, Hermes personifies a civilized form of rebellion that tempts rather than forces change. Yet in the case of *House*, while Hermes is evoked through allusions to the caduceus, the daimon trickster is also embedded in the central character as he becomes increasingly relentless in his attacks on, and resistance to, a world view that insists on vulnerability and self-reflection for emotional/psychological development.

Jung talked about Mercurius, derivative of the Italian Mercury, from the perspective of the medieval alchemists who saw him as 'duplex and utriusque capax ("capable of both")' (Jung, 1967: para. 481). What is meant here is that the god functions as a daimon, a symbol of opposing forces in the psyche that can inspire the lowest depths and highest potential of human behavior. Through the archetypal energy of Mercurius, Jung argues that we are able to bring the more disparate aspects of the unconscious together as if in dialogue, and by way of this exchange, work through the process of *individuation* or psychological maturation. The duality of Mercurius, though, is also a source of inner conflict and self-destructiveness likened to the dualities of good and evil, Christ and the devil. For Jung, he is 'akin to the godhead' and 'found in the sewers' (Jung, 1967: para. 269). Mercurius embodies the messiness of the collective unconscious. He personifies our attempts to grapple with the impacting minor and critical contradictions of our lives that can become a source of havoc or healing. We see such archetypal discomfort in almost every episode of *House*. This aspect of the series will be discussed later, but for the moment it is necessary to examine the symbolism of the staff that has become enmeshed in the framework of the series. Not only can the walking stick represent the fusion of Asclepian and Hermetic energy, it also signifies House's 'mercurial' struggle; his desperate need to be relieved of pain, and his dependence on woundedness as a form of permission for recklessness and misanthropy.

The fusion of staffs

Basel publisher Johann Froben began to use the caduceus as a printer's mark in 1516. A number of printers have since adopted the symbol, most probably, according to Friedlander, because they 'saw a strong link between themselves as printers and Mercury . . . the messenger of the ancient gods and certainly the printed word was a message' (1992: 111). Friedlander also suggests that the name *Mercury*, adopted by a number of newspapers from 1620 onward, supports this idea of the caduceus as an established insignia for those who courier information. It was not until 1837, when Londoner John Churchill, a printer of medical books, adopted the symbol, that the caduceus more concretely became associated with medicine. Friedlander explains how Churchill justified his use of the dual-snake caduceus over the single-snaked staff: 'On one of the two snakes is the word *Medicina* and on the other one there is the word *Literis*. In other words, medicine and literature are here entwined and thus united or bonded' (1992: 114).

From the use of Churchill's mark, the most significant association of the caduceus with medicine came with its adoption by the United States Army. In 1817 the staff of Asclepius was appropriated by the US Medical Department, but in 1902 the department claimed the caduceus as the insignia for its official badge at the insistence of an Assistant Surgeon, Captain Frederick Reynolds, who confused the meaning of the Asclepian and Hermetic symbols (Friedlander, 1992). When confronted about the inappropriate nature of the change by the then Surgeon General (G. W. Sternberg), Reynolds refused to retract his suggestion. His letter justifying the caduceus as 'associated with things medical' and 'more graceful and significant than the present emblem' found its way to Sternberg's successor, the more sympathetic W. H. Forwood (Friedlander, 1992: 131–2). Reynolds, it would seem, was more concerned with aesthetics than the mythological import of the iconography. The Asclepian staff though, has always remained the official seal for the American Medical Association (see www.ama-assn.org).

The single-snake coiled image is still used globally to signify the medical associations of Greece, Britain, Australia, New Zealand, Canada, Italy, Switzerland, China, South Africa and Germany, while the Anglo French Medical Society, the US Public Health Service, and the Indian Medical Association, for instance, adopt the caduceus. Although it seems appropriate for commercial industries servicing medicine to claim the hermetic symbol, an argument can also be made for its use, particularly in the United States, by medically related organizations, when one considers the state of the country's health care; a system not available to all, but run on the basis that only those with 'adequate' medical insurance can receive treatment. This social failing was most popularly exposed in filmmaker Mike Moore's documentary *Sicko* (2007).

House's insignia

House's walking stick renders him wounded, dependent and armed. It is a libidinal prop that not only becomes associated with his body-image and inner state of mind, but also his indispensability to an urban teaching hospital, that while committed to treating the poor and 'incurable', is dependent on stringent budgets and benefactors to survive. This wounded healer, then, whose sense of self incorporates the cane-cum-medical caduceus, acts as a filter for the energies of Asclepius (healing) and Hermes (commerce), as well as representing the difficulty of reconciling their respective ethical and moral positions.

According to Elizabeth Grosz's reading of Paul Schilder's work on body-image, the psychological 'map' we have of our body can extend beyond the skin:

> External objects, implements, and instruments with which the subject continually interacts become, while they are being used, intimate, vital, even libidinally cathected parts of the body image . . . Part of the difficulty of learning how to use these implements and instruments is not simply the technical problem of how they are used but also the libidinal problem of how they become psychically invested.
>
> (Grosz, 1994: 80)

To illustrate her point she cites Schilder's example of the stick, which we can apply to House's cane:

> When we take a stick into our hands and touch an object with the end of it, we feel a sensation at the end of the stick. The stick has, in fact, become part of the body-image. In order to get the full sensation at the end of the stick, the stick must be in more or less rigid connection with the body. It then becomes part of the bony system of the body, and we

may suppose that the rigidity of the bony system is an important part in every body-image.

(Schilder, in Grosz, 1994: 80)

Schilder also argues that our body-image is developed from the touch of others and the importance certain body parts assume, particularly those invested with prime importance through injury and pain. Through pain, 'the model of the body changes in its libidinal structure' and our concept of how we position the body, the body schema or the postural model, 'is overloaded with narcissistic libido in the aching part' (Schilder, 1970: 126). One might argue that House fetishizes his wounded leg. Attention is continually drawn to the injury. It is pampered, commented upon by others, and in the episode *Three Stories* (1: 21), where the details of his infarction play out in flashback, the wounded leg becomes a source of debate, desire, and much physical touching and probing. Schilder continues:

> With the erotic change, a change in the perception goes. The hand returns again and again to the aching organ, when the pain is not immediately present, pressure provokes it. There is a feeling of swelling, of dryness, of moisture in the aching part . . . The aching organ becomes a centre of renewed experimentation with the body. It takes a part usually taken by the erogenic zones . . .
>
> Pain, dysaethesia, erogenic zones, the actions of our hands on the body, the actions of others toward the body, the interest of others concerning our body, and the itching provoked by the functions of our body are therefore important factors in the final structuralization of the body-image.
>
> (Schilder, 1970: 126–7)

Similarly the cane/caduceus, as an extension of the body-image and a focus of intense attention, also becomes libidinally invested. In Freudian terms this object may be considered an erogenous zone, but in the Jungian idiom where libido is not purely associated with sexuality, but understood more as a life force (Jung 1956, para. 194), it becomes the energy hub of House's inner self-map.

A fusion of Hermes and Asclepius

The role of psychopomp or ferryman/woman of souls, a trait Hermes and Asclepius share, is one of House's distinguishing features. In mythology the psychopomp was largely associated with figures, such as Charon, Hermes, Xolótl, Anubis, or the Valkeries, who guided dead souls through the life–death passage. In analytical philosophy, though, a psychopomp is also seen as an actual person or energy that guides the subject from one state of awareness to another, most commonly from an ego-based worldview to one able to tap the unconscious. As mentioned earlier, Asclepius began to practice raising the dead, and was punished with death for this flirtation. Similarly, in the more dramatic episodes of *House*, we also see the nearly or just dead being raised by House's diagnostic expertise, often grounded in logic and empiricism, but occasionally guided by intuition. It is a fitting character trait, when considering that Hermes, the 'appointed messenger to Hades' (Hesiod, 1950: 405), used the caduceus to lull souls to sleep and enliven the dead (Lempriere, 1949). As a nerve centre for the most puzzling of life-threatening medical anomalies, the fictional Princeton-Plainsboro Teaching Hospital is not known for its fatalities. A patient rarely dies without being revived on House's watch. Like Asclepius, unable to rouse himself after death, House's skill in allowing patients to transcend the seemingly terminal nature of their illness, even rousing them from death-like states, doesn't extend to his own physical and psychic injuries. It is a character quirk that grounds him in the sludge of human suffering.

All three mythic figures (Asclepius, Hermes and House) can be read as saviors: Asclepius most obviously for his healing powers, empathy and generosity towards the sick; Hermes for his ability to shift awareness and force change; and House for his powers of deduction and willingness to risk personal safety, sanity and reputation to rescue the seemingly damned. Jung understands the trickster figure and the trickster archetype in general (not just Hermes) as capable of transforming 'the meaningless into the meaning-ful', raising a level of awareness about certain situations in order to gain insight into how they might be approached and possibly resolved (Jung, 1969: para. 458). Trickster figures, generally speaking, rarely take moral or ethical positions (unlike Asclepius). It is in this very ambiguity and boun-dary straddling from one position to another, or reality to another, that trickster energy, embodied in the various figures of mythology, allows those it works on and for to arrive at their own moral/ethical positions. In other words, trickster facilitates the development and consolidation of cultural and individual conscience. In this way it functions as a transformer-savior.

As mentioned earlier, Jung most passionately talked of trickster in the form of Mercurius, so venerated by the medieval chemists because of his/its promise of transformation. The alchemists were governed by the concept of turning base metals into gold, finding the elixir of life and so making one's life whole (finding the 'gold') by working through the indi-viduation process. Mercurius, Asclepius and House are therefore embedded in medical/pharmaceutical origins and share a common, curative purpose. The caduceus, staff and walking stick are bound into one therapeutic wand. In line with the *duplex* nature of Mercurius, the facility to heal and harm are not easily separated, and often include considerable suffering. For trickster, there is no care as to how perceptions are altered, or regard for the accompanying distress change often involves. As a multidimensional, unconscious daimonic force, it is without morality and so capable of havoc. By displaying the qualities of this dominant energy, House looms large as the alchemist's poster boy in another guise.

Embodiment and disavowal

Given that the Asclepian/medical aspects of House and the series are fairly obvious, I am going to look at the caduceus connection by highlighting the ways in which House emulates and rejects the trickster paradigm. The puerile nature of the character and his self-conscious attempts to buck the system for his own ends are fairly stock trickster tactics. House neither follows standard medical procedure nor abides by the 'do-no-harm' dictum of the *Hippocratic Oath*. His invasive medical explorations often reduce those he treats to seizure-prone specimens, of interest only for their potential to feed his love of physiological anomalies. As is often mentioned by practically all the main cast characters, House is fixated on the puzzle of finding a cure rather than actually curing. Once patients are healed, he seeks out the next medical quest, much like the infant Hermes who sought one adventure or object after another, not because he needed or desired the object of his quest, but, one suspects, for the illicit, anti-authoritarian play it involved.

Trying to conquer the labyrinth of the body, decode its every function and malfunction, even overcome death (which gave Asclepius so much grief) is a form of divine intervention that, as Greek mythology warns us, should be left to the gods. Yet House, a passionate atheist, even prone to defy science (at whose altar he worships), imagines himself a force to be reckoned with: a rare intellect beholden to neither mortal nor god. Far from the narcissistic personality whose unjustified sense of self-importance and grandeur stems from an inability to transcend infantile narcissism, every character and the series itself validates House's ego-inflation. He rarely loses patients, always cures the most incurable of diseases, is kept on at the hospital because of his unique healing skills, illicitly manipulates the system without being seriously called to account, and is allowed to place patients in near-death situations to test his theories. In this sense House channels Hermes' teflon nature. There are only two story arcs in the entire five seasons where we see him served with any tangible comeuppance. Both are related to drug addiction rather than egocentric exploits.

The 'fleet-footedness' attributed to Hermes via his winged sandals and helmet is another marker of the series. Each episode is built on the speed with which House must find the source of a rare illness before his patient dies. The narrative begins with a two-minute teaser culminating in the subject of the episode either convulsing or collapsing. The cause of these seizures is always unknown and so predictably begins a rapid flow of inexplicable bleeding, skin discoloration and/or rashes, MRI scans, unnecessary surgery, vomiting, occasional soiling (not necessarily in this order), and finally the restoration of well-being. House is forced to competitively pit his rapid-fire thought processes against each patient's swiftly ailing body as it invariably combats invasive forces or shuts down organ by organ. His motorcycle fetish, occasional flirtation with skateboards, and the unexpected pace at which he hobbles around the hospital using his walking stick as a fifth limb, also highlights this need for speed. His young team of protégés (Foreman, Cameron, Chase, Taub, Hadley, and Kutner), who add diagnostic suggestions to a whiteboard when they are not lounging around their office, adequately compensate for his quadricep infarction by sprinting to and from the patient of the day with all the histrionic urgency of stock prime-time medicos.

The lying and cheating aspect of House's trickster persona is perhaps a more convincing link to Hermes, who, according to the Homeric hymn, when only an infant, dashed from his crib to steal, lie, swindle, and convince Zeus of his usefulness. With the infantile ruthlessness of little Hermes, House blackmails fellow surgeons, habitually deceives the long-suffering administrator Cuddy, pits his diagnostic team against each other, and breaks into patients' homes. He consistently compromises the reputation of his best friend, the cancer specialist Wilson, by appealing to his empathetic nature and then abusing his gestures of compassion. House is not heroic. In trying to emulate the more stereotypical traits of generalized trickster figures, Hermes in particular, the character is sadistic and ruthless. When in bullying mode, his attempts at humor are almost always at the expense of others. In trying to emulate trickster, though, *House* and House provide a sage lesson – one cannot consciously out-trick the trickster aspect of the unconscious.

As much as House may try to claim god-like status through his conscious uptake of trickster (and I am arguing that is it a conscious emulation rather than an unconscious eruption), the archetype is beyond ego control. There are many aspects of House's character that are decidedly untrickster-like. The concerns of commerce personified by Hermes are left to Cuddy, while House continually dismisses monetary matters by constructing himself as a force beyond materialism. He's also devoid of charm, whereas the more slippery Hermes emulator is an unknowable character skilled in enchanting those from whom s/he benefits without having to reveal any inner self or sleight of hand. House doesn't easily fool those around him. While his backslappers revere his talent, they're also aware and wary of his foibles.

In the mode of Hermes and other trickster-lechers, House gestures toward nymph chasing but does not have the finesse to pull it off. He remains sexually frustrated, reduced to the odd prostitute and crude sexual ogling/harassment of female patients and colleagues. Trickster figures, by comparison, are often characterized as sexually fixated *puers* who not only lust after, but seem to revere women, even morphing from male to female in their capacity as shape-shifters: the West African Ananse has a 'monthly period' (Pelton, 1980: 52); 'Wakdjunkaga' of North American Winnebago culture fashions a vulva for himself (Radin, 1972: 22–3); and 'Sitconski' and 'Inktumni', the Asiniboine tricksters, birth rabbit litters (Radin, 1972: 101–3). House, however, openly belittles women (Cuddy, Cameron and ex-partner Stacy [Sela Ward] in particular) for their ability to see through and emotionally rupture the outer shell of his trickster persona.

Despite these more superficial discrepancies he distinguishes himself most clearly from classical and antiquated tricksters by his resistance to change. Tricksters are, after all, most at home in liminal spaces – playing with the in-between, always in flux and exciting transformation. House's inability to shift perspectives (and the unadventurous predictability of the series itself) shows us how mortal and untrickster-like the character and the series really are. This flaw most clearly reveals itself in the ongoing cycle of House's drug addiction. It is a disabling behavior that I will argue is combated by an unconscious trickster element woven into the narrative, in an attempt to tease him toward transformation.

Addicted to the status quo

In this last section, I would like to talk about two story arcs (flagged earlier) that focus on House's addiction, retribution, and internal trickster. Although he develops a dependence on Vicodin to relieve the residual ache of his leg (with sundry other narcotics thrown into the mix), he is also reluctant to imagine himself without pain, as if he has incorporated the wound and its sensations into his body-image. In a perverse and almost superstitious way, he also feels that this ongoing suffering contributes to his medical virtuosity. Losing his intellectual edge by throwing away the walking stick seems akin to discarding the caduceus/Asclepian staff: it is a prop that completes his 'wounded healer' persona, aids his emotional isolation, and connects him to the decedents of Apollo (his son Asclepius, and half-brother Hermes). This signifier of personal suffering and the suffering of others is affixed to House's self-concept as a defense against change. So while he is addicted to painkillers, he is even more addicted to the pay-off of pain.

The cycle of addiction (weaning himself off Vicodin and resuming the habit) has kept the series buoyant for five seasons. In season three's story arc, the clash between House's trickster-persona and the unconscious flaring of trickster energy is clearly on show. When working clinic duty, he has words with patient 'Michael Tritter' (David Morse), who consequently accuses House of bullying behavior before kicking the precious walking stick from under him: 'You're rude . . . and you're smart and you're funny, but you are bitter and you're lonely so you treat everyone around you like they're idiots and you get away with it . . . treat people like jerks and you get treated like a jerk' (*Fools for Love*, 3: 5). In attacking the cane, Tritter has, in effect, dismissed House's disability (the libidinally invested wound) and the staff/caduceus twinning of healing and trickster energies that define him. The slight is a form of castration. In retribution House inserts a thermometer in Tritter's rectum, makes an excuse to exit the examination room, and never returns. Revenge comes when Tritter, a detective, later pulls House over for speeding, frisks him, draws handfuls of un-prescribed Vicodin from his bomber jacket pocket, and arrests him for possession. Threaded through the season where this story is played out, House becomes increasingly desperate for drugs, stealing a dead patient's prescription, conning hospital pharmacists, and forging from Wilson's prescription pad. Tritter searches his apartment, questions his diagnostic team, and confronts Cuddy about the hospital's negligence in allowing a doctor to practice while addicted.

When House willingly checks himself into PPTH's rehab unit to avoid a jail sentence, we see him slide into the disheveled persona of the stereotypical de-toxing junkie (*Words and Deeds*, 3: 11). The seemingly heartfelt self-recrimination and apologies he makes to Wilson, who placed his career on the line to cover for House's theft, were, we discover, ruses to gain sympathy and conceal his resumption of Vicodin. For the first time in the series there is a teasing delight in House's initial comeuppance. Although it is tempting to think that the only way to contain a bully is via another bully, Tritter cuts a fine line between calm self-assurance and ethical conviction; there is an Apollonian sensibility about him. In House's case, though, the prime objective is to satiate desire. He may offer an Asclepian duty of care to patients, but he does not apply the same (even skewed) nurturing to himself. He dupes his colleagues with the assurance of his trickster-persona, a teflon mask that blocks all attempts at emotional penetration.

If we adopt the idea that the archetypal trickster is also at play in the narrative as a catalyst for transformation, then we have an interesting contest of energies. As the drug-taking/detox aspect of the series is cyclic, it can be argued that the unconscious trickster is working *for* House, always moving him towards confronting addiction by tricking him into situations that force him to contend with his demons. Self-reflection, though, is usually thwarted. It is as if the ego tries to out-trick the unconscious, which repeatedly flares until addressed. Having the archetypal trickster in conflict with a very conscious trickster persona (a trickster complex perhaps) is a canny way for the series and its principal character to maintain a compelling edge.

The fifth season also plays around with this idea. House is plagued by hallucinations of Wilson's dead lover. She regularly appears to him as a personification of his unconscious trickster, trying to outmaneuver him on matters personal and diagnostic in an attempt to emotionally and intellectually move him towards change. He finally concedes that his drug addiction is responsible for the visions. The two-part cliffhanger episodes *Under my Skin* (5: 23) and *Both Sides Now* (5: 24) have us believing that Cuddy, the ever manipulated brunt of House's mood-swings, has set herself up in his apartment to shepherd him through the detox process, and in a fit of Mills and Boon-esque surrealism, becomes the willing recipient of his 'sexual magnetism'. Next day back at the hospital, Cuddy is aloof. As a means of forcing her to attend to his feelings, he yells her down as she confers with colleagues in the busy reception area by announcing that they had sex the previous night. He is subsequently fired. We discover that the sexual encounter was hallucinatory. Cuddy was never in his apartment. He never sweated the night away coming down off narcotics and venting his long-repressed sexual frustration, but spent it tripping on Vicodin. At the close of the final episode, he cuts a pathetic figure as he looks towards the entrance of the Mayfield Psychiatric Hospital. As poignant as this scene is, and if the last five predictable seasons are anything to go by, even an enforced and agonizing abstinence will not stymie his will to reuse and relive the pain of detox.

Conclusion

If we think of the ubiquitous walking stick/crutch in *House* as a symbolic fusion of the caduceus and the Asclepian staff, it helps us unpack the series and its emotionally crippled central character. While drawing on the pathologies of the human body/psyche as its backdrop and prime source of visual spectacle, the show can also be a surprisingly slippery package. Having survived five seasons, geared up for launching the sixth at the time of writing this chapter, and currently celebrating its status as the most watched program on television for 2008 by Eurodata TV Worldwide ratings (2009) (with a viewing audience of 81.8 million), *House* seems to have tapped the global zeitgeist. Although the character is often cited by cast members and Laurie himself as a figure who refreshingly speaks his mind, unrestrained by the rigors of workplace politeness (forced upon us mere mortals), House, it would seem, is less feral than this kind of promotion would lead us to believe. For trickster there is no regard for retribution, morality, ethics, or repercussions. House, on the other hand, while attempting to emulate the archetype, cares too much about being emotionally caught out, is far too vulnerable, and, it would seem, substantially ill-equipped to genuinely speak his mind. As a clichéd narcissist-bully, this un-evolved puer is yet to transcend his crippling infantile self-aggrandizement. House, a would-be Hermes and a gifted ancestor of Asclepius, stews in the liminal twilight between these oscillating energies. His caducean walking stick, a signifier of all he is and pretends to be, heralds both suffering and healing.

References

Currie, B. (2005) *Pindar and the Cult of Heroes*, Oxford: Oxford University Press.

Eurodata Television Worldwide (2009) Press Release, Eurodata Worldwide, Winners of the 4th International Audience Awards. Retrieved from www. mediametrie.com/eurodatatv/communiques/winners-of-the-4th-international-tv-audience-awards.php?id=81

Friedlander, W. J. (1992) *The Golden Wand of Medicine: A History of the Caduceus Symbol in Medicine*. Westport, CT: Greenwood Press.

Froman, C. R. and Skandalakis, J. E. (2008) One snake or two: The symbols of medicine. *The American Surgeon*, Vol. 74(4), 330–4.

Graves, R. (1960) *The Greek Myths: 1*. London: Penguin Books.

Grosz, E. (1994) *Volatile Bodies: Toward a Corporeal Feminism*. New South Wales: Allen & Unwin.

Habicht, C. (1985) *Pausanias' Guide to Ancient Greece*. Berkley, CA: University of California Press.

Hart, G. D. (2000) *Asclepius: the God of Medicine*. London: The Royal Society of Medicine Press.

Hesiod (1950) *The Homeric Hymns and Homerica*. (Trans. G. Evelyn-White). London: William Heinemann.

Hillman, J. (1983) *Archetypal Psychology: A Brief Account*. Dallas, TX: Spring.

Homer (1991) *The Iliad of Homer*. (Trans. E. Rees). New York, NY: Oxford University Press.

Jung, C. G. (1956) *Symbols of Transformation, Collected Works 5*. London: Routledge & Kegan Paul.

Jung, C. G. (1967) *Alchemical Studies, Collected Works 13*. London: Routledge & Kegan Paul.

Jung, C. G. (1969) *The Archetypes and the Collective Unconscious, Collected Works 9i*. London: Routledge & Kegan Paul.

Lempriere, J. (1949/1788) *Classical Dictionary of Proper Names Mentioned in Ancient Authors, with a Chronological Table*. London: Routledge and Sons.

Miles, S. H. (2004) *The Hippocratic Oath and the Ethics of Medicine*. New York, NY: Oxford University Press.

Neville, B. (1992) The Charm of Hermes: Hillman, Lyotard, and the Postmodern Condition. *Journal of Analytical Psychology*, Vol. 37, 337–53.

Pelton, R. D. (1980) *The Trickster in West Africa: A Study of Mythic Irony and Sacred Delight*. Berkeley, CA: University of California Press.

Radin, P. (1972) *The Trickster: A Study in American Indian Mythology*. New York, NY: Schocken Books.

Schilder, P. (1970) *The Image and Appearance of the Human Body: Studies in the Constructive Energies of the Psyche*. New York, NY: International Universities Press.

Waddell, T. (2006) *Mis/takes: Archetype, Myth and Identity in Screen Fiction*. London and New York, NY: Routledge.

Waddell, T. (2009) *Wild/lives: Trickster, Place and Liminality on Screen*. London and New York, NY: Routledge.

Wilcox, R. A. and Whitham, E. M. (2003) The symbol of modern medicine: Why one snake is more than two. *Annals of Internal Medicine*, Vol. 138(8), 673–7.

Film and television references

CSI: Crime Scene Investigation [television] (2000–present) Bruckheimer, J. and Zuiker, A. E. (creators), CBS Productions, Alliance Atlantis Television Productions, Jerry Bruckheimer Television, USA.

House, MD [television] (2004–present) Shore, D. (creator), Heel & Toes Films, Bad Hat Harry Productions and the Fox Broadcasting Company, USA.

Sicko [film] (2007) Moore, M. (director), Dog Eat Dog Films and The Weinstein Company, USA.

Note

1 This glitch is mentioned in *Whac-a-Mole* (3: 8), when a psysiotherapist urges House to hold his cane on the *left side* so that he can ease the weight from his right leg. When she's out of sight he immediately switches the cane to his right hand.

Chapter 5

Anatomy of genius
Inspiration through banality and boring people

Lucy Huskinson

HOUSE: I need an epiphany.

WILSON: There are other oconologists.

HOUSE: Better oconologists, but I need you . . . Let me describe the symptoms, problems, issues and you say whatever you feel like saying till something triggers an idea in my head.

WILSON: That's not the way it works.

HOUSE: It's another way of thinking about things. It's sloppy, it's undisciplined, it's not very linear, but it complements mine, drives me down avenues I wouldn't ordinarily . . .

WILSON: House, just go away.

(*Not Cancer*, 5: 2)

Introduction: House does not have a 'problem' relating to people

Dr Gregory House is an enigmatic character undoubtedly steeped in neuroses, and the temptation to psychoanalyze him and to account for his behavior is great. A superficial interpretation of his compulsion to alienate people, an impulse he has had since he was three years old (*Detox*, 1: 11[1]); his insistence that you 'Can't get angry if you don't feel anything' (*Histories*, 1: 10); his 'Rubik's complex' – his 'need to solve the puzzle' (*DNR*, 1: 9); and his addiction to the painkiller Vicodin are just a few of several neurotic traits. We could interpret these as symptoms of his unresolved anger towards his 'bastard' of a (non-biological) father, in relation to whom House admits, 'If he had been a better father I would be a better son. I am what I am because of him' (*Birthmarks*, 5: 4; cf. *Daddy's Boy*, 2: 5). Such speculative analysis is, however, all too easy. Furthermore, it spoils our fun. A diagnosed House is a boring House: House's neurotic disposition steals the show and makes *House* the captivating program that it is.

In this chapter I am seduced by a slightly different temptation – one that is, hopefully, less of a spoiler – and that is to dissect House's genius. In the course of doing so I shall reveal that House's supposedly 'neurotic' compulsion to alienate people, to objectify and trivialize them, is not symptomatic of a maladjusted personality per se, nor indicative of a 'problem' that would benefit from years of psychotherapy. Rather, I argue, such behavior is integral to the thought processes that enable him to 'think' his inspired diagnoses, or his self-professed 'epiphanies'. To put it another way, House needs to keep people at a distance and to find them banal so he can put them to good – healthy – use. People, as banal and trivial objects, evoke within House unrealized possibilities that facilitate both the development of his personality and intelligent insights that enable him to save the lives of others. Trivializing people – even insulting them[2] – is part of House's thinking process, and I claim that if he did not do so, he would not be the brilliant diagnostician that he is, but just another very good doctor. Indeed, in response to House's betrayal of his desire for intimate union with another (reunion with Stacy, his ex-girlfriend), Wilson asserts: 'You are so afraid that if you change you will lose what makes you special' (*Need to Know*, 2: 11).

House's distance from others is integral to his genius, and yet, as I shall argue, despite this apparent distance that House enforces, House *needs* other people to enable his intuition and inspired thinking. Moreover and more controversially, I assert that the genius in House needs to converse with the banality of boring people for its own realization. I therefore reject outright Jill Winters' claim that House can arrive at his diagnoses without other people. In Winters' opinion,

> One might like to imagine that House needs Foreman, Cameron, and Chase, that he "couldn't do without them". . . But the reality is, we have no evidence that they are integral. As individual doctors they might be valuable, but within the structural context of the show, they are not necessary. As viewers, we have every reason to believe that House *could* do it without him [*sic: them*] since week after week it is House having the final epiphany about a patient's condition.
>
> (2007: 41)

I undermine Winters' claim by providing the evidence that she could not find and implicitly calls for: I explain how the people around House – notably through their banal conversations with him – are integral to the realization of his epiphanies. It is no anomaly and no coincidence that when House finds himself without his team on board a flight with a sick passenger, he is compelled to construct a mock team comprised of flight passengers that resemble Foreman, Cameron and Chase respectively. Through conversations with this mock team, House can order his thoughts and arrive at an appropriate diagnosis. In contradistinction to Winters' opinion, I therefore concur with that of Cuddy, who orders House to hire a new team of colleagues when his thought processes stagnate shortly after his team disband. Cuddy rightly states: 'You need someone to bounce ideas off. You need a team' (*Alone*, 4: 1).[3]

In addition to the banter supplied by his colleagues, House finds in the clinic patient a rich source of banality to inspire the epiphanies of his diagnoses. The clinic is the drop-in centre in which House is forced against his will (by his boss, Cuddy) to treat people who walk in off the street with illnesses that are all too easy to diagnose. For House, the clinic goes by the other name of Hell. It is where House is 'condemned to useless labour' – a punishment Wilson identifies as 'the sixth circle of Hell' (*Damned If You Do*, 1: 5) – and where there is 'melancholy without hope' – a statement House follows with the question, 'Which circle is that?' (*Damned If You Do* 1: 5).[4] In Jungian terms, we would regard the clinic as the *shadow* to Jung's diagnostic practise, for during his clinic work the genius of House is repressed, made redundant and reduced to the inanity of treating what House considers 'boring' symptoms (such as common colds, sore throats, or in some cases, no illness at all). True to Jungian dynamics, House attempts to distance himself from this shadow aspect. He tries to escape its encounter by gambling away clinic hours in bets with Cuddy (*Detox*, 1: 11); he ridicules and belittles it by giving false diagnoses (*Joy To The World*, 5: 11), dodgy prescriptions and treatment (*Damned If You Do*, 1: 5; *One Day, One Room*, 3: 12), and by paging his colleagues for emergency consultations in order to mock the case with them (*Meaning*, 3: 1), or to put the joke on them by running out of the room when they arrive (*Skin Deep*, 2: 13; cf. *Occam's Razor*, 1: 3). In Jungian terms, the clinic is a 'house of Hell' – or, indeed, a portrayal of House in Hell – because it is within the clinic that House is forced to negate his genius and embody a regular (or, 'boring', as House would say) doctor and general practitioner. The shadow-clinic has an effect on House similar to that of kryptonite for Superman. However, as the Jungian cliché contends, the shadow is 'pure gold', as its integration within the self facilitates individuation and the wholeness of being. Therapeutic healing from a Jungian perspective requires one to engage with one's shadowy aspects and to learn from one's harrowing descent into Hell. If we accept the compensatory model of the Jungian psyche with its *enantiodromic* cycles, we must concede that House's genius requires the banality of the clinic patient for its realization.

House is certainly drawn to the trivial on both a conscious and unconscious level, to its pleasures and irritations. In addition to enjoying banter with his colleagues, he is devoted to his favorite hospital soap opera; he is an avid player of computer games, reader of comic books, follower of *Monster Jam* (entertainment that usually involves trucks crushing other trucks) and performer of practical jokes (*Safe*, 2: 16; *Saviors*, 5: 21); and he even has a television subscription to *The New Yankee Workshop*, where the presenter plays around with power tools (*Clueless*, 2: 15). Likewise, in his frustration with the triviality of the hellish clinic patients, we find rich pickings for his unconscious attraction to them.[5] What is not obvious, however, is how House's encounter with the trivial facilitates the profundity of his inspired diagnoses. In other words, how exactly is the banal integral to House's epiphanies of the correct diagnosis? By addressing the theories of Jung, cognitive psychology and object relations (particularly Christopher Bollas's ideas of the evocative and aleatory object), this paper will both answer this question, and also proffer the ironic hypothesis that it is through his relationship to people – including the boring, hellish clinic patient – that enables House to do his work, and to realize the genius that he is. In illustration of Foreman's claim that House likes 'contradictions piling up left and right' (*Dying Changes Everything*, 5: 1), I argue that House is fascinated by that which bores him; and that far from relating ineffectively to people by distancing himself from them, House engages with them to profound implication.

How House thinks

House's genius is in his ability to diagnose obscure illness accurately and quickly – before the patient dies, or before the patient undergoes an unnecessary life-debilitating medical procedure. But how exactly does House arrive at his diagnoses? And what are the underlying thought processes of his genius? Our answers begin with Jung's two designated pathways of thinking: *directed* and *undirected* thinking. These are ways of thinking to which we all subscribe, but House, I contend, does the latter particularly well.

According to Jung, we think 'with directed attention' when our thoughts 'imitate the successiveness of objectively real things'; that is to say, when 'the images inside our mind follow one another in the same strictly causal sequence as the events taking place outside it' (1911–12/1952: para. 11). Simply put, directed thinking is conscious, logical, causal deduction: a form of thinking that no effective diagnostician like House can afford to be without. Indeed, most of us would probably presume that House relies on directed thinking to figure out the correct diagnosis of his patient's illness. Certainly in almost every episode House uses a method of differential diagnoses to try to deduce, through elimination, the most reasonable diagnosis. To this end he consults his team and encourages them to debate the validity of the competing diagnoses in order to ascertain which is most likely and which empirical test will help to corroborate their choice. More often than not, House uses a whiteboard upon which he writes his differential diagnoses and further deductions. Occasionally we find House alone, staring intently at the board as if consciously willing the correct diagnosis to make itself known; and we even see him talk to it – 'We give you so much, and you give us so little' (*Distractions*, 2: 12). House uses other props to help direct his thoughts, such as his large red and white ball, which he bounces, catches, balances, juggles, and throws rhythmically as if attempting to initiate a parallel ordering of his thoughts – in much the same way as Detective William R. Somerset in the film *Se7ven* (1995) uses a metronome, the regular ticks of which, Somerset maintains, 'helps me think'[6] – and in very early episodes we find House consulting textbooks and computer files (*Pilot*, 1: 1; *Occam's Razor*, 1.3).

Non-directed thinking, by contrast, is a non-linear 'automatic play of ideas' that 'leads away from reality into fantasies of the past or future' (Jung 1911–12/1952: para. 18–19). We think without direction when 'we no longer compel our thoughts along a definite track, but let them float, sink or rise according to their specific gravity' (ibid.). In contrast to directed thinking, which comprises logical deduction in correspondence to perceived reality, non-directed thinking comprises a mental collage of unconscious associations: of 'images piled upon images' and 'feelings upon feelings' arranged 'not as they are in reality but as one would like them to be' (ibid.). To think without direction is to think non-rationally, beyond the concentrated focus of the ego. It therefore requires one to abandon the active pursuit of ideas and withdraw or dissociate from logical chains of reasoning, so that associated thoughts from a perspective untainted by the ego's prejudice can make themselves known. That which is beyond the ego's orientation is unconscious, and non-directed thinking is an unconscious activity; it is, Jung says, a form of 'dreaming' (1911–12/1952: para. 19).

Non-directed 'dream' thinking tackles conscious problems from perspectives not yet conceived by the ego, and can point to ideas and possible solutions that the ego has not been able to think. Thus, although non-directed 'dream' thinking appears to be disorganized, a composition of ideas and feelings linked by obscure associations, it is not without purpose, and leads often to conclusions of a rational and practical nature. Jung makes efforts to emphasize the teleological nature of non-directed thinking by referring to – what he construes to be – the authoritative sources of William James and Freud (1911–12/1952: para. 18, n. 16).

Despite its capacity to lead to rational conclusions, House is not convinced – on a conscious level – of the value of non-directed thinking, and he openly dismisses it. In response to Cameron's assertion, 'You are, apparently, afraid of discovering something you can't rationally explain,' House angrily snaps: 'Shut up!' (*Top Secret*, 3: 16). And yet, not only does House adopt both types of thinking (as we all do), he seems to become more dependent on non-directed thinking from the second season onwards, as his spontaneous insights or epiphanies likewise become more frequent. Whichever type of thinking he adopts depends on what he is doing and with whom. For House to begin to think with non-direction he must walk away from his whiteboard and turn on the television to watch a soap opera, or interrupt the intellectual debate of his colleagues on differential diagnoses to gossip about their personal, social and emotional lives. And, of course, these are the kinds of things House does. Time and again we see House move between directed and non-directed thinking, and, I contend, it is his switching between them – of distracting himself from the often 'difficult and exhausting' (Jung 1911–12/1952: para. 20) process of logical deduction – that enables House's epiphany of the correct diagnosis. House's capacity to realize and order his non-directed thoughts makes him the genius that he is. And House seems to be aware of this, for he proclaims as a categorical imperative of practical reason: 'Work smart, not hard: that's my philosophy' (*Deception*, 2: 09; *Act Your Age*, 3: 19), which is supported by his related imperative: 'Read less, watch more television' (*Control*, 1: 14). Indeed, when his team demonstrate their ignorance of this ethical law by asking him to turn off the television and return his directed attention to the problematic diagnosis, House overrules this, saying that 'I'm multi-tasking' (*No More Mr Nice Guy*, 4: 13).

'Work smart not hard': loaf about

In parallel to Jung's notions of directed and non-directed 'dream' thinking, Guy Claxton describes the 'hare brain' and 'tortoise mind' (1997). Claxton argues that intelligence and the capacity to solve problems increases when rational thought (the hare brain) is more readily abandoned to allow the unconscious (the tortoise mind) to think for us. Claxton writes:

> [I]t is sometimes a good idea to pull off the Information Super-Highway into the Information Super Lay-By; to stop chasing after more data and better solutions and to rest for a while . . . it is sometimes more intelligent to be less busy . . . there are mental places one can gain access to by loafing which are inaccessible to earnest, purposeful cognition.
>
> (1997: 14)

In an echo of Claxton's words, House himself says of the creative potential of non-directed thinking: 'It's another way of thinking about things. It's sloppy, it's undisciplined, it's not very linear, but it complements mine [and] drives me down avenues I wouldn't ordinarily [go down]' (*Not Cancer*, 5: 2). Claxton maintains that 'often our best, most ingenious ideas do not arrive as a result of faultless chains of reasoning. 'They "occur to us". They "pop into our heads". They come out of the blue' (ibid.: 49). They are, in House's words, 'epiphanies'.

The anecdotal evidence for such intellectual and creative enlightenment is abundant and often astounding. Claxton cites an array of historical figures who are regarded as 'icons of creativity and wisdom', and yet in actuality 'spent much of their time doing nothing' (ibid.: 4). Thus,

Einstein, it is said, would frequently be found in his office at Princeton staring into space. The Dalai Lama spends hours each day in meditation. Even that paragon of penetrating insight Sherlock Holmes [on whom Dr Gregory House is modeled] is described by his creator as entering a meditative state 'with dreamy vacant expression in his eyes'.

(ibid.)

To these figures we can add many more, including August Kekulé, the chemist who apparently discovered the molecular structure of benzene through a dream-like vision; the mathematician Henri Poincaré, who visualized the Fushian functions during caffeine-induced sleep; Giuseppe Tartini, who apparently dreamt of the devil playing the most beautiful violin score, which formed the basis of Tartini's technically demanding violin sonata in G minor; Otto Loewi, the pharmacologist who dreamt an experiment that would prove nerve impulses are transmitted chemically and not electrically, and so on.

The dormant period that follows the abandonment of focused, directed thinking about a problem and which precedes the spontaneous realization of its solution is often referred to in cognitive psychology as 'incubation' (see Wallas 1926). The role and effects of incubation for problem solving has been examined widely, and empirical evidence demonstrates that in most cases a period of incubation enables successful problem solving. Several explanations have been given for this. For instance, it is thought that incubation facilitates the cathartic release of mental or physical fatigue that accumulates during the more strenuous efforts of problem solving – efforts that Jung associated with directed thinking (1911–12/1952: para. 11). In this scenario, 'Underlying knowledge structures might remain constant, but the processing capacity available to deal with the problem might increase as the fatigue disappears' (Yaniv and Meyer 1987: 201). The beneficial effect of a period of distraction from the problem therefore results from the disruption of non-productive conscious thought rather than active unconscious processes. In other words, such distraction encourages one to abandon inappropriate approaches to the problem:

[P]eople often approach a problem with wrong cues, wrong heuristics, and/or wrong information. Following a period of distraction, such wrong approaches become less accessible or are forgotten altogether.

(Bos et al. 2007: 1115)

(Just as Wilson says to House: 'Now you've distracted me I think I might change my mind' [Saviors, 5: 21]). However, as I shall argue, the incubation period for House involves much more than a simple 'fresh look' alternative. House does not benefit from distraction simply because it interrupts his misguided conscious thought and releases psychic energy to allow for a new, unbiased orientation to the problem. When House is, to use Claxton's term, 'loafing' about and distracting himself from the diagnostic problem, he is not merely directing his conscious attention to something else that inadvertently refreshes his mind or that erases or negates the results of his previous efforts to figure out the diagnosis with directed thinking. Rather, House continues to think about the problem within this incubatory period, and he continues to think unconsciously through his previous deductions. Thus, when House plays his video games, watches banal programs on television, plays pranks on Wilson and Cuddy, reads comic books while eating his lunch sitting with coma patients, and so on, he is most likely engaged in an unconscious attempt to solve his case. For it is through his preoccupation with such apparently trivial activities that House is able to detach himself from the life-threatening problem posed; and consequently, is more likely to discover the sought-after solution. By engaging in these kinds of activity House is indeed 'multi-tasking' as he claims, for his mind is busy tending to the problem in its incubation, trying to tease out the answer that directed thinking could not. Not only does House's unconscious think, but its thoughts often prove to be more productive than those he thinks consciously.

How to have an epiphany

> No wonder you are such a renowned diagnostician. You don't even need
> to actually know anything to figure out what's wrong.
>
> (Wilson, *Pilot*, 1: 1)

The trivial activities with which House engages are integral to the realization of his epiphanies, and thus also to his genius. To call them trivial is, strictly speaking, inappropriate, for they facilitate the incubation of profound, life-saving diagnoses. When House loafs about, he is not doing nothing. Likewise, the incubation period that gives rise to the epiphany of the solution sought is not a passive vacuum of non-activity: House's epiphanies do not really emerge 'out of the blue' or in isolation from previous conscious attempts to discover them. Rather, the incubation period is merely one interdependent stage among others in the development of creative thought, and House's epiphanies are a complicated product of this developmental process.

Graham Wallas in his seminal work *The Art of Thought* (1926) postulates a four-stage developmental model of creative thinking, which can be traced clearly within the thought processes revealed by House's behavior. The first stage is 'preparation'. This is equivalent to directed thinking, where House attempts to answer the problem with logical deduction. When this attempt fails, the second stage comes into play. This is the 'incubation period', where we find House has abandoned his directed thinking about the problem and is now engaged in 'loafing' activities. The incubation period is difficult to enforce (likewise, non-directed thinking cannot be consciously willed), as it occurs after the limitations of directed thinking have been realized. Bollas makes the following point when writing about Poincaré's discovery of mathematical Fushian functions:

> Nor would he have achieved his breakthrough if he had not tolerated his ignorance, which I liken in the psychoanalytic situation to the capacity to tolerate not knowing what one is doing, so that uncertainty becomes a useful feature to the private work of the receptive process.
> (1992: 77)

The incubation period is an active time for the unconscious as it revises the ideas that were realized by directed thinking in the first stage. Later I shall both explain and illustrate how House's unconscious does this in its tendency to rearrange his directed thoughts through the 'dream-work' procedures of 'condensation' and 'displacement'. But for now we need only to note that House's inspired epiphanies are the product of this unconscious refiguring of directed thoughts. The epiphany comprises the third stage of Wallas's model, to which he gives the name 'illumination'. This stage marks the moment when the creative thought (such as the diagnostic solution) enters consciousness. This occurs when the person is still engaged in distracting activity and is thereby less influenced by the judgment of ego-consciousness and more receptive to unconscious communication. The fourth and final stage is 'verification', which involves the re-employment of directed thinking in order to test and corroborate the validity of the epiphany.

The process described by Wallas is apparent in House's behavior and can be traced in those episodes where he arrives at his diagnosis as if out of the blue. I shall outline several instances later, but for now let us look at one from the episode *Meaning* (3: 1). Here we find House trying to ascertain why surgery for a brain tumor has left a patient paralyzed for eight years, non-communicative and confined to a motorized wheelchair. The patient appears to attempt suicide by intentionally driving his wheelchair into a swimming pool. House and his team open their investigation by trying to determine what, if anything, other doctors have failed to find over the years. They yield no answer. This investigatory process constitutes the 'preparatory' stage of Wallas's model. Following recognition of their failure to arrive at an answer, House embarks on a loafing activity, which comprises the second stage of the creative process: the incubation period. Thus, while on Ketamine treatment to eliminate the pain and weakness in his leg, House goes for a long, sweaty run. He jumps into a water fountain to cool himself down, and it is at this moment that he has his epiphany (stage three: illumination). He realizes his patient has hypothalamic dys-regulation, which is to say he is unable to regulate his body temperature, and consequently he sought the waters of the pool not to kill himself but to cool himself down. A malfunctioning hypothalamus can lead to a variety of other problems, and House suspects that it is the cause of his patient's paralysis. House then seeks to work with his team to corroborate his inspired diagnosis, by rescanning his patient's head and repeating every blood test the patient has ever had.[7] This further investigation constitutes the fourth stage: verification.

In addition to Wallas's quadripartite model, House's creative thinking process reveals an additional – and, arguably, more interesting – pattern. And this is the intimate connection between stages two and three: between the incubation period and the moment of illumination or epiphany. Thus, in the example above we find that the loafing activity – of jumping into the cool fountain water – is analogous to the solution to the problem that is sought; and it is the content of this analogy that triggers the epiphany. In other words, House's unconscious employs mechanisms of association to communicate its work (i.e. the refiguring of House's directed thoughts) to conscious awareness. We shall examine these mechanisms of association later to expound on their role in House's inspired thinking.

House's epiphanies are a re-figuring of his conscious deductions, which means his unsuccessful attempts to solve the problem with directed thinking are integral to the realization of the correct solution. Both directed and non-directed thinking are essential to the realization of the epiphany. Thus, although the limitations of directed thinking need to be recognized if non-directed thinking is to be enabled, it is only through directed thinking that the productive ideas of non-directed thinking can be acknowledged. Poincaré expresses their interdependence when he claims of non-directed thinking: 'It is possible, and of a certainty it is only fruitful, if it is on the one hand preceded and on the other followed by a period of conscious work' (1915: 27).

House's astonishingly rapid incubation period

House is extraordinarily proficient in processing creative thoughts. Most astonishing is his capacity to navigate rapidly through the incubation period. Arguably, House's genius in problem solving resides not so much in his impressive intellect and vast reservoir of medical knowledge, but in his capacity to nurture unconscious thinking and allow his non-directed thoughts to reveal themselves to consciousness at the right time. In other words, his capacity for directed thinking makes him a great doctor, but his ability to tolerate uncertainty and to enable his unconscious to think for him makes House a genius. And his unconscious thinks for House at an alarmingly fast pace.

House is often criticized for being formulaic in its structure. We can reduce episodes to the following formula: a patient with unusual symptoms comes under House's care; House's team break into the patient's house to discover clues that help with the differential diagnoses of the illness; the patient's symptoms become mysteriously aggravated; an – often contingent – event occurs that leads House to discover the correct diagnosis; the patient is cured. In those episodes where House has an epiphany, it usually occurs approximately 34–38 minutes into the 40–43-minute episode. The majority of these episodes are therefore taken up with stages one and two of Wallas's model of creative thinking. In other words, the events in the episode comprise the incubation of the successful diagnosis: the twists and turns of the plot are ingredients for House's unconscious play and comprise a composite of associations that lead House to discover the hidden diagnosis. Luckily for House, his unconscious works incredibly quickly to rethink his rational deliberations and to project its refiguration of this material on to and into the objects that surround him (thereby animating them in such a way that House cannot fail to be drawn to them and ever so deftly discover their latent, associative meaning). The rapidity with which House is able to harness his non-directed thoughts (that is, to both solve the problem unconsciously and then have his unconscious convey the solution in such a way that it can be decoded easily by House's conscious mind) is astonishing. But is it implausible?

Of course we cannot answer this definitively, as we cannot apply time frames to the atemporal unconscious, and we cannot therefore predict the likelihood of an epiphany's occurrence (except, of course, within the formulaic reality of *House*). However, there is evidence to suggest the implausibility of House's super-efficient incubation period. Indeed, even Dijksterhuis and Meurs (2006) – who maintain that the unconscious *can* be measured – have found epiphanies (or what they call 'eureka moments') difficult to test and to monitor on the basis that

> [T]he period of incubation experimental participants are given in a lab experiment is often very short compared to real life creativity. After all, sometimes creativity can take months of even years.
>
> (ibid.: 136)

Furthermore, there is compelling evidence to suggest a direct correlation between the length of the incubation period and successful problem solving, with a greater chance of success happening after a longer incubation period.[8] If we were to examine House's remarkable success at problem solving alongside the evidence gathered from other test cases, we would expect the length of incubation required for him to obtain his results to be considerably longer – months or years longer – than the average length of time he himself took. As Bollas notes:

The unconscious play work that a subject devotes to any set of received 'issues' incubates an internal organization derived from and devoted to such effort. A scientist working on a scientific task, for example, plays with many ideas; years may pass before he has an inspired idea that heralds an important discovery.

(1992: 75)

However, the evidence to suggest the implausibility of House's short incubation periods is less compelling when we appeal to House's strong receptivity to his unconscious communications generally. Although, as we have noted, House is consciously resistant to irrational sources of information, he enables his unconscious to think for him with relative ease. Indeed, if we accept Jung's assertion that consciousness and the unconscious are related by compensation, House's conscious resistance to non-rational sources makes him particularly susceptible to being 'ambuscaded by them' (1950: para. 620) and having them take control of his mind to alter the way he thinks. Indeed, as we witness in the course of seasons three to five, House's unconscious becomes increasing forceful in its capacity to think on behalf of his ego-consciousness. Thus, in season three we find House a recipient of prophetic and lucid dreams, in which he both learns the identity of his next patient and the coded diagnosis of his patient's condition (*Top Secret*, 3: 16). Then in season five, we see the unconscious take over House's thinking in more startling ways. Thus, in *House Divided* (5: 22), we find House conversing with a persona of his split personality (the hallucinatory figure of Amber, Wilson's recently deceased girlfriend and a student of House, over whose death House seems to harbor guilty feelings). This possessing complex recalls with ease facts House's ego-consciousness had otherwise forgotten and makes decisions contrary to House's ego-judgment (cf. Jung 1948: para. 203). Amber, as a personification of House's autonomous unconscious, appears to have a more efficient intelligence and a greater reservoir of knowledge at her disposal than his familiar ego-consciousness. Amber is the thinker of House's unthought thoughts, and the personification of his non-directed thinking processes. She herself cannot rationalize how she thinks; when she attempts to do so she says its 'just a glimmer, I couldn't put it into words.' Amber's presence does not diminish, and by the end of season five the unconscious overturns House's ego-orientation almost completely by instigating psychotic episodes from which House seeks relief by checking himself into the local sanatorium.

The affective presence of Amber within House's mind leads to the thought that House's rapid incubation periods are not as implausible as one might first have thought. The forcefulness with which House's unconscious thinks on behalf of his personality obscures the dividing line between his madness and his genius. For House, the unconscious capacity to think is the source of both his inspiration and his mental breakdown.

House, master of condensation, or 'the guy who sees connections between everything' (Wilson, *No Reason*, 2: 24)

We have so far outlined the general developmental process through which House realizes his epiphanies. Let us now turn to specific examples of House's epiphanies to deconstruct them according to this process. We will focus on the incubation period, to elucidate those unconscious processes that enable the moment of epiphany.

We have already noted that House's epiphanies arise out of his unconscious capacity to sift through the mass of knowledge and directed thoughts that he has accumulated and to rearrange it rapidly and in accordance with associative patterns that elude the judgment of the rational ego. We have also mentioned that House's unconscious tends to rearrange his directed thoughts through the 'dream-work' procedures of 'condensation' and 'displacement'. Now we shall turn our attention to these procedures of association to explain exactly how House's unconscious employs them to reorder his directed thoughts about the problematic diagnosis, and to communicate its solution to ego-consciousness in the form of epiphany.

Condensation and displacement in dream thinking

House's unconscious is particularly masterful in its employment of condensation and displacement, which is nowhere better illustrated by House's inspired moments of epiphany. For House's epiphanies are ideas that have been refashioned and remolded according to these mechanisms of association.

Jung described condensation as the underlying dynamic of non-directed thinking when he noted that the unconscious piles image on image, 'feeling on feeling, and . . . shuffle[s] things about and arrange[s] them not as they are in reality but as we would like them to be' (1911–12/1952: para. 19). In order to better understand condensation and displacement, however, we would do well to turn from Jung to Freud.

According to Freud (1900), the dream is 'the royal road to the unconscious', and it is through an awareness and examination of the different aspects of the dream's construction – which, collectively comprise the 'dream-work' – that we are able to interpret more effectively the meaning of the dream. Thus, in order to make better sense of House's dream-thoughts – of which his epiphanies comprise – we would do well to begin with an examination of the dream-work that underpins it.

At this point it is important to emphasize that we are not here concerned with the meaning of the particular 'dreams' that House has when he is asleep – such as the prognostic dream mentioned above – rather, we are concerned with the general 'dream-like' process that underlies his non-directed thoughts and associative thinking.[9] According to Freud, the dream comprises a distortion of reality through four different unconscious 'dream-work' processes: condensation, displacement, representation, and symbolism. Of these, I am concerned with the first two. Thus, condensation distorts reality (and thus reorders directed thoughts) by merging together a number of associated ideas and feelings into one condensed image. Condensation explains why dreams 'are brief, meager, and laconic in comparison with the range and wealth' of meanings that are concealed within its narrative (ibid.: 383). Displacement, on the other hand, distorts reality by replacing one idea with another which in some way is closely associated with it. By this process, the emotional signification of the real object or idea is separated from it and is attached to a different, unexpected one. Condensation is a form of displacement in so far as, 'instead of *two* elements' effectively exchanging places, 'a single common element intermediate between them' is found (ibid.: 454).

According to William James, the underlying connections that inform general associative thinking – and thus those associative connections of condensation and displacement – are 'empirical concretes, not abstractions' (cited in Jung 1911–12/1952: para. 18). They are therefore gleaned from our observations and experiences, and are from rational deduction.[10] Amusingly, William James further notes that associative thinking is 'a sort of spontaneous revelry of which it seems likely enough that the higher brutes should be capable' (ibid.). And Dr Gregory House undoubtedly exemplifies such a 'higher brute'! For House demonstrates with great consistency the realization of practical and theoretical truths through the collation and reshuffling of empirical concretes.

Once we are aware of the solution of the correct diagnosis revealed to House in his epiphany, we are able to trace the paths of associations – the condensations and displacements – that his unconscious mind probably took to enable its realization. These paths of thought develop during those periods of loafing about; when House is not trying to conceptualize the diagnosis abstractly through directed thinking. Thus, if we pay attention to the sub-plots and the apparently superfluous occurrences within relevant episodes of *House* – and particularly to the apparently mindless conversations and trivial activities to which House is drawn – we find the diagnosis that House seeks in condensed and displaced form. Let us now turn to specific examples for illustrations.

Examples of House's condensed thinking

House arrives at his inspired diagnosis by engaging with those objects within his vicinity that convey the identity of the diagnosis through their associative meaning to it. This meaning is conveyed to House through a variety of mediums, including visual images, tactile sensation, and – as

Freud himself may well have predicted (1900: 403–13)[11] – through word-play in conversation with others.

On screen we find the patterns of association vary in complexity. They may, for instance, be relatively short, so that a fleeting glimpse of an image is enough to trigger the identity of the diagnosis. This is exemplified in *Informed Consent* (3: 3) where House watches a flirtatious daughter of a patient walk past, whose red thong attracts House's attention not merely for their obvious conscious appeal to him, but for the importance of their associative meaning to the diagnosis that has been incubating within him. The red thong captivates House and trigger the epiphany of the diagnosis: 'Congo Red!' (A dye, which is itself indicative of amyloidosis). To this Foreman replies, 'How the hell did you pull that out of your mind?' 'Not out of mine,' House says, 'I had a muse.' Another example of a visual stimulus providing an apparently brief associative link arrives courtesy of the crotch of House's handyman. Thus, in *Painless* (5: 12), we find House captivated by the sight of his handyman, who grabs and scratches his crotch. Yet within this banal action House finds the associative link to the profound diagnosis: by drawing attention to his crotch, the handyman enables House to realize that his patient is having epileptic seizures in the sensory area of the brain that controls muscular support of the testicles. Further examples where House's epiphanies appear to result from immedi-ate associations made to external stimuli include the time he watched wrestling on television and subsequently realized that his patient has an 'out of his head hormone-aggressive' problem (*Act Your Age*, 3: 19) and the occasion we cited earlier of the tactile sensation of cooling water, which led House to realize that his patient was unable to regulate his own body temperature (*Meaning*, 3: 1).

There are, likewise, occasions where the realisation of the diagnosis takes relatively longer. For instance, where House is unable on his first attempt to engage with the associative meanings presented to him, but is able to after successive promptings. This is illustrated in *House's Head* (4: 15) when House is desperate to recall the identity of the person he was with in a bus crash. His unconscious conjures up a hallucination of a woman whom several times asks House 'Who am I?' 'What does my necklace mean?' When House notices it is made of amber, he realizes the person he seeks is Amber. Similarly, in *Lines in the Sand* (3: 4), we find the diagnosis – a worm parasite swimming in the young patient's eyes, contracted from his sandpit – implied throughout the episode in various images. Thus, before House realizes the diagnosis upon observing the patient's drawings of wavy, 'worm-like' lines, we twice see House draw wavy lines in Wilson's 'sand-play' tray; we also find House sitting in front of a conspicuous artistic water feature – where water moves in wavy ripples; and House makes the pertinent comment (to his self-proclaimed 'muse': the girl with the 'Congo-Red' thongs): 'Here's looking at you kid.'

The realisation of the diagnosis can also take longer when the inspired thought employs a *series* of associations for its expression. A good example is in *The Greater Good* (5: 14) where House's epiphany follows a train of associations within conversation with Cuddy. The associative links in this example are more complex than those already noted partly because House has a complicated personal investment in the person of Cuddy. Cuddy represents to House a potential love interest. She therefore evokes in him a complex network of associated thoughts and feelings. By the time of this episode Cuddy and House are aware of yet resistant to their growing mutual attraction. Cuddy's confused feelings for House – and her indecision as to whether to return to work full time or stay at home to care for her (adopted) baby – causes Cuddy to take out her frustration on House. When Cuddy attempts later to apologise to House they strike up a particularly crass conversation that leads to House's epiphany. The case that House has been struggling to diagnose is a female patient who continually bleeds from a lung lesion and from within the pericardinal sac (which compresses her heart, and prevents it from beating correctly). In his conversation with Cuddy, House rebukes her apology: 'Are we gonna have to do this dance again in 28 days?' Cuddy responds angrily: 'What the Hell is wrong with you?' House replies: 'Yesterday you hate me. Today you're practically weeping on my shoulder. I can only assume that what I'm hearing is your Aunt Flow telling me . . .' House then withdraws momentarily to have his epiphany. It is House's apparently banal and offhand PMT jibe at Cuddy that reveals to him the correct diagnosis. Aunt Flow is indeed telling House the answer, for at this moment House realizes his patient is bleeding heavily because she is menstruating, and her 'flow' is aggravated by ectopic endometriosis. House continues to think in associative terms, though perhaps more consciously at this time,[12] for in response to Cuddy's next remark, 'When I was being a jerk you suddenly act human, but when I act human, you turn back into a jerk', House continues the menstrual analogy and says, 'Guess our cycles aren't matched up yet.' This throwaway comment is suggestive of House's desire for Cuddy and his potential 'match up' with her. Furthermore, it implies a parallel process where House's condition is identified with his patient's: in both cases the '(menstrual) cycle' refers to a compressed heart that is unable to beat correctly.

Why House needs others to think for him

'I've just given you the answer, haven't I?'

(Wilson, *Joy*, 5: 6)

I will now continue to deconstruct those epiphanies of House that appear to be triggered in his conversation with others. I shall do so in order to expound the integral role other people play in House's creative thinking process, and also to explain why House's genius is reliant on the banality of others.

As we have seen, House's engagement with trivial and banal activities provides the incubation for his creative thinking on problematic diagnoses. House's unconscious, I have claimed, often thinks for him and realizes the correct diagnosis through its non-directed or associative thinking. The seemingly trivial objects in House's environment are selected – according to their association to the answer – and animated by House's unconscious projections onto and into them so that those external cues that trigger House's epiphanies of thought are given affect by the unconscious itself.

Christopher Bollas's notions of the evocative and aleatory object are particularly useful to us for elucidating the importance of other people within this creative thinking process of House's, and especially of those clinic patients who embody the shadow-aspects of House's genius. Let us now explain how.

Bollas develops Winnicott's concept of the 'use of an object' to give an account of non-directed thinking from an object-relations perspective. He argues that

> [O]ur encounter, engagement with, and sometimes our employment of, actual things is a *way* of thinking . . . we select objects because we are unconsciously grazing: finding food for thought that only retrospectively could be seen to have a logic . . . whether we are pushed to thought by objects arriving or we seek objects to use them as forms of thinking, it is clear to us all that such existential engagements are a very different form of thinking from that of cognitive thought.
>
> (2009: 92–3)

Whether House selects other people or is selected by them is not apparent. What is clear however is that House unconsciously employs other people to evoke those ideas that cannot be ascertained through directed thinking. Indeed, as one commentator of Bollas writes, 'Unconscious thinking initially requires the facilitating presence of others who make available to us what would otherwise be unthinkable' (Beck 2002: 13). Indeed, by using others to think, House is psychologically fusing with the other in 'an intimate rendezvous' (Bollas 1987: 31); he maintains a 'deep subjective rapport with the object' (ibid.: 28) so that he can use it to incubate an undiscovered part of himself. House must therefore 'lose himself' in his projective identification with the object in order to allow it to transform him and furnish him with a new perspective. Thus, far from not needing other people to help him with his diagnoses, as Jill Winters asserts, we find House seeking intimate connection with others to enable him to think, and to become the genius of a diagnostician that he is. Bollas summarises such seeking and need to think through the other thus:

> . . . a person projects a part of himself into the object, thus psychically signifying it. This gives the object meaning, converting it into a tool for possible thought: the thinking that is special to the dream state. To do this, however, the subject must 'lose himself' in moments of experience when he projects meaning into objects, a type of erotic action that must be unconscious and one in which the person is not being, as it were, thoughtful. Indeed, he must be a rather simplified consciousness, even out of touch with himself for a moment, in order to invest the object world with psychic potential. Viewed this way, this type of projective identification is ultimately self-enhancing, transforming material things into psychic objects, and thus furnishing an unconscious matrix for dreams, fantasies, and deeper reflective knowings.
>
> (1992: 22–3)

This applies well to what House does. Those moments where House withdraws momentarily from his conscious activity before the epiphany occurs illustrate well Bollas's description of the moment of projective identification: when House engages with those objects into which he has projected his unconscious thoughts, and realizes the associative meanings (to his diagnostic solution) that are latent within them.

The evocative object facilitates the transformation of House from knowledgeable diagnostician to inspired genius. In the illustrations above we saw that House occasionally projects aspects of himself into objects other than people (such as the red thong, fountain water, and sand). However, it is in his conversations with people – especially those of a banal nature – that we find particularly rich pickings for the unconscious dream narrative that House creates to facilitate his transformation. In the following section I outline several illustrations of what is arguably the favoured medium of object-relating of House's unconscious: the banal conversation.

Constructing genius through banal conversation

The majority of House's epiphanies appear to be triggered by condensed and displaced patterns of association that arise in his conversation with others – notably with Wilson and Cuddy.

I have identified occasions where House's epiphany follows a conversation with Wilson.[13] Thus, in *Damned if You Do* (1: 5), House is convinced his patient – a young woman who lived a wild life before becoming a nun – has had a severe allergic reaction, but he cannot ascertain what she is allergic to. When Wilson asks him how the case is going, House replies: 'She has God inside her. It would have been easier to deal with a tumor.' Wilson responds crassly: 'Maybe she's allergic to God,' and walks off. House appears to have a (somewhat subdued) epiphany on the basis of the condensed meaning of his comment merged with Wilson's (that is to say, that she is allergic to something – to God – inside her). Consequently House calls his team to look for an allergic reaction *within* the patient. A CT scan subsequently reveals an old copper intra-uterine device (a contraceptive) in the shape of a *cross*, to which, it transpires, the patient is allergic.

In *Hunting* (2: 7), House's epiphany occurs during an increasingly confused conversation with Wilson where three subjects of the conversation – House's pet rat, called Steve McQueen, his patient and the patient's father – become condensed into one. In response to Wilson's dismay with House for bringing his infected rat into work, House says, 'His infection is not contagious to humans.' House and Wilson walk as they talk, and they pass the father of House's patient sitting outside the room of his sick son. They talk briefly about the patient before Wilson conjectures, 'Who knows what else he might have: parasites, bacterial infection.' House responds: 'The kid doesn't have parasites.' Wilson replies: 'Not the kid, the rat.' At this point an epiphany appears to be dawning on House. House asks Wilson: 'Was he still sweating?' To which Wilson responds: 'Rats only sweat through their tails.' House says: 'Not the rat, the dad.' House then withdraws into himself for a moment and has his epiphany. Walking back to the patient's room, House asks: 'Where are they from?' Wilson says: 'Er, Montana. Why?' House responds: 'You were right, it was a parasite. Cancel the biopsy it will kill him.'

Freud notes that the 'construction of collective and composite figures is one of the chief methods by which condensation operates in dreams' and thus also in 'dream-thinking' (1900: 400). And, in addition to the example above, we can cite another conversation about a composite identity that fuels House's epiphany. This time the condensation is a merger of Wilson's feelings towards his schizophrenic brother, Danny, and the symptoms of House's patient. Thus, in *The Social Contract* (5: 17) Wilson reveals to House that he is still racked with guilt over his neglect of Danny and Danny's subsequent compulsion to run away from home without his medication. House responds tactlessly: 'Talk about an overreaction to a single event!' Wilson retorts: 'It was a pretty big event!' House insensitively notes: 'Of course he [Danny] overreacted too, but . . .' At this point House withdraws from the conversation as his epiphany emerges. He says quietly: 'His glucose was normal.' Wilson responds: 'We're not talking about my brother anymore are we?' When describing the patient's illness House later says: 'He has Doege-Potter Syndrome. *This whole thing is an overreaction.* That one small fibroma [cyst], it's benign. His body is acting like it's an invader. His antibodies went to war against it; they *got carried away* and attacked his other systems.'

The last illustration I will describe from House's conversations with Wilson is perhaps the most amusing, as House is identified – through associations made by his unconscious – to be a greedy parasitic worm. Thus in *Insensitive* (3: 14) House steals Wilson's sandwich. In response Wilson asks: 'Do you get some primeval thrill out of beating the other hunters to the food?' At this point House realizes his patient has a 25-foot parasitic worm feeding off her within her gut. The other eight examples appear in: *All In* (2: 17); *House vs God* (2: 19); *Resignation* (3: 22); *Alone* (4: 1); *You Don't Want to Know* (4: 8); *Joy* (5: 6); *Unfaithful* (5: 15); and *Saviors* (5: 21).

We have already described an epiphany that occurs in conversation with Cuddy. There are two further examples, which both revolve around babies.[14] Thus in *Cane and Able* (3: 2) House chastises Cuddy for lying to him by pretending to talk to her unborn child inside her womb: 'Oh your mummy is in such trouble. She is such a liar. That's why you don't have a daddy. That's why she had to. . .' House has his epiphany and realizes that his patient is a chimera – 'he has two sets of DNA. He's two persons in one' – and his brother is deceiving him with hallucinations, and is generally 'like a bad doubles' partner . . . who just takes up space and gets in the way.'

In *Big Baby* (5: 13) House unsuccessfully deduces a diagnosis through directed thinking as we find him late at night bouncing his ball while staring at his whiteboard, before Cuddy appears with her baby. When the baby vomits on House's neck, Cuddy laughs, and House asserts: 'Some people have evolved to find baby puke cute. Cos otherwise we'd kill 'em all before they became functional.' House then has his epiphany and says, 'Bonding is over. I've gotta go see another baby.' The diagnosis is revealed to House through his verbalization of the threat to babies who are not yet functional, for House realizes that his patient's problems are due to her dysfunctional ductus arteriosus (a shunt that enables the blood of the foetus to bypass the lungs) which did not close properly after birth.

In addition to the six epiphanies House has in conversations with clinic patients – which I treat separately below – three can be discerned in conversations he has with others, including a young girl in the canteen (*Merry Little Christmas*, 3: 10)[15]; Lucas, the private detective House hires to spy on his colleagues (*Not Cancer*, 5: 2); and Cameron (*The Itch*, 5: 7).

In the next section I explain the particular significance of the boring clinic patient for House's associative thinking process, in order to convey both House's attraction to and his need for this shadow personality in the realization of his genius.

House's aleatory objects: The genius's need for boring people

For Bollas, some objects evoke a greater awareness of self; they 'release us into intense inner experiencings which somehow emphasize us . . . lift us into some utterance of self available for deep knowing (1992: 29). Like House, Bollas describes this moment of insight as 'an epiphany' (2009: 30); and as 'a surprise' (1987: 31) that feels 'revelatory' (1992: 88), and which 'sponsors a deep conviction that such an occasion must surely be selected for us' (1987: 32). And such moments need to be surprising if they are to evoke a new perspective. Insight cannot be anticipated or desired (Grotstein, 2002: 78; Bollas, 1992: 37; 2009: 93).

In Jungian psychology there is, arguably, nothing felt to be more surprising than the irony of becoming enlightened by engaging with one's inferior shadow traits, and thus seeing light in the shadow (1959: para. 872; 1945/1954: para. 335). I have argued throughout this chapter that House's epiphanies are born ironically from out of the trivial loafing activities to which he is unconsciously drawn. Now, we see how House's genius is likewise facilitated by his encounters with those 'idiotic' clinic patients, who inhabit the 'Hell house' of House's shadow. The most surprising source of intelligence for House is also the most unlikely: the banal conversations of those people who have no interesting illness to diagnose. The 'boring' clinic is both the (Jungian) shadow to House's genius, and House's (Bollasian) aleatory object. On both counts, House's engagement with the boring clinic patient enables his insight and self-transformation.

Time and again we find House complain that various things are 'boring'. Yet there are also times when House is receptive to the creative potential of boredom. Thus, in *Birthmarks* (5: 4) we learn that if House 'hadn't been bored one weekend' then his friendship with Wilson 'wouldn't exist'. In philosophical discourse boredom is often been regarded as a prerequisite for creativity. Furthermore, as Heidegger contends, profound boredom reveals being and subsequently allows one to open up to oneself and to grasp one's possibilities for being (1929/1930). Arguably, House's unconscious comes close to illustrating Heidegger's notion as it finds within boring patients, and banality in general, the means to realize the profundity of the sought-after truth (and, as Wilson maintains, 'House's [diagnostic] work is who he is').

Boring clinic patients do not test House's directed thinking, but they are food for thought for his non-directed thinking. While they themselves have nothing interesting to be diagnosed, they often suggest the diagnoses for House's more 'interesting' problematic cases. Let us now end this chapter with examples that demonstrate the power of the boring clinic patient to facilitate House's genius.

Final illustrations: Inspiration through boredom

As the seasons of *House* progress we find House less involved with on-screen clinic duty. Consequently, the clinic patient is a medium for House's epiphanies in the first two seasons only. In the following five scenarios the associative link between clinic patient and problematic diagnosis seems glaringly obvious and requires minimal decoding by House's consciousness.

In the first two episodes of season one, House realizes invaluable information for the diagnoses of his problematic cases when he berates his idiotic clinic patients. Thus, in *Pilot* (1: 1), while reprimanding the mother of a boy for not allowing him to use his asthmatic inhaler daily as prescribed, House begins to lecture her on the value of steroids for her son's condition, and stops mid sentence to have his epiphany. He rushes out of the clinic to tend to his problematic patient, who, he claims – like the clinic patient – 'needs steroids'. In the next episode, *Paternity* (1: 2), House encounters a mother in the clinic who refuses to vaccinate her baby on the basis that vaccinations make money for large national pharmaceutical companies. House undermines her opinion with great sarcasm. Later, when it transpires that his problematic patient is an adopted child, House's earlier conversation with the clinic patient prompts House to ask whether the biological mother of his patient had been vaccinated against measles as a child. It comes to light that the patient has a mutated measles virus caught from his mother.

In *Fidelity* (1: 7) House encounters in the clinic a woman with breast implants bought by her for her husband's birthday present, whose husband is putting his own blood pressure medication into her oatmeal breakfast to decrease her sex drive. When she asks him for advice on what she should do, House says: 'If you care about your husband at all, I'd do the responsible thing. Buy yourself some condoms, go to a bar and find . . .' House stares into the distance as he has his Epiphany. 'Huh,' he says, before leaving to consult with his team over the diagnosis of his problematic patient. To his team he announces: 'Luckily I have the answer.' The patient has caught African sleeping sickness from having sex with someone – other than her husband – who has been to Africa.

In *Love Hurts* (1: 20) House meets in the clinic an old couple. After bickering with each other, the couple make up in front of House. When the man squirts breath freshener into his mouth before kissing the woman, House says to himself: 'Welcome to Hell' – at which point he has his epiphany. He reaches into his pocket to bring out a packet of *Tic Tac* mints – one of a whole drawer full that Chase found in the house of the problematic patient. House realizes the patient was trying to cover his bad breath, and he diagnosis the symptoms as fulminating osteomyelitis (infected jawbone).

In *Skin Deep* (2: 13) a man comes to the clinic twice to be treated by House for his 'sympathetic pregnancy'. The clinic patient has too much estrogen in his body, which causes him to grow breasts. Later, when his wife goes into labor, the patient pages House to help him through it (as he, too, appears to have gone into labor). In response to the wife, who complains about her husband's behaviour, House says: 'Shut up! You have the perfect man – a woman! He's got more estrogen coursing through his veins than . . .' It is then that House has his epiphany. He sets out to prove the diagnosis that he now has in mind for his problematic patient (a 16-year-old supermodel, who he calls 'the ultimate woman'). House is correct and says to his patient: 'You've got male pseudohermaphrodism . . . You're immune to testosterone. You're pure estrogen . . . The ultimate woman is a man. Nature's cruel, huh.'

Finally, in *Clueless* (2: 15) House's problematic patient is a man who comes under House's care after suffocating for no apparent reason during sexual role play with his wife (House consequently names the wife 'Mrs Nympho'). While working on his case, House attends clinic duty, where he encounters a man who needs treatment for herpes. When the man asks House how he could have contracted it, House gives him the impression that his wife must be cheating on him. Later we discover his wife has been tested for the disease. When Cuddy gives House the wife's test results he asks both her and Wilson whether one would ordinarily tell one's partner that one has herpes or wait till he or she contracts it to shift the blame. House continues to hypothesize: 'Then maybe it was the wife. Maybe she was the one who . . .' House stares into space and has his epiphany, as he realizes his words apply equally to 'Mrs Nympho', who he realizes is poisoning her husband. After failing to corroborate his new theory with empirical evidence, House is forced by Cuddy to meet with the husband and wife, who both have herpes. The couple fight and accuse each other of sleeping around. The wife throws her gold wedding ring on the floor. As House picks it up he has a further epiphany: 'Mrs Nympho' is poisoning her husband with gold sodium thiomalate!

References

Beck, J. (2002) Lost in thought: The receptive unconscious. In J. Scalia (ed.), *The Vitality of Objects: Exploring the Work of Christopher Bollas*. London and New York, NY: Contiuum (pp. 9–37).

Bollas, C. (1987) *The Shadow of the Object: Psychoanalysis of the Unthought Known*. London: Free Association Books.

Bollas, C. (1992) *Being a Character: Psychoanalysis and Self Experience*. London and New York, NY: Routledge.

Bollas, C. (2009) *The Evocative Object World*. London and New York, NY: Routledge.

Bos, M. W., Dijksterhuis, A. and van Baaren, R. B. (2007) On the goal-dependency of unconscious thought. *Journal of Experimental Social Psychology*, 44, 1114–20.

Claxton, G. (1997) *Hare Brain Tortoise Mind: Why Intelligence Increases When You Think Less*. London: Fourth Estate.

Dijksterhuis, A. and Meurs, T. (2006) Where creativity resides: The generative power of unconscious thought. *Consciousness and Cognition*, 15, 135–46.

Freud, S. (1900) *The Interpretation of Dreams*. Trans. J. Strachey, The Penguin Freud Library Vol. 4. Penguin Books, New edition. Middlesex: Penguin. 1991.

Fulgosi, A. and Guilford, J. P. (1968) Short-term incubation in divergent production. *American Journal of Psychology*, *81*, 241–6.

Grotstein, J. S. (2002) 'Love Is Where It Finds You': The Caprices of the "Aleatory Object'. In J. Scalia (ed.), *The Vitality of Objects: Exploring the Work of Christopher Bollas*. London and New York, NY: Contiuum (pp. 78–92).

Heiddegger, M. (1929/1930) *The Fundamental Concepts of Metaphysics: World, Finitude, Solitude*. Trans. W. McNeil and N. Walker, Studies in Continental Thought. Bloomington, IN: Indiana University Press, 1995.

Jung, C. G. (1911–12/1952) Two Kinds of Thinking, *Collected Works* 5. London: Routledge & Kegan Paul.

Jung, C. G. (1945/1954) The Philosophical Tree, *Collected Works* 13. London: Routledge & Kegan Paul.

Jung, C. G. (1948) A Review of the Complex Theory, *Collected Works* 8. London: Routledge & Kegan Paul.

Jung, C. G. (1950) A Study in the Process of Individuation, *Collected Works* 9i. London: Routledge & Kegan Paul.

Jung, C. G. (1959) Good and Evil in Analytical Psychology, *Collected Works* 10. London: Routledge & Kegan Paul.

McMahon, J. L. (2009) House and Sartre: 'Hell Is Other People'. In H. Jacoby (ed.), *House and Philosophy: Everybody Lies*. Blackwell Philosophy and Pop Culture Series, Oxford: Blackwell (pp. 17–29).

Poincaré, H. (1915) Mathematical Creation (Trans. George Bruce Halsted). In B. Ghiselin (ed.), *The Creative Process*. New York, NY: Mentor. California paperback edition, 1985 (pp. 22–31).

Se7ven (1995) directed by David Fincher, written by Andrew Kevin Walker. Time Warner/New Line Cinema.

Sio, U. and Omerod, T. C. (2009) Does incubation enhance problem solving? A meta-analytic review. *Psychological Bulletin*, *135*, 94–120.

Smith, S. M. and Blakenship, S. E. (1989) Incubation effects. *Bulletin of the Psychonomic Society*, *27*, 311–14.

Wallas, G. (1926) *The Art of Thought*. New York, NY: Harcourt, Brace.

Winters, J. (2007) Dysfunctional Family in Residence. In L. Wilson (ed.), *House Unauthorized: Vasculitis, Clinic Duty, and Bad Bedside Manner*. Dallas, TX: Benbella Books.

Yaniv, I. and Meyer, D. E. (1987) Activation and metacognition of inacessible stored information: Potential bases for incubation effects in problem solving. *Journal of Experimental Psychology: Learning, Memory, and Cognition*, *13*(2), 187–205.

Notes

1 References to episodes of *House* are to season number followed by episode number.

2 As Cuddy notes, 'Go to your office. Play with your ball. Write on your whiteboard. *Insult your team*. Do whatever it is that you do to figure things out!' (*Euphoria, Part 2*, 2: 21).

3 My opinion is further corroborated in *Team Work* (6: 7), an episode of season six that went to air in America just before the completion of this chapter. Here House is seen to stalk both 'Thirteen' and Taub to try to coerce them to rejoin his team after it breaks up once again. House needs to work in a team and he goes to great lengths to regroup his team after it disbands. Indeed, as Cameron remarks (to House) in this later episode, 'You risked another patient's life to bait your old team.'

4 I concur with Jennifer L. McMahon's (2009) well-argued assertion that House's relationship with others – especially with his clinic patients – is tantamount to a Sartrean Hell.

5 Amusingly, we can employ the dichotomy of Heaven–Hell to highlight the difference between House's respective attraction and aversion to the trivial. While Hell for House is personified by the boring clinic patient, we learn that, 'two all-access passes to . . . the biggest official monster truck jam in the history of New Jersey' comprises 'passes to paradise itself' (*Sports Medicine*, 1: 12).

6 House also walks rhythmically in circles. Such exercise, as Cameron asserts, relieves his leg pain, and prevents his thoughts being distracted by it (*Who's Your Daddy?* 2: 23). The converse is also true: when captivated in thought by interesting cases, House is distracted by his pain (ibid.). However, a hallucinatory figure of House's mind notes a direct correlation between the reduction of House's pain with House 'getting dumber' (*No Reason*, 2: 24).

7 Although in this instance Cuddy denies House the necessary treatment that would prove him correct (on the basis that his epiphany 'is a wild guess that came to you while sweating'), she herself treats the patient accordingly and refrains from telling House he was – yet again – correct, in an attempt to teach him a lesson in humility.

8 See for instance Fulgosi and Guilford 1968; Sio and Ormerod 2009; Smith and Blakenship 1989; Yaniv and Meyer, 1987.

9 A concern shared by Christopher Bollas, who argued that Freud's model of dream work underpins all of our unconscious thinking (Bollas 1992, 2009).

10 Bollas similarly notes that 'this play with the elements [is] prior to logical construction . . . a combinatory play that leads to the eventual establishment of a new perspective' (1992: 76); and the contemporary psychologists Yaniv and Meyer corroborate the empirical construct of such associations when they claim that the incubation or 'dormant' period 'offers opportunities for an individual to experience new environmental stimulus inputs, which may trigger chains of associations and suggest analogies toward a good solution (Yaniv and Meyer 1987: 189).

11 On the basis that the ambiguity of words makes them well disposed to the play of displacement and condensation.

12 Indeed, when House later explains the diagnosis to Drs Kutner and Taub he alludes again to the number 28: 'There's about a 3 or 4 in 28 chance [the menstruation] is a coincidence. Which leaves a much bigger chance that the diagnosis is ectopic endometriosis.'

13 This chapter was written before season six aired in America. I have since watched the first ten episodes of season six. Two of these episodes depict House having an epiphany following a conversation with Wilson: *Instant Karma* (6: 4); *Known Unknowns* (6: 6).

14 Interestingly, Cuddy has an epiphany of her own when discussing a 'baby-related' theme with House in *Joy to the World* (5: 11). When complaining to House of his faked miraculous diagnosis of a clinic patient's virgin birth (human parthenogenesis), which he staged to win a bet with Wilson, Cuddy realizes that

House's more problematic patient has eclampsia (a life-threatening complication of pregnancy) and not leukemia, which means, she says, 'we don't have one dead patient, we have two.'

As mentioned above, since writing this chapter I have had the opportunity to watch season six, episodes 1–10. Of these there is one further instance of House having an epiphany following conversation with Cuddy (in *Brave Heart*, 6: 5). Their conversation is flirtatious. Cuddy says to House, 'You press my buttons, I press yours.' House replies, 'But by buttons you mean . . .' at which point he has his epiphany. The displaced theme of 'pressing buttons' is later revealed in House's diagnosis of his patient, to whom House says, 'You have also inherited a self-destruct button.'

15 This instance is a particularly good illustration of the associative link with the diagnostic answer sought. Thus, when the girl introduces to House her toy bear, called 'Bill', as a dog, House begins to explain her faulty syllogism: 'Just because you call Bill a dog doesn't mean he is a . . .'.It then suddenly dawns on House that his problematic patient is not in fact a dwarf (like her mother). To his colleagues he echoes his conversation to the girl, asserting that: 'Just because we called her a dwarf doesn't mean she is a dwarf.' Rather, as House reveals, the patient has a growth hormone deficiency caused by a pituitary tumor.

Chapter 6

Limping the way to wholeness
Wounded feeling and feeling wounded

Angela Cotter

> Why is it always acceptable in House-land to take an emotional problem
> and sidestep it by turning it into a mechanical problem?
>
> (Wilson, *Both Sides Now*, 5: 24)

Wilson's question to House in the last episode of Series 5 encapsulates a key
aspect of House's character and is the central thematic facet of what I will
explore in this chapter.

At home with the mechanics of modern medical health care, and
undoubtedly functioning brilliantly as a diagnostician within this framework, House remains curiously unschooled, indeed almost inept, in the
world of emotion (*Both Sides Now*, 5: 24). Indeed, his boss, Cuddy, tells him
in this episode that people who get close to him get emotionally battered. I
will dwell on this episode longer because it marks a turning point in House's
televisual journey. The primary patient in this episode appears at first sight
to have a split between right and left brain functioning. This dysfunction
allows House the opportunity to decry the right brain in a most unmitigated
way. House insists that he is a man of the left brain, i.e. valuing cognition,
thinking and intellect, those very qualities privileged in current Western
society. By his and society's insisting on the advantages of these qualities, the
right brain is inevitably cast into shadow. The right-brain world concerns
basic survival by means of emotion and intuition; it is primarily non-verbal.
Indeed in this episode, House finds the right brain to be pure encumbrance
(despite the fact, as I explore later, that a good argument could be made for
his being an intuitive, right-brain character!). In an ironic twist at the end of
Series 5, we see the doors of a psychiatric hospital, a huge old-style institution, close in on House. He has committed himself as a voluntary patient
after realizing the depth of his hallucinations and his need for help in freeing
himself of them. The viewer is left to wonder how he will manage in this
uncanny role of being a patient after so many years.

Whatever the future holds at that point, it could be said that House has
pushed his left-brain world too far – that he has always been on the edge of

sanity but now has moved beyond that edge. This chapter argues that "House-land", at least as portrayed up to the end of Series 5, is indeed a polarized, one-sided world but one that is not so far away from the practices of the current medical system. Indeed, it is a world that many health care workers also enter at the cost of their mental or physical health.

Yet there is another salient factor to be considered to point out the comprehensive dilemma this trend presents. In current Western society it is significant to note that the virtues of the left brain are associated with male characteristics – i.e. thinking and cognition, analytical or logical aspects of understanding – while the right brain is accorded the traditional feminine ones – i.e. the emotional aspects also associated with a more diffuse, holistic dimension. What I propose to explore is the nature of the kind of healer House is in light of his lopsided practice. My scrutiny of this character affords me the opportunity to consider how he reflects what Robert Johnson has argued about the vicissitudes of the development of Western "civilization" and its privileging of left-brain functions. This development has been made at the cost of a serious collective wounding to the feeling function which both men and women now carry (Johnson 1993). A scientific explanation of brain functions is beyond the scope of this chapter, but my argument focuses on the thinking and feeling functions.

As a corollary to this disjunction, the first part of the chapter will briefly reflect on the current biomedical model of health care with a particular focus on the so-called "curing-caring" divide. Central to my argument is that modern health care practice no longer enshrines the split between "curing" and "caring" that took firm hold in the nineteenth century. Doctors were perceived as those who cure, and nurses as those who care. It has now gone beyond this. Actually, caring in the sense of "bedside nursing" has almost vanished from the picture, at least in acute general hospitals.

As a nurse and now a Jungian analytical psychotherapist, I have always been interested in how caring and emotion have been seen within medicine and all disciplines associated with medicine. Relevant aspects of my own experience are woven into the commentary throughout the chapter, which will end with reflections on House's experience as he is treated in a psychiatric hospital in the first (double) episode of Series 6.

In response to these tensions, I consider alternative concepts of the "wounded healer" as part of a counterculture movement towards wholeness rather than perfection in health care. Although I will specifically explore later in the chapter what kind of "wounded healer" House is – if he is one at all, although it seems evident on the face of it that he is one. To provide the framework, I will describe four different strands of the healer concept, evidenced in practice by research undertaken in 2005–2006. Throughout, my discussion will return to where House is situated within these strands.

Before continuing an assessment of the caring dimension of health care, it must be pointed out that there are certain ways in which House seems to offend against the *prima facie* concept of the wounded healer despite some salient attributes. The wounding is evident in his limp, which was caused by an infarction, and his addiction to Vicodin is a running sore. Clearly he is a brilliant diagnostician and healer in the allopathic arena. I would argue, in line with my themes, that House's core wounding is actually in the feeling function, symbolized by the wound in his thigh, similar to the Fisher King's wound that Johnson (1993) associates by analogy to the wounded feeling function. In this aspect, House overcompensates with his one-sided left-brain approach within the current biomedical model and even though he exaggerates the approach, the right-brain nevertheless emerges.

It has long been noted that current reductionist, mechanical models of biomedicine produce a fragmented picture of the human being, increasing specialization, and producing a failure to grapple with the existential problems encountered by the ill person (see, for example, Dubos 1959), Heron and Reason 1985, Illich 1975, Kidel and Rowe Leete 1988, Price 1984). Relevant to the argument here, Kidel (1986), for example, has commented on the fact that the Western model of medicine leads to us being trapped inside a model that rigidly separates "physical" from "emotional" or "mental" events and struggles with understanding the link between them. Cartesian dualism is often seen as lying behind this split, which is enshrined in the medical system by the curing/caring divide. In the past, medicine was seen as dominating the field of health care with a model of "curing" that was technological, positivist and reductionist. "Caring" was ascribed to women as their innate "natural" role (*qua* being mothers) with the subsequent conclusion that nurses did not need training to nurse (Davies 1980, Salvage 1985).

Presumably, the appeal for House in the "House-land" model is that it apparently manages to avoid difficult emotional and existential issues by focusing on the diagnostic physical end of the spectrum. Although at times House appears to get emotionally involved (especially when he is dealing with children), the emotion soon gets in the way for him, and it is brushed aside as an uncomfortable aspect rather than as an integral aspect of the healing (as indicated above by his brushing aside right-brain functions).

House reflects a dis-ease, un-ease, that perpetuates the deep problems of our current health care system. Nowhere is this more sharply illustrated in my view than in the current situation of nursing. The documentation on nursing history has often lamented the emphasis on the "moral" aspect of nursing as it concerns the lack of recognition of nursing skills and knowledge (e.g. Rafferty 1996). Coupled with the growth of evidence-based practice in health care – those practices informing NICE (National Institute of Clinical Excellence), based in the UK, for example – and changing demographic issues leading to a shortage of and an ageing population of nurses, this has in turn led to an emphasis on the "science" of nursing and the importance of nursing skills (e.g. Nelson and Gordon 2006).

These distinctions have been interpreted in a narrow way on the political and policy stage, in the UK at least, whereby evidence-based practice in general has come to be seen as encompassing mainly technological interventions that can be made manual and therefore can be researched using randomized controlled trials. So, for example, the relational aspects of care fall outside this bracket. In short, as medicine has become more technical so has nursing. This has tended to lead to a focus on nursing as a series of technological tasks, like undertaking the dressing of wounds, while such fundamental nursing care needs such as feeding patients and assisting them with toileting and personal hygiene, are delegated to care assistants and at worst neglected. In August 2009, the Patients Association published a report called *Patients Not Numbers, People Not Statistics* to raise awareness of the failings in hospital care being highlighted every week through phone calls to their Helpline, emails and letters. This report contains 16 illustrative descriptions of poor care received, nearly all of which centre on concerns over basic nursing and personal care. The report hit the headlines because it mentioned that nurses sometimes appeared cruel, but the general findings were not new to those monitoring health care, at least in certain specialties.

For example, in 2001, I was a researcher on a Department of Health Nursing and Midwifery Committee (NMAC) report into standards of acute care for older people. This derived practice guidelines in response to concerns then expressed about these same issues (NMAC 2001). The Patients' Association report (op. cit.) does include the caveat that, if the National Inpatient Survey results are taken into account, only two per cent of patients rated their care as poor, with 43 per cent rating their care as excellent in 2008. However, this 2 per cent held constant over the six years of the survey (2002–2008) and equates to over a million patients. This is despite an increase in nursing staff of 26.2 per cent between 1996 and 2008.

Coincidentally, while writing this chapter, my partner was admitted to hospital with very severe sickness and a possible intestinal obstruction. This allowed me the opportunity to observe caring at first hand. The compartmentalization of the work was very evident – all the staff were only intent on their own particular job – and, though helpful when stopped and asked a question, they usually replied that you needed to see another person (e.g. "your" nurse). Patients sometimes assisted other patients with personal care, such as when a man with oedematous legs had his dressings done and the nurses just left, so he requested another patient to help him on with his surgical shoes. The nurses did come back but it was not at all clear whether they would have assisted him with his shoes. They rather seemed to accept without any comment that the other patient had assisted.

Two other episodes stood out. One night my partner was sick on a bed sheet, covering an area of about eight inches in diameter. The nurse who came in simply wiped the sick off the sheet and said "We'll change that in the morning." He was too ill to argue. Second, he was sick on the floor and a nurse came in who wiped a cloth round with her foot then left. Admittedly she came back a bit later, rather shamefacedly saying "I've been told to do it properly." It was not clear to him whether these were qualified or unqualified nurses, but the point remains that they saw this care as acceptable. Arguably the health care system and nursing itself seems to have forgotten in practice that this fundamental care has an effect on patient recovery and infection rates, and can be seen as a part of nursing. Perhaps they do not see it as the job of a nurse to clear up and clean. It is true that all patients, visitors and health workers are encouraged to wash their hands in chemical soaps but basic caring tasks may have become subsumed under the weight of medical and nursing technology. A one-sided view of curing is the order of the day a higher value is put on the technological tasks and caring is undervalued.

The wounded healer – aspects and definitions

In this context, the concept of the wounded healer provides a framework that goes against the grain because it is fundamentally about a holistic approach to healing and health. The wounded healer archetype, also describes the archetype of the doctor–patient, and it is activated every time a person becomes ill (Guggenbuhl-Craig 1971). For the illness to heal, the intra-psychic or inner healer has to be contacted by the patient as well as being projected onto the external doctor. Within the doctor, by contrast, inner illnesses are awakened by the patient, and the patient/illness side of the archetype is projected onto the external patient. If neither can acknowledge the existence of the other pole within themselves, the relationship prevents a real cure taking place. Both repress one pole of the archetype, project it onto the other and then attempt to reunite the archetype through power. The doctor

> objectifies illness, distances himself [sic] from his [sic] own weakness, elevates himself [sic] and degrades the patient. He [sic] becomes powerful through psychological failure rather than through strength.
>
> (ibid.: 94–5)

In this model, the key to breaking the circular relationship is that the doctor must allow the patient's potential for self-healing to flourish. In other words, the doctor must be able to acknowledge her/his own wounds to reunite the split archetype of the wounded healer. Doing this, however, means stepping down from the pedestal of (assumed) omniscience, acknowledging vulnerability, and allowing the patient to participate in the healing process (Jess Groesbeck 1975). Now clearly Gregory House is not a wounded healer in this sense, which is based greatly on an acknowledgement of the importance of the self-healing powers of the patient, drawing on a homeopathic understanding of disease and concepts such as the placebo effect. Granted he is wounded, but he would be more neatly classified as an archetypal physician of Western allopathic technological medicine. However, an exploration of the wounded healer in depth may prove illuminating here.

In my PhD thesis, I differentiated four different strands of the wounded healer (Cotter 1990). The first is the healer who both wounds and heals. The second is the healer who has walked close to death and recovered. The healer who bears a permanent wound is the third, while the fourth is the healer who heals through their wounds. These are not mutually exclusive in that it is possible to belong to more than one category.

The healer who heals and wounds

The first strand goes back to the earliest views of disease, which often attributed religious causes to it: disease was divinely created and so must be divinely cured. The goddesses and, later, gods of pre-Christian times were often seen as having a dual role:

> In the older Goddess representations, such as the Egyptian Sekhemet, or the Indian Kali, we still find the complementary aspects of engendering life, love and joy as well as reveling in suffering, destruction and death.
> (Whitmont 1983)

Later Apollo, frequently seen as the paradigm of this kind of wounded healer, was seen as the god who kills, yet also purifies and heals (Kerenyi 1959). A saying of Apollo is that "the wounder heals". This is often referred to as the knife that wounds also heals. It is paradoxical because it relies on an idea that the divine physician was the sickness and the remedy (Jess Grossbeck 1975). Because he/she was the sickness, he/she was afflicted and because he/she was the divine patient he/she also knew the way to healing. House's wounds – in the thigh from the infarction and his addiction to Vicodin – give him the claim to being in this category, since having the wound is the way in. But there is a more subtle consideration. Ultimately, this notion of the wounded healer as both the one who wounds and the one who heals is an analogy for the surgeon, and underlies much of our allopathic medical practice, such as surgery. There is often little recognition of the impact that having to wound patients has on doctors and those in the professions allied to medicine. The surgery or cutting into a patient, i.e. the wounding, may create a wound in the doctor or nurse. When I worked in health promotion in the 1980s, I remember talking to student nurses about their work. One talked of how difficult it was to pass a naso-gastric tube into a patient. She said that it felt like torturing the patient and then added,

"But of course you get used to it." My response was that of course while it is true that you get used to it, this does not detract from the fact that it remains a very difficult thing to do.

The 30 interviews which I conducted during my time as Ferguson Fellow at Woodbrooke Quaker Study Centre in Birmingham contain several different examples of health workers, at all different points in the current hierarchy of health care, all caught in this conundrum. There was the care assistant who feared that her administration of orally administered morphine regularly to a patient who was dying had hastened their death – which in an unsupported and untrained situation is quite a burden. Those who know about pain management at its best will say that regulated and controlled administration of pain-relieving opiates should not hasten death because the build-up of the dosage allows it to be tolerated. But this may or may not have been such a case. There was also the nurse who administered the final dose of an opiate knowing that it would ease the passage to death. There was the medical student on a specialist course whose work involved animal experimentation, which was abhorrent to him, but he had to do it as part of the degree. There was the medic whose work involved imparting details of a poor prognosis – or, not to put too fine a point on it, was the one who says, 'Actually, you are dying.' A doctor in their thirties at the time of the interview revealed the impact of this aspect of the work:

> And I actually think that as a group the defence of most doctors against this kind of thing, [they] even the nice and caring ones, have blank patches. Often around death, and often around sexuality, and you know areas that are . . . and I can think of a number of doctors who I think are great, good doctors . . . the number of really caring doctors I've worked with who cannot ever bear to tell people that somebody is dying . . . I think the doctors, who come back to the profession and say, "Let's look at our feelings. Let's get help", you know, like Elisabeth Kubler Ross . . . the people who come back are almost deliberately discredited, because it's too dangerous, you are threatening our collective defence, our collective defence is not just that exactly like the nurses [you researched], "they're the patients we're the well ones", but "We don't have feelings, they're the people with feelings, we need to help them with their feelings".

The interview continued:

> Modern doctors' communication skills [training] in breaking bad news [emphasize] we must help patients with their feelings. No wonder it is difficult. And the reactions I have seen in groups of young doctors when someone running a workshop calls for a response and says,

"How did you feel about that". People just go completely into, almost absolute denial and repression: "I have no feelings about that". "How does that make you feel?" "Well, nothing."

House discusses the issue of breaking bad news in the episode (*Three Stories* 1: 21). He asks a student how they are taught to tell someone they are dying, adding: "It's kind of like teaching architects how to explain why their building fell down." It is, in other words, an admission of failure on the doctor's part. House continues by asking whether the students are graded on supportiveness and gentleness, pointing up the irony in having to break bad news with compassion: "The weird thing about telling someone they are dying is that it tends to focus their priorities. You find out what matters to them. What they're willing to die for." For House, the main point of interest in delivering bad news is not how the patient is affected emotionally but rather how they are affected in a specifically medical sense. And we see throughout the series the ways in which this holds true for him. He delivers such news in very brutal ways, at times with no seeming concession to the shock that may be felt on the receiving end. Sometimes he uses that reaction to get a more specific diagnosis. Despite his explanation of how to deliver such news to patients in *Three Stories* (1: 21), he highlights the difficulties of doing so. Yet the very fact that medical students are trained in breaking bad news is an acknowledgement that this is a situation that affects both parties.

A participant in my research who was a social worker spoke about the impact of receiving bad news delivered in a cold way:

> I asked about my prognosis, and the response was, "If you're lucky, you will still have some sight in five years." Now that was about 1981, so this person was saying you might be blind by 1986 . . . So I was absolutely gobsmacked by that. That for me was the emotional wall really, I just hit the wall . . . and I remember being very, very, very distressed. I don't remember that person as a person at all, I just remember that assault really . . . there was no sense of care at all about what was being said or how it impacted on me.

They continued:

> And in three weeks I'm going to an annual conference. There will be people there all with my . . . type of problems. They will talk from 30 years ago, or 40 years ago, [about] what was said at the time of diagnosis, and just occasionally people with speak with warmth, and often tears about a good experience, and at other times people will still talk of pain, anger and tears about what was destructive.

Presumably underlying the concept of the wounded healer is the idea that the experience of the wounding somehow will increase the empathy of the healer. In many of the interviews which I undertook, this clearly related to a reported increase in "experienced sensitivity" among my interviewees because they had experience of being both "wounded" patients and "healers".

But despite his experience of illness, this increase in empathy does not seem to hold true for House. He delivers his diagnoses or prognoses with great brutality. Whether or not this is a defensive strategy, the effect on the patient remains the same. However, there is nothing in the described first strand which says that it is necessary to wield the wounding/healing knife gently to be a wounded healer of this type. Indeed the earlier concepts would not appear to entertain this as part of the idea. It is a later requirement as we have moved towards a greater recognition of the importance of attending to patients' feelings led by research into patient experience.

The healer who walked close to death and recovered

How does House fit within the second strand of the wounded healer? The second strand is the wounded healer who has walked close to death and recovered. In Greek mythology Asklepios is hailed as providing the blueprint of the divine physician and indeed of the wounded healer. His "wounding" was that he was snatched from the jaws of death. His father was the God Apollo and his mother the mortal Coronis. Apollo abandoned her when she was pregnant and she took a mortal lover, being tired of waiting for Apollo to return. Apollo took revenge by slaying her. However, seized with remorse for his unborn son, he delivered Asklepios by Caesarian section when Coronis was on a funeral pyre.

Asklepios became a renowned physician during his lifetime but was only raised up to divinity as a physician after his death. He was killed by Zeus, who hurled lightning at him either for over-reaching himself when he raised a mortal from the dead or for simply being too successful as a healer and depriving the underworld of the dead. There were such terrible cries of anguish from humans after his death that Zeus raised him from the dead and immortalized him. This appears as his second encounter with death and rebirth and this time into immortal life. John Sanford in *Healing and Wholeness* (1977) says that this brush with death is common among those who are closely involved with successful healing. Such people, he says, "live, and work, close to death, and they themselves . . . are people who have felt the hot breath of death or illness, and have narrowly escaped destruction" (43).

Already we see two different components of this strand. The first is the healer or helper who has walked close to death and recovered. The second is the healer or helper who, perhaps following the initiatory experience of being close to death, continues to walk within that arena and to that extent constantly keeps the experience of being close to death alive. This may result in having a permanent wound. To that extent, this strand and the next one are closely allied. However, let's start by looking at the first aspect: the experience of very acute illness.

This component is closely allied to the shamanic initiation in tribal societies where the person (often a child, but it may also be an adult) who experiences either acute or ongoing illness is marked out as the one with the vocation to be a healer – a vocation that is not always received as a positive one. It is argued that this kind of experience often contains an initiatory aspect whereby a new window on the world is opened for the person experiencing the illness. To give an example from my research, a psychiatrist who underwent mental health treatment for depression both in hospital and as an outpatient commented on the effect it had on their work:

> Well I suppose I wasn't particularly dogmatic in my attitudes because I felt that I'd been very vulnerable myself, and that this person who was a patient now, not me but someone else, was in that same situation; and I couldn't, I don't think I could have easily said, "Oh you must have ECT, you know, that's the thing for you" . . . or "You must be on this sort of medication and you better keep to it" – this sort of thing, these attitudes of being the director and the patient being the recipient and I think because I'd been a patient I, particularly when there was no alternative, I felt I was in a situation that I had to accept it and I couldn't get out of it. But in my talking to patients afterwards, I think this is true, I was more ready to listen than to lay down the law, as it were. It was more a two-way process but again if you're working in an institution, the other staff are not particularly willing to accept this more liberal situation where you share more rather than impose on a person.

In this example, the initiation involves someone already involved with health care, for whom a new window opened on the patient's perspective. This again links with an empathic and closer relationship with how it feels to be a patient. House has experienced very acute illness, where he, so to speak, walked close to death, when he suffered an infarction in his leg. The resultant pain (probably caused by the medical attempt to bypass the circulation to the dead muscle) was at one point so severe that he had to be put into a chemically induced coma. However, there is one important enduring symptom, an enduring wound that may impede his empathic responses. This is the chronic pain that was left and that is ongoing. Whether because of this or, as is sometimes implied, because of his addiction to Vicodin, which he takes to relieve the pain, House is presented as often irascible and blunted. Again he appears to be a wounded healer with the marks of being wounded and the marks of being a healer but perhaps not (yet) being a "wounded healer" as conceived in the Jungian canon. The learning from this is that being wounded *qua* being wounded does not a wounded healer make.

The healer who bears a permanent wound

Let us turn to the third strand of the wounded healer to see whether House fits within this category. This concerns the healer who has a permanent wound. Chiron the centaur is the mythological figure often cited here. It was to Chiron that Asklepios was sent for instruction in the art of healing and indeed for his upbringing. Chiron's wound is said to have been caused by an arrow of Hercules and remained incurable, until he traded immortality for mortality. He was later taken from Hades and immortalized. He is a strange figure in Greek mythology because he is a god and yet he has an incurable wound. Having this wound, however, seems to have led him to a great knowledge of herbal medicine as he searched out cures. In the legend of the Holy Grail, the Fisher King is similarly permanently wounded in his thigh. However, rather than this propelling him to search for a cure, the Fisher King is permanently wounded until he can pass on his guardianship of the Holy Grail to another. There is one obvious parallel between the Fisher King and Gregory House: both are wounded in the thigh. Therefore, I want to look at Johnson's (1993) interpretation of the Fisher King legend to see if there are further parallels. Johnson discusses the sad character of the Fisher King who is the guardian of the Holy Grail, yet unlike the others in the castle he alone cannot receive the nourishment and healing it can provide because of his wound, which causes him to lie on his bed groaning. To be near something beautiful or precious but be unable to experience it is, Johnson claims, the subtlest form of torture (ibid.: 35). Because the feeling function gives a sense of joy, worth and meaning to life, a wounded feeling function can lead to a depressed and flattened state. To be clear, a wound in the feeling function does not mean that feeling is not experienced at all but rather that it is undeveloped and in the shadow. For Johnson, this is the collective price we have paid for the "cool, precise, rational, and scientific world" (ibid.: 17).

It could be argued that the narrow evidence-based world of health care informed by business targets and measurable standards is conducive to the development of a wounded feeling function in both its male and female workers. As a young doctor among my research interviewees said about ill-health in their workplace:

> And the department itself has its problems with sick leave: one of the consultants had six months off herself recently, one of the health advisers has been off, one of the nurses has been off. I mean, people go on and off with depression, it's a stressful job but it's acknowledged, you know. In my last department, from talking to the registrars, four

out of five of them had depression, three of us were on medication. I was not the only person off on sick leave. One of the consultants was in hospital having ECT, several consultants had been off in the past but nobody ever would mention it.

This sounds like ongoing wounding, a permanent wound, in part arguably generated by a system that has a wounded feeling function. It is possible that the situation of House at the end of Series 5, where he is admitted to a psychiatric hospital, is not so unusual for health workers.

The healer who heals through their wounds

Turning, finally, to the fourth strand of the wounded healer: this is the aspect where the healer heals through their wounds or takes on the wounds of others. This is also a shamanic conception of healing and perhaps easier to see in societies where the boundary between individuals is different. As one interviewee said about this idea of relationship:

> A lot of years ago, I met a phrase and it said – it was an African phrase – and it says not "He's got the flu", or "He's poorly", but this particular tribe uses the phrase which translates as "I am sick in my brother". And it sort of breaks down this division between you know "he's ill, I'm not" . . . it's sort of; it creates an image of the bond, doesn't it? I think it's a beautiful phrase, absolutely lovely and it's not just on an individual level but to me it translates globally as well really.

In a very alienated or individualistic society, which I am positing here, it is hard to imagine what the experience of this kind of connection may be. Sadly, however, this often means that some experiences of energetic connection between individuals may be left unexplored. I recall teaching massage to student nurses and one saying, "Sometimes you feel you could drown in someone else's soul," to which another reacted quickly with, "You mustn't say that." The way that House portrays this fourth strand is not however in these kinds of dimensions. He is extraordinarily careless about his own health in many ways. He treats himself like an experimental laboratory at times in that he is prepared to try medication and surgical interventions on himself. While sometimes this is seeking after a cure for his own health issues, at others it is clearly done for his patients. The most striking example of this is in *Wilson's Heart* (4: 16) where he undergoes electrical stimulation of the hypothalamus to evoke his memories of being with Amber on the bus so that he can find the clue to what is wrong with her. This leads to him going into a coma following a partial seizure that affects most of his temporal lobe, widening his skull fracture and leading to a brain bleed. In a sense, the extremes he goes to in relation to using himself as the experimental field are at times so unusual (injecting himself with patients' blood, injecting himself with nitroglycerine to cause a migraine) that one wonders whether they must be there to emphasize a point. Yet what could that point be? Could it be that the one-sidedness of his brilliantly rational and cognitive mind is offset by a shamanic aspect that, unbalanced by a strong feeling function, leads him into recklessness?

To recap, the fourth strand of the wounded healer described here is about the healer who takes on the wounding of others and heals through processing it themselves. Jung's discussion of the psychology of the transference and his parallels of the therapeutic relationship with alchemy put him in this domain (Jung 1966/1954). This work has been further developed by Jungian analysts (e.g. Sedgwick 1994, Schwartz-Salant 1998, Stein 1984, Schaverien 2002, among many others) with a focus on the implications of neuroscience for the relationship entering their explorations recently (Paris 2007, Wilkinson 2006). However, House is unusual in that he is working within the general medical field, and it is not the therapeutic relationship with which he is working, but physical medicine. Again he is an unusual kind of wounded healer.

House, the wounded healer

Gregory House MD would appear to sit uneasily among the congregation of wounded healers as traditionally explored within the Jungian context. Yet, there may be changes afoot. At the time of writing, the first episode of Series 6, *Broken* (6: 1) had been aired in the UK. This covers House's admission and discharge from psychiatric hospital, alluded to at the start of this chapter. A different dimension of House appears in my view during the second hour of that episode. He seems much more vulnerable and more connected relationally. In particular, the relationship with his psychiatrist, Dr Nolan, is interesting here. Their sessions cover a lot of ground in between a challenging exchange of banter. There is an interesting point in their exchanges where Nolan tells "Greg", as he is known in the psychiatric hospital, that "You're not God, House; you're just another screwed up human being who needs to move on." This follows an interchange where House is berating himself for encouraging Steve "Freedom Master" in a delusion that he can fly to disastrous effect. It seems that House's idea of justice is that if he hurts someone he has to suffer equally. Hence Nolan makes the earlier comment. This underscores House's vulnerability by indicating his inflated view of himself. Later in this same session, Nolan encourages House to apologize to Steve. He adds, "Apologize to him. Let yourself feel better. Then you can learn to let yourself keep feeling better." The double entendre of "let yourself feel better" is germane to my argument. House needs to be better at feeling. Indeed the episode ends with Nolan saying that House can be discharged because he was emotionally hurt and came to him to talk about it rather than rejecting everyone. This is a more relational perspective and therefore a breakthrough for House. It remains to be seen whether Greg can continue to learn to let himself feel better, and let the wounded feeling function be healed, or whether his re-entry into the medical system, which could be said to perpetuate it, will swamp the learning.

References

Cotter, A. (1990) *Wounded Nurses: Holism and Nurses' Experiences of Being Ill.* PhD Thesis held at London South Bank University.

Davies, C. (ed.) (1980) *Rewriting Nursing History.* London: Croom Helm.

Dubos, R. (1959) *Mirage of Health.* New York, NY: Harper.

Guggenbuhl-Craig, A. (1971) *Power in the Helping Professions.* Dallas, TX: Spring Publications.

Heron, J. and Reason, P. (eds) (1985) *Whole Person Medicine: A Co-operative Inquiry.* London: British Postgraduate Medical Federation.

Illich, I. (1975) *Medical Nemesis: The Expropriation of Health.* London: Marion Boyars.

Jess Groesbeck, C. (1975) The archetypal image of the wounded healer. *Journal of Analytical Psychology*, *20*(2), 122–45.

Johnson, R. (1993) *The Fisher King and the Handless Maiden.* San Francisco, CA: HarperSanFrancisco.

Jung, C. G. (1966/1954) *The Practice of Psychotherapy.* Collected Works, Vol. 16. London: Routledge & Kegan Paul (see especially The psychology of the transference, Part Two, III, 163–323).

Kerényi, C. (1959) *Asklepios: Archetypal Image of the Physician's Existence.* New York, NY: Bollingen Foundation.

Kidel, M. (1986) The meaning of illness. *Holistic Medicine*, *1*(1), 15–26.

Kidel, M. and Rowe Leete, S. (eds) (1988) *The Meaning of Illness.* London: Routledge.

Nelson, S. and Gordon, S. (2006) *The Complexities of Care: Nursing Reconsidered.* Cornell: Cornell Paperbacks, Cornell University Press.

Nursing and Midwifery Advisory Committee (2001) *Caring for Older People: A Nursing Priority. Integrating Knowledge, Practice and Values.* London: Department of Health.

Paris, G. (2007) *Wisdom of the Psyche: Depth Psychology After Neuroscience.* Hove: Routledge.

The Patients' Association (2009) *Patients Not Numbers, People Not Statistics.* London: The Patients' Association.

Price, L. (1984) Art, science, faith and medicine: The implications of the placebo effect. *Sociology of Health and Illness*, *6*(1), 61–73.

Rafferty, A. M. (1996) *The Politics of Nursing Knowledge.* London: Routledge.

Salvage, J. (1985) *The Politics of Nursing.* London: Heinemann.

Sanford, J. (1977) *Healing and Wholeness.* New York, NY: Paulist Press.

Schaverien, J. (2002) *The Dying Patient in Psychotherapy: Desire, Dreams and Individuation.* Basingstoke: Palgrave Macmillan.

Schwartz-Salant, N. (1998) *The Mystery of Human Relationship: Alchemy and the Transformation of the Self*. London: Routledge.

Sedgwick, D. (1994) *The Wounded Healer: Countertransference from a Jungian Perspective*. London: Routledge.

Stein, M. (1984) Power, shamanism and maieutics in the countertransference. In N. Schwartz-Salant and M. Stein (eds), *Transference/Countertransference*. Wilmette, IL: Chiron Publications (pp, 67–88).

Whitmont, E. (1983) *The Return of the Goddess*. London: Routledge & Kegan Paul.

Wilkinson, M. (2006) *Coming into Mind: The Mind-Brain Relationship: A Jungian Clinical Perspective*. Hove: Routledge.

Chapter 7

Our inner puer and its playmates, the shadow and the trickster

Sally Porterfield

Life is a comedy to those who think.
Life is a tragedy to those who feel.
Horace Walpole

He is no cheerful marching to the pipe
Like a shepherd with his flock.
No, a bitter cry.
Socrates' *Philoctetes*

Like Philoctetes, another cripple whose leg was the cause of his woes, House interminably bewails his fate. But unlike Sophocles' master archer, who has been cast away on an island, House remains in the world, where he punishes both colleagues and patients with his cantankerous behavior. Philoctetes, son of Heracles, is a hero of the Trojan War in which his miraculous bow, a gift from his divine father, has earned him the title of master archer. When bitten by a snake, Philoctetes is cursed with an agonizing wound that will not heal, and which drives all away with its appalling stench. Understandably bitter when he is abandoned on a remote island, left to die alone, he somehow manages to survive for ten years, with the help of the marvelous bow which provides him with sufficient food to keep him just barely alive. Eventually Odysseus tricks him into returning to save the Greeks and Philoctetes is returned to his former glory with the help of his great father, Heracles, in a *deus ex machina* finale.

House, unlike Philoctetes, has not been banished because of his wounded leg, but is suffered by all around him because he is the master diagnostician whose talents are indispensable. Week after week he solves the medical problem of the moment with uncanny instincts and knowledge. Week after week he abuses everyone around him, including patients, by his miserable disposition and complete lack of compassion. His bitterness is not caused by human betrayal but rather by anger at an unjust fate, which he expresses by cruelty to all around him, as if making others suffer might somehow alleviate his own pain.

Whatever can be the source of his popularity, this unpleasant, insulting, insolent, arrogant, disheveled, and apparently brilliant diagnostician? He is consistently rude, inconsiderate, inappropriate, brash: in short, everything we dislike in our physicians, or in anyone else, for that matter. Our notion of the *Healer* conjures the image of a being who is wise, kind, gentle, and *mature*, especially mature in that we want him/her to be a nurturer, care-taker, an iteration of the childhood projection of parent as all-powerful healer, one who is able to keep dangers at bay and cure ills, both physical and emotional. We want him/her, above all, to care, and because of that care to protect us from the evils that beset us in a bleak, inhospitable world.

House, of course, upends all of these expectations with his adolescent narcissism, caustic tongue, and lack of compassion or dignity. He is a typical *Puer Aeternus*, Jung's archetype of the eternal child, an adult who refuses to grow up. He clings stubbornly to his bad boy persona, reveling in his behavior like a teenager intent on thumbing his nose at the world. Meanwhile, he shows the stuffy adults around him that he is far superior because of his surpassing brilliance and ability to solve problems that elude the brightest of them. One episode, in which his parents come to visit, shows this adolescent trait in a particularly egregious way (*Daddy's Boy*, 2: 5). He avoids seeing his family by every ruse he can concoct, and finally is forced to share a meal at which he continues to act like a sullen child, despite the fact that his parents appear to be perfectly normal people. We are left to wonder what unresolved issues cause him to behave in this way. But the question is not answered and watchers must continue to puzzle over the enigma he seems bound to create of himself. Perhaps his ego cannot stand the notion that he is not a superman, but in fact, like all of us, was born of woman and has a father to boot. Most people get over that stage a great deal earlier in their development. In later episodes we learn that his father's rigorous and unreasonable demands as he was growing up are responsible for his hatred toward his parents.

The *puer*'s dream, as anyone who has ever been or been exposed to a teenager in his omniscient stage will know, is to be recognized for what he perceives himself to be, a person infinitely wiser than those who have gone before him, whose opinions should be honored as sacred truth, and treasured as such. Fortunately for the ordinary adolescent, this is not to be. His sacrosanct pronouncements are greeted as the callow uttering of inexperienced youth, his astute opinions derided as foolish or even worse as absurd.

Where is the individual who has never been humiliated by the scorn or even the kindly amusement of his elders when as a budding philosopher or pundit he committed some *faux pas* that provided no end of amusement for the adults around him? We all have such incidents embedded in our memories, or possibly stored beyond reach in our unconscious, that can trigger a reflexive pang of humiliation when some incident triggers the memory. The mature response is to deflect the embarrassment if another hapless victim has been the occasion for recall and attempt to rescue the sufferer by a change of subject or some other verbal ploy. The *puer* response is to join in the merriment, glad that he is past the point of being the butt of adult humor. Probably most of us fall into both categories depending on the situation, but the constant *puer* never considers the possibility that kindness might be an option. He is still on the defensive, quick to wound and quick to be wounded.

One of the gifts of maturity is the ability to accept individual limitations, but the *puer* cannot accept his own because he has never grown past the stage of needing to be revered and honored for his perceived uniqueness; his ego still rules. Thus House appeals to the *puer* in all of us, the irreverent wit who is also a whiz kid. He thinks he knows it all because he does. He is living the adolescent dream, behaving like a child while being venerated for his superior wisdom.

The puer

Much has been written about the *puer* by Jung and his followers. Marie-Louise von Franz (1985, 2000) used the term *puer* to describe men who had difficulty settling down, were impatient, unrelated, seemingly untouched by age. Andrew Samuels *et al.* refer to the *puer* as being unable to be in a perpetually evolving state (1986: 125).

We see examples of the *puer aeternus* all around us in a society that worships youth and aspires to be forever young. The notion that one must change and grow is anathema to the *puer*, who wishes nothing more than to stay within the protective walls of childhood while being granted all the privileges of adulthood without assuming the responsibilities that accompany those privileges. In our popular idols and heroes we see these childlike creatures, whether they be athletes, performers, or simply "personalities" whose claims to fame are often obscure.

This youth cult is certainly a factor in the popularity of the show, since House embodies that ideal in terms of his personality and his attitude. He is unquestionably funny, with the cruel humor beloved of adolescents, a sort of pie in the face approach that denies the humanity of the other and recreates him as simply the butt of a joke. It is a sort of childhood hangover which denies seriousness and by extension, mortality. One of House's paradoxes is this denial coupled with the dead seriousness of his quest to cheat death, and to declare himself the victor.

An early attempt to describe this phenomenon of the *puer aeternus* in our society was the popular psychology volume, *The Peter Pan Syndrome*, by Dan Kiley. The book discusses the difficulty many men have in settling down and assuming the responsibilities of adult life, and is subtitled *Men Who Have Never Grown Up* (Kiley 1983). In the opening of his chapter on

Narcissism, Kiley muses about the exchange between Peter and Wendy when he tells her he can't help crowing when he's pleased with himself. Wendy finds it queer that his favorite stories are those about himself.

That, of course, is the crux of narcissism, a quality of the *puer aeternus*. Like a child who has never grown past the point of self-obsession, the *puer* finds it quite natural that his favorite subject should be himself. House, of course, is equally unrepentant about his self-absorption. Although his obsession is to solve the mystery of whatever disease confronts him, the zeal with which he approaches the task is less about the patient than about his own ability, which has become his sole identity since he is unable to form relationships with other human beings. We see only the vaguest hints of concern for those whose lives depend on him and that is covered by a facade of indifference that protects him from emotional involvement.

Perhaps one of the chief explanations for House's popularity is the desire to see the man behind that facade. The show occasionally allows us a glimpse of House in his meditative state, moodily gazing into the distance or playing the piano. Most of the time, though, he keeps himself so thoroughly steeped in various pain medications that he is effectively shut off from his own feelings.

The meds are a constant presence in House's life, yet another symptom of the *puer aeternus*. Like many people both public and private, for whom the refuge of drugs and alcohol keeps them from attempting to solve their problems and move on toward individuation, House walls himself away from reality by numbing himself to anything that might intrude on his self-imposed exile. Philoctetes languished on his island through no choice of his own, while House chooses to set himself apart and creates his own isolation through pills and often through alcohol as well. In *House's Head* (4: 15) his drunken refusal to leave a bar causes the death of his friend Wilson's partner Amber through a complicated series of events. The show maintains its posture of detachment despite this tragedy because the character of Amber is problematical due to her aggressiveness and self-interest. It is interesting that House manages to kill her off, when she is in many ways very much like him. Jung might speculate that House has managed to annihilate the bad anima, leaving room for the good anima, often personified by Cameron, one of his permanent staff members whose humanity he constantly seeks to quash. Cameron also has secrets in her past, but she chooses not to share them with her colleagues and attempts to treat her own pain by attending to the misery of others.

Other members of his coterie – notably Wilson, the oncologist, who clings to the notion that House is redeemable, and Foreman, a member of his team who continues to strive for professionalism – are, like Cameron, decent people and dedicated physicians, despite personal foibles. One of the comic staples of the program is the attempts by others to avoid the traps that House sets by his childish conduct, but they often fail and fall into immature behavior themselves when they lose their tempers and consequently their better judgment. Cuddy, the hospital administrator, is a case in point. Although she does her best to maintain a tight ship she is constantly bedeviled by House and occasionally descends to his level of trickery and deceit in an effort to survive. In one episode (*Whac-A-Mole*, 3: 8) she hides his cane and he is forced to hop around painfully until she finally restores it. This is clearly a juvenile, actually quite cruel act, but House has the ability to bring out the worst in his associates.

Again, this situation plays into adolescent fantasies of the *puer* as being in charge of the adults around him because of his superior abilities. We see the Peter Pan syndrome here in full flower, except, of course, that Pan is merely childish and not malign, as is House. House might better be compared to Heathcliff or Mr Rochester or other dark gothic animus figures, the outlaw, the demon lover who is invariably irresistible to women. Unfortunately for House, that darkness does not make him alluring to women, except for the occasional flirtation or missionary zeal of would-be female redeemers, like the hapless Cameron, who longs to save him from himself.

The program consistently avoids that kind of affect by making his negative *puer* qualities consistently primary. He seems determined to avoid any serious relationship by clownish behavior, and a typically adolescent demeanor toward women. The sexual mystery and intensity of a Heathcliff or a Rochester is created largely by the smoldering passion suggested by their silence. House is more of a leering Groucho, waggling his cigar as he makes suggestive comments to colleagues and patients alike. In his relationship with Cuddy, which he tries ineffectually to advance, the crux of the matter is that House seems to purposely avoid the possibility of any real connection with a woman by his crudeness in expressing sexual interest. An excellent example is his dream of her as a pole dancer in *House's Head* (4: 15). Again, we see the *puer* at work, continuing on the path he started when he found a little girl attractive in elementary school. How does a young boy signify interest in a girl? He teases her and frequently makes her uncomfortable and angry. As he grows into adolescence, if he is unable to relate to girls in a comfortable way, often he becomes the sexual braggart, in a clumsy attempt to cover his own embarrassment and sense of inadequacy. Still, House is undoubtedly an attractive man, whose behavior frustrates and exasperates those around him, especially the women, who often find him attractive despite his intolerable conduct.

Black humor

What is going on here is, of course, what we call gallows humor or black humor, which causes us to laugh in order to avoid crying. By setting the story in a hospital and dealing with life and death cases, we could easily find ourselves drawn into a weekly medical drama that keeps its audience glued to the set in suspense over the outcome. Such dramas have a long record of success with television viewers, looking back to such classics as *Dr Kildare*, *Ben Casey*, and more recently such favorites as *ER* and *Grey's Anatomy*. Of course some of the more recent ones do have their moments of levity but the overall tone of the programs is a serious one and it is the drama that draws its audience in. The appeal of House is clearly not the drama but the comedy and, of course, the weekly puzzle of discovering what is killing the current patient.

The dramaturgical method at work in House is what Berthold Brecht called *Verfremdung*, which is loosely translated into English as "alienation effects" (1964: 99). Brecht, a supreme political polemicist, wanted to instill in his audiences a "long anger" rather than a "short anger". By that he meant that he wanted his plays to inspire thinking, rather than feeling, so that the audience did not experience an emotional catharsis, which Aristotle describes as the "pity and terror" that allowed the Greeks to leave the tragedy behind them when they left the theatre. That, to Brecht, would have constituted a short anger, which is quickly dissipated by the catharsis and which he felt was possible only through an emotional connection to or identification with the play. For him, a long anger was made possible by an emotional detachment that permitted the individual to think, unhampered by feelings. Thus his political messages made his audiences form a more thoughtful and longer anger that stayed with them and he hoped would lead to political action. With this end in mind, Brecht introduced devices into his plays that prevented the viewer from what Coleridge called "the willful suspension of disbelief". By that he was referring to the phenomenon in which audiences accept theatre conventions and agree to accept as truth what is happening on stage despite other audience members, visible stage lights, and scenery. It is a tacit understanding between artist and audience that allows theatre to become real for that moment and to make the emotional connection that permits us to become invested in the action.

One of the tricks used to accomplish this emotional disengagement was Brecht's practice of telling the audience what was to occur in the scene to come in order to remove the surprise. If you know that a character is going to die in the following scene, the actual death is less shocking than it would be otherwise. Kurt Weill's music was also intended to exacerbate the alienation effects. Much of it is harsh, disturbing and grating to the ear or the sensibilities, a familiar example being *Mack the Knife*, from *Threepenny Opera*. He also used voices that assaulted the ear, rather than soothing it. Lotte Lenya, Weill's wife, was known for her harsh, abrasive voice, which she used to good effect in *Mother Courage*. In that play, when Lenya, as Mother Courage, learns of the death of her son, she pretends not to recognize the body and then goes downstage left, a position that creates emotional distance, and, facing the audience, lets out a silent scream that is a classic moment in Brechtian drama. A normal reaction would be to scream aloud at the sight of her dead son, but this woman, Brecht's icon for the mindless pursuit of profit in wartime, thinks it more important to dissociate herself from her dead child in order to get on her way and make more money as she peddles her wares to both sides of an endless war.

House accomplishes the same alienation effect when he is rude to colleagues and particularly when he is cruel to patients. His apparent lack of interest in humanity creates much the same kind of comedy as a clown does when his boutonnière squirts one in the eye. It is the jolt of the unexpected that causes laughter, as when a passer-by slips on a banana skin. The unexpected is nearly always an element of comedy. But in order to laugh at another's misfortune, it is necessary to deprive the situation of its emotional content, as Brecht did with his drama. With House, of course, the audience is trained to expect him to behave in a certain way, so the surprise depends on another element of comedy, which is repetition.

In his essay *Laughter* (1911), Henri Bergson notes that

> Contemporary light comedy employs this method in every shape and form. One of the best-known examples consists in bringing a group of characters, act after act, into the most varied surroundings, so as to reproduce, under ever fresh circumstances, one and the same series of incidents more or less symmetrically identical.
>
> (Bergson 1911: 50)

Bergson referred to the theatre and the action within one play, but television comedies are more akin to the old Commedia dell'Arte, in which a group of stock characters acted out different scenarios, largely improvised, but always similar in that each character had his or her role to play so that the results were predictable, but all the funnier for being so since the audience was in on the joke, being familiar with each character.

This tendency to laugh at repetition plays in to the *puer's* world with perfect ease. The first laughter that comes from an infant is often inspired by a game of peek-a-boo, in which repetition of the same action over and over again makes the baby scream with laughter. That primitive source of humor continues into childhood and particularly into adolescence, when groups of teenagers are convulsed repeatedly by the same keyword or phrase that has become a sort of talisman guaranteeing laughter among those who are in on the joke, whatever it may be. Comedy is profoundly influenced by its time and place, dependent upon a collaboration of minds, a social bond that is forged by the society in which it is born. That quality is clear when we watch old sitcoms or encounter Shakespeare's clowns. The comedy is no longer funny because it does not strike a chord of recognition in its audience, unlike drama or tragedy, which remains much the same throughout the ages. It is that quality of being current, of being part of the here and now, that makes it so vital to the adolescent, who needs to be part of a group in order to feel safe.

Much can be learned about a culture from knowing what makes it laugh. In addition to repetition, the forbidden is always a basis for laughter. Countries that are under repressive regimes often find release in political humor that pokes fun at those in power. If the oppression comes from religious tyranny the wit is often centered on the sacred cows of whatever religion is in power. The United States, still clinging to Victorian prudery, often finds levity in sexual jokes, because the subject is a forbidden one. *The Ik*, by Colin Higgins and Denis Cannan (1985), a play based on an ethnographic work by Colin Turnbull entitled *The Mountain People* (1972), deals with the life of a Ugandan tribe sometimes called *The Teuso*, which was driven from its land to make way for a park. Their humor is about food since they are a starving people, former hunters forced to live by attempting to farm a barren area.

Martyn Green (1899–1975), a British actor known for his agility as a song and dance man, particularly in Gilbert and Sullivan operas, lost his leg in an elevator accident while living in Manhattan. His leg was pinned between the car and the shaft and badly mangled. The leg was amputated on the spot by a young resident doctor from one of the nearby hospitals, using a penknife. After this grisly incident Green was asked by one of the hospital officials to sign a release to have the limb disposed of. He replied that he told the man he would sign his release but he was damned if he'd go to the funeral (*Time* magazine, December 7, 1962). This, according to Green, was what had inspired his interest in black humor. Here is another story about the terrible loss of a limb, but this time it is true and Martyn Green's response was much more akin to House than it was to the long-suffering Philoctetes. Sometimes humor is our only defense against despair; for the politically and religiously oppressed, it is a way to deny the power of the oppressor over one's mind. For the starving Ik it becomes a bitter weapon against the fate that brought them to that state, and for the sexually repressed it allows them to laugh at the conventions that make a natural function shameful.

The same principle obtains to some degree in humor that is inspired by what Bergson refers to as "topsyturvydom" (Bergson 1911: 51). We become accustomed to certain conventions and ways of seeing our world so that when those expectations are overturned it sometimes results in absurdity. An English professor once illustrated this principle to a graduate class in Victorian Literature when discussing Jane Eyre's proper education in terms of what was expected of a lady at that time. Jane is described as being proficient in playing piano, speaking French, and painting in water colors, all skills that made her a desirable governess for a young girl. "On the other hand," noted the professor, "If she had played bassoon, spoken Hungarian, and painted large murals it might have been a different matter." The thought of modest, self-effacing Jane in that situation made the class break into laughter at the absurdity of the suggestion (personal account).

House provokes mirth for the same reason. Certain things are expected of both nineteenth-century governesses and twenty-first-century physicians. When actions fly in the face of convention and habit, we have an example of Bergson's "topsyturvydom". The sheer incongruity of the thing moves us to laughter. Doctors are not supposed to make light of their profession or of their patients and when they do, there is an element of the outlaw and the forbidden that plays into our buried desires to break the rules ourselves

Shadow and trickster

There are two other of Jung's archetypes here that work in conjunction with the *puer* much as they do in actual experience. Both the *shadow* and the *trickster* are very much present in the adolescent psyche. The *shadow*, the part of our personality that we choose to suppress because we dislike those qualities, is a force that needs to be recognized and integrated in the process of individuation. We are taught what is good and bad as we progress through infancy to adulthood and in most cases we attempt to choose the good over the bad. The difficulty occurs when we refuse to see that the qualities we reject are also a part of who we are as a part of the human family. Often we project those traits onto those we dislike because we cannot own them as part of ourselves. That kind of self-delusion can lead to a judgmental attitude inspired by the belief that we are free of such unsavory qualities.

The adolescent, on the other hand, often revels in those qualities, in a search for self-identification. Those bad boy and bad girl personas adopted by many high school students are part of their passage into adulthood, very often left behind as the individual matures and begins to take on adult responsibilities. In many cases that stage of development allows them to own that part of themselves in a way that those who are more concerned with "good" behavior are unable to do. Part of the rebellion that is neces-sary for passage into a more autonomous being, this stage has been well known to anxious parents over the ages. Some adolescents often fail to integrate their shadows because they have never formed the capacity to view themselves with objectivity, having lived a provisional life based on the belief that they have not yet begun their adult experience, which is still far off, they think, in their future.

The bitterness House feels over the misfortune of his leg allows him to project every angry thought onto everything and everyone around him, thus freeing him to ignore any faults of his own. The adolescent rebellion he indulges in abuses and denigrates any conventional adult values and excuses him in his own eyes from judgment. If you never try it is impossible to fail, and House makes no attempt to behave like a mature adult, so therefore no judgment touches him. He makes himself completely obnoxious, like many teenagers who use this camouflage to hide from judgment that might damage their frail, undeveloped egos.

As for the *trickster*, Jung described this archetype as related to the *shadow*: "The trickster is a collective shadow figure, a summation of all the inferior traits of character in individuals" (Jung 1954: para. 484). He also refers to it as a part of the psyche close to the animal level, but also, because of the *trickster's* abilities as a shape-shifter, he relates him to the savior image, an interesting parallel with House in his savior role as the worker of medical miracles. The *trickster* appears in many guises and many cultures from the coyote of American Indian lore to Brer Rabbit to Mardi Gras and circus clowns. There is much literature on this figure not only in Jungian volumes. Although there are female tricksters, House embodies many attributes that are common to the trickster. He is the bringer of laughter, sometimes innocent and at other times malign, as in various myths and folk tales that deal with the subject. Clowns have been the occasion for both laughter and fear historically, as evidenced by the number of children who become terrified at the sight of them. They are the subject of phobias in adults as well and have been featured in fictional plots as a disguise for evil masquerading as entertainment. Batman's Joker is a ready example of the *trickster* figure in popular culture. Part of the terror or unease that the clown inspires is the lack of humanity caused by the make-up or mask behind which he stays hidden.

House hides behind that same mask, poking, prodding, and belittling everyone around him with the skill of a practiced clown. Often, when a colleague nears the point of actually making contact with him, hoping for some human response, the clown mask goes on and what looked like the possibility of a human emotion emerging becomes just another pratfall, accompanied by a vulgar or obscene comment. The *trickster* is House's constant companion in all his various permutations and, of course, that is the very core of the show's humor. House is completely inappropriate nearly all the time, and that is the ingredient that makes the *trickster* both maddening and funny. As Bergson tells us, we laugh at what is inappropriate and particularly at what is forbidden. What could be more illicit than to laugh at illness and the possibility of death? House breaks a universal taboo week after week, thereby allowing his audience to laugh at those things that most frighten all of us; to laugh at death and illness takes away some of its power, at least in the abstract.

A friend tells the story of visiting friends and relatives during the Christmas and New Year holidays, a custom in many Latin American countries. Whole families go to visit all their contacts during the festive season and are able to catch up on what has happened during the previous year. The level of excitement is high and everyone talks at once, asking about absent family members and loved ones. On one occasion, while visiting a family whose son, José, had died the previous year, a hapless guest gushed on with her questions, going through the whole litany of names belonging to the large brood and finally asked, "And how is José?" Then realizing her horrible gaffe she quickly added, "Still dead?" causing her mortified listeners to fall into a deathly silence while subduing a wild urge to break into hysterical laughter.

Like Martyn Green's refusing to attend the funeral of his missing leg, the situation was so horrific that those present were struck dumb and found it almost impossible to keep a straight face, despite the tragedy that had occurred. For most of us, such idiotic mistakes would be a nightmare, but for House, and for the *trickster*, these gaffes are simply another way of upsetting the status quo and therefore perfectly legitimate. The same can be said for the *puer*, whose sensibilities about the forbidden are often non-existent. To adolescents anything is fair game for humor and the more outlandish the better. They can be cruel about situations that have no reality for them and therefore are unable to comprehend the effect that such remarks might have on others. Because of that inability to empathize, they go on with their tactlessness and often need to be brought up short by an adult who can explain the damage they are doing.

House seems to fall into this category as well, except that he, as an intelligent adult who knows personal suffering, seems unlikely to be so obtuse. His behavior is clearly meant to annoy and to hurt others and that is the mystery that keeps his audiences coming back. The question is will House ever grow up and allow the formation of human relationships, feel compassion for others, be a normal human being? Perhaps there are at least two schools here, one that hopes for his growth and another that fantasizes about being able to live as House does, say anything that comes to mind and not to care about the sensibilities of others. In fact it is likely that this dichotomy is present in most of his audience for a host of valid reasons.

Chase, a young Australian surgeon, is one House's original team and his personality clashes with House's. He shares some of House's traits, in that he also has chosen to separate himself from a father whose personality has oppressed him and therefore demonstrates some of the adolescent rebellion that House manifests (*Cursed*, 1: 13). Because of his youth, Chase also rebels against House's tyranny in an Oedipal sense and shows less tolerance for his childish behavior than the others. Chase also demonstrates some of House's emotional distance and lack of empathy for his patients in his professional drive to find answers and to solve problems. Their relationship is interesting in that it mirrors much of what transpires in our present cultural situation in which the *puer* is a familiar figure regardless of age or position. Chase, in attempting to separate himself from the father, in the form of House, finds himself frustrated by the role reversal in which the older man plays the part of adolescent, thus forcing the younger man to step into the position of elder himself, but an elder who lacks the power that should go with the responsibility.

Again we see an example of Bergson's topsyturvydom, the state that House is expert at maintaining and one that creates a constant sense of unrest in everyone around him. His colleagues expend huge amounts of energy in maintaining their own sanity in the face of an insane situation that House willfully creates.

I have written elsewhere about the ways in which drama creates an instant connection to the unconscious because we are viewing our inner archetypal theater made flesh (Porterfield 1994). Suddenly our inner players are there before us on screen or on the stage, an experience that can often be numinous, in great classics such as Shakespeare or the Greek tragedies. But even lesser works bring that shock of recognition when we experience something that has the power of psychological truth in that its archetypal elements are familiar to our ever busy unconscious. It is that recognition that creates memorable characters who are instantly recognizable and powerful in ways that we often fail to understand. Thus House speaks to our own experience of the *puer*, what might be referred to as our inner child in current usage. He also stands for the arrogant ego that trips us up occasionally when we become inflated over some real or perceived triumph. He is, of course, also the *trickster*, a familiar voice in the unconscious who allows us to laugh and manages to keep us from becoming too impressed with ourselves in the way in which he often causes us to fall on our faces when our necks become too stiff to see what's underfoot. But perhaps more than any other archetype, House evokes the *shadow*, whose presence is strong in the adolescent mind with its rebellions and refusal to fulfill the requirements that life demands. We revel in its repudiation of all civility and virtue, while allowing ourselves to rationalize that genius can be forgiven all.

The other players in this drama also speak to their counterparts in our psyches, as when Cuddy, who in her professional role invokes the archetype of the *persona*, attempts to discharge her responsibilities in a professional way but rarely succeeds due to House's constant subversion. We recognize and sympathize with her efforts but in the end laugh at her failures because the comedy is ultimately about subversion of all authority.

Cameron could be categorized as an *anima* figure not only because of her youth and beauty, but because she combines these attributes with a capacity for love and empathy, which are clearly feminine aspects that are missing from House's personality. House, as a *puer*, has never begun to individuate so has never integrated many of the other archetypes. He is fixated in the adolescent stage in which his masculinity would be threatened by an *anima* integration, or indeed by acknowledging the necessity of a *persona* in his professional life. Cameron also incorporates the *mother* archetype because of her nurturing nature but House, of course, wants nothing to do with that, since as an adolescent he needs to get away from parental authority.

The *father* is very much present in Wilson, House's only real friend, who cares about him and attempts to guide him towards a more rational way of living. Wilson is a kind of Horatio to House's Hamlet, but House is a Hamlet who has not returned from his sea journey into the unconscious, so is unable to appreciate the quality of Wilson or of any of his other colleagues. He is also a classic *raissoneur* character, a dramaturgical device that is most familiar to us in the plays of Molière. In each of Molière's works the title character, who is an extreme of one quality or another, like the miser or the misanthrope, has a close friend who provides the voice of reason that the badly skewed title character cannot hear, since he has crippled his thinking processes by his lack of temperance. Molière is a useful reference here since his works are all comedies of character, a style that plays very well into our current fashion of sitcom humor, in which I loosely include *House*. Unlike some of the other theatrical categories, such as the comedy of intrigue or the comedy of manners, the comedy of character remains fresh in any age, since these extreme characters are always a part of life in a less exaggerated form. We can laugh at House when we watch the program, but would not want to work with him. Like the horror film that brings us a vicarious terror, sitcoms often bring us vicarious aggravation, but at a remove, so that we watch others cope with difficulties that we do not have to solve.

Finally, we share in House much of the entertainment that has always been the reward of cheering for the bad guy. The shadow has a powerful hold on us because it does represent those elements of ourselves that we have attempted to subdue in the interest of becoming well-balanced people. That's the secret of much comedy, like pie-in-the-face slapstick, the charming gangster, the rebel without a cause, the bad boy or bad girl. We find this quality featured since early times when the Greeks leavened their festivals with Satyr plays, which followed their serious dramas and gave free rein to a wild, scatological humor that seems impossible to connect with the somber majesty of the myths retold by the great dramatists Aeschylus, Sophocles, and Euripides. That's the appeal of Richard III and of Iago, because in seeking balance in our lives, we allow ourselves to enjoy the vicarious thrill of cheering for the shadow that does things we would not dare to do. Nor do we actually want to do the villainous things that these shadow figures do, but by enjoying them at a remove we keep ourselves intact safely, without resorting to actual shadow behavior. By this harmless ploy perhaps we avoid the pitfall of becoming too self-righteous, like the sanctimonious television minister or the politician who is found in a compromising position sexually, financially, or ethically. By allowing ourselves to see the shadow at work in a character like House, perhaps the lure of childish behavior is seen as the comedy it is and we can devote ourselves to the task of attempting to live our own lives as conscious adults intent on becoming more balanced in a world that often seems intent on tripping us up.

References

Bergson, H. (1911) *Laughter: An Essay on the Meaning of the Comic.* London: Macmillan.

Brecht, B. (1964) Alienation effects in Chinese acting. In J. Willett (ed.), *Brecht on Theatre.* New York, NY: Hill and Wang (p. 99).

Higgins, C. and Cannan, D. (1985) *The Ik.* Woodstock, IL: Dramatic Publishing.

Jung, C. G. (1954) On the Psychology of the Trickster Figure. In *The Archetypes and the Collective Unconscious, CW 9i.* London: Routledge & Kegan Paul.

Kiley, D. (1983) *The Peter Pan Syndrome: Men Who Have Never Grown Up.* New York, NY: Dodd Mead.

Porterfield, S. (1994) *Jung's Advice to the Players: A Jungian Reading of Shakespeare's Problem Plays.* London and Westport: Greenwood Press.

Samuels, A., Shorter, B. and Plaut, F. (1986) *A Critical Dictionary of Jungian Analysis.* London: Routledge & Kegan Paul.

Turnbull, C. (1972) *The Mountain People.* London: Macmillan.

von Franz, M.-L. (1985) *Puer Aeteurnus: A Psychological Study of the Adult Struggle with the Paradise of Childhood.* Boston, MA: Sigo Press.

von Franz, M.-L. (2000) *The Problem of the Puer Aeteurnus.* Toronto: Inner City Books.

Part III

Dissecting House

Chapter 8

House not Ho(l)mes

Susan Rowland

CSI borrows heavily from the compelling elements of Sherlock Holmes stories: their generic innovation in the serial format, their sensational plots cloaked in rhetoric of rationality, their conception of the body as a scientific text to be read, and their ideological significance in the conception of the nation.

Ellen Burton Harrington (2007: 379)

All patients lie.
Gregory House

Introduction

It is widely known that the medical series *House MD* is based upon the Sherlock Holmes stories by Arthur Conan Doyle (1859–1930). Indeed the co-creator of the show, David Shore, admits that his fascination with Holmes was central to the characterization of the eponymous Gregory House (Shore 2006). A diagnostician extraordinaire, Dr House shares more with the great detective than a pun on his name, Ho(l)mes. Both House and Holmes claim to pursue scientific truth; they intellectually and psychologically dominate their colleagues, and both suffer from drug addiction. Moreover, *House* is also like Holmes and *CSI* as analyzed by Ellen Burton Harrington. *House* adopts the now customary series format of continuing characters 'housed' in complete stories in each episode. Also like *CSI*, *House* takes detecting as its paradigm, although it seeks to unravel the material traces of the crime of illness.

On the other hand, this chapter is going to explore the ways in which *House* is *not* like the world of Sherlock Holmes. To take the list of common features between the comparably conservative *CSI* and Holmes given by Harrington, is to begin the diagnosis of the problematic equation of House equals Holmes. After all, unlike House, Holmes is not violently unhappy. For the permanently troubled House, Holmes's comfortable serial format becomes a kind of circle of hell. Moreover, where the Holmes stories disguise their irrationality in the language of scientific reason, the House stories unpick the very notion of detached scientific reason and replace it with logos related to mythos (as shown below). In effect, if a body is a scientific text to be read for Holmes, it is a text to be *mis-read* by House and his disciples. This persistent trope of mis-diagnosis is emphasized by significant story space devoted to the onrush of medical language, a descent into jargon that is incomprehensible to 99 per cent of the audience. By contrast Holmes habitually *teaches* Watson, and by extension the audience, his superior reasoning. Finally, where Holmes and *CSI* are dedicated to shoring up the social status quo, *House*, principally in the character of maverick Gregory House, undermines it. In *House* social meanings are opened up for debate, leaving a crucial part of the action to the imagination of the viewers.

As House puts it: 'All patients lie.' Such typical 'Housean' disdain is straightforward and logical only if the text is framed by a wholly rational scientific paradigm. Derived largely from the work of Isaac Newton, modernity's scientific paradigm argues for an essential gap between subject and object. Related to this ethos of detachment, Newton espoused *reductionism*. Here reality was to be studied in its minutest possible parts. Eventually, by following this path, all the different pictures of reality would add up to a whole. Hence Gregory House and his team often begin by ignoring everything about the patient except the portion of the body exhibiting abnormal phenomena. However, I am suggesting that *House* does not simply validate modernity's science. The most obvious clue to this troubling of scientific reductionism and rationality is the oft referred to, 'All patients lie.'

'All patients lie' says House, the physician. Yet, if we recall that within the framework of the series *he himself is a patient*, then this accusation stops being the proclamation of a disillusioned doctor-scientist and becomes the utterance of a trickster. House cannot escape the role of a patient. We often see him in pain greater than he can bear. The viewer cannot avoid the repeated visual image of House as a patient as he limps down corridors, poking colleagues verbally and physically with his stick. He criticizes other patients over their ways of taking medication while ingesting dangerous quantities of Vicodin.

House is a sick man. He is not a wholly rational doctor because he is not objectively and 'scientifically' detached from the painful dependence of a patient. Put even more simply, he cannot pretend successfully to be a great mind untroubled by its 'other', the physically grounded body. Holmes, by contrast, manages, for at least parts of the stories, to maintain an attitude of cerebral detachment.

So if all patients lie and House is also a patient, then is that statement itself a lie? What begins to emerge here is an alternative framework to the scientific paradigm of rational doctor objectively scrutinizing his patient.

Rather, the series *House* structures a 'field' in which the observer is forced to recognize his own participation in what is observed. Like the new scientific paradigm of quantum reality in which a wave or particle changes according to how it is measured, *House* begins a shift from medicine as Holmesian detached science, to medicine as new science of the interactive field. *House* moves from diagnosis to *gnosis*. The narratives enact a shift from a knowing based upon reductionism to parts, to a knowing based upon ideas of a whole that offers the audience a hope of collective transformation, for we, too, are *implicated*. Gregory House wants to evade the psychological exposure demanded by the field by clinging to the reductionist paradigm. He is shown to live in hell.

Oedipus detects 'House'

House is far from the first doctor to take on the role of the detective. Before considering his relationship to psychoanalysis as a modern framework linking doctoring the mind to the analysis of psychic traces, it is worth recalling its antecedent myth of Oedipus (Sophocles 429 BCE, 1984). For Oedipus is another would-be detective who discovers that the distance between righteous detective and guilty quarry is not what he thought. King Oedipus declares that he will cleanse the stain of dishonor corrupting his city of Thebes by hunting down the murderer of his father. He will not listen to anyone who tries to deflect him from his implacable thirst for justice. Tragically, what is finally uncovered is the double identity of both detective and killer: Oedipus himself, unwittingly, slaughtered his father and married his mother.

So in ancient times, there is a profound challenge to modernity's paradigm of separation and objectivity. For here, the detective is not separate from the base matter he detects. There is no detachment for Oedipus, who begins aiming to be a good ruler by taking on the role of impartial, rational detective. Oedipus thinks that he can be an observer who is uninvolved with what he observes: he cannot. In this, Sophocles's *Oedipus Rex* is perhaps both the first detective story and the one that encapsulates a crucial dynamic of the future genre: an assessment of how far the detective is implicated in the crimes. Put another way, one of the most persistent tragic ingredients of detective fiction is the question of distance and the (im)possibility of objectivity in the detective. Even Sherlock Holmes, contrary to usual assumptions, does not manage complete and objective, as in unbiased, neutrality.

Sherlock Holmes: The fallible infallible detective

In the Holmes stories, a belief in the possibility of a great and rational detective is provided by the rhetoric of his fictional biographer, Dr Watson. The mind of Holmes is a magnificent machine, Watson avers in 'A Scandal in Bohemia': 'He was, I take it, the most perfect reasoning and observing machine that the world has seen' (Doyle 1892/1992: 3). Yet in the same story, Holmes is thwarted by the intelligence and resources of a woman, Irene Adler. Even more than admiration for her mental brilliance, Holmes is impressed by her honorable treatment of her erstwhile lover, the King of Bohemia. Approaching her, first of all, armed with the King's assertion that she is a blackmailer, Holmes tricks his way into her house. In order to do so, he stages a riot, aided by his Baker St Irregulars. He fails to retrieve the incriminating photograph, which is returned to the King by Irene Adler via a dignified letter to Holmes. As payment from the King for this far-from-glorious success, Holmes asks for the photograph. He makes it clear that Irene Adler is now for him not a blackmailer but a woman whose courage and sense of fair dealing exceeds the King's social cowardice.

Watson ends the story by telling the readers that Irene Adler kept a permanent place in Holmes's imagination: thereafter she was always *the* woman (ibid.). Not only does Holmes not continue to separate himself from his quarry as a 'criminal', and so the object of the virtuous 'detective', she actually seems to stand for some feminine part of him. In 'A Scandal in Bohemia', there is more resemblance to *Oedipus Rex* than is at first apparent. The criminal proves finally to be an-Other to the strong-minded detective. For not only is Irene Adler's agile mind recognized by Holmes as equal to his own, he also perceives her deviance to be socially imposed upon her.

In part, she is a guilty woman because of the King's social position and his conventional anxieties about it. By taking the photograph as payment, Holmes refuses to be slotted back into the existing social system as a paid hireling. He thereby refuses to accept the King's assessment of Irene Adler and the 'danger' she poses. Ultimately, he aligns himself with 'The Woman' who is on the margins of society. So his internal otherness is acknowledged and no longer entirely projected onto the (feminine) Other.

Oedipus, as the detective who discovers he is also the murderer, haunts detective fiction more deeply than he haunts it as lover of his mother. As Harrington describes them, the Sherlock Holmes stories are ideologically and paradigmatically devised to uphold modernity, and by extension the politics of patriarchy and empire (Harrington 2007: 380). They give the appearance of offering a supremely rational detective who is unencumbered by personal or even professional relationships. In fact, close examination of the stories show otherwise. More truly, even for Holmes, the intimacy of detective and criminal, the impossibility of completely separating observer from observed in the form of detective and detected, is maintained only by repressing and re-articulating aspects of Holmes himself.

On one level, detective fiction as a genre may have been invented in the nineteenth century as a doomed attempt to counter the anti-modernity success of the irrational in Gothic literature. From the murky and criminal depths of Gothic itself, the figure of the detective arises to proclaim the possibility of rational, objective truth (Rowland 2001). Holmes spearheads a cultural attempt to shore up rational modernity and its epistemological basis on Newtonian science. However, his descent from Oedipus is only concealed by devices such as the appearance of Dr Watson. In the emotional and admiring doctor we find one man all too likely to become personally involved with suspects. Also showing the presence of the Gothic is the prevalence of the occult in Holmesian plots. What is for a large portion of the narrative beyond rational explanation, displays the full potential of the invasion of the self by forces apparently immune to scientific investigation.

True, Holmes always disposes of the supernatural, but what is revealed in its place is a terrifying and mysterious otherness embedded in human nature itself. Holmes can neither remove from existence, nor wholly account for, the criminal ingenuity that adopts the trappings of the 'beyond nature, super-nature' for crime. So the occult in the stories becomes a theatrical display of what is literally un-image-able in rational science about human nature. The deathly hound of the Baskervilles is shown to be a large brutalized dog only after readers have been thrilled by its spooky presence on the haunted moor. That 'otherness' is for the reader part of the horror of the crime in which the interior of the criminal is never directly examined.

Detectives and the Gothic

Gothic is a literature that trespasses over boundaries such as self/Other that are celebrated by rational modernity. In the Gothic, boundaries prove to be liminal or terrifyingly fragile. Beginning with eighteenth-century novels of haunted castles, by the next century it had developed more domestic and generic genres, eventually giving birth to science fiction, fantasy and detective fiction (Botting 1995).

So the detective could be regarded as Gothic's attempt to test itself by generating a figure supposedly devoted to re-instating boundaries of self/ Other. The detective is supremely charged to restore order, principally by rebuilding through investigation the social roles of the detective versus the criminal, and by founding them on a moral order of innocence versus guilt. However, detective fiction continually struggles to escape from the contingency of detective and perpetrator roles. Indeed, Sherlock Holmes himself has to admit that the gaping body of the earth is willing to swallow virtuous and wicked alike!

Sherlock Holmes, Lord Peter Wimsey, and the bog

In *The Hound of the Baskervilles* (Doyle 1902), the horror of the supposedly supernatural hound is compounded by the active malignancy of the earth.

'Grimpen Mire' is the moor's bog that swallows dogs, ponies and at last, the villain, Stapleton. The would-be murderer's gruesome death occurs just at the moment when Holmes and Watson catch up with him. Described as a place of sickness and decay, the bog is the earth itself in Gothic mode, for it refuses to respect its own boundaries in calling the living to its depths.

> Its tenacious grip plucked at our heels as we walked, and when we sank into it, it held us. It was as if some malignant hand was tugging us down into those obscene depths, so grim and purposeful was the clutch in which it held us.
>
> (Doyle 1902/2001: 153)

Holmes and Watson can only listen as their lawful prey is sucked down, for fear that they too will become Grimpen Mire's victims. The story ends with the detectives very much aware that they too could share the fate of the criminal. In many societies that produce detective fiction, this trope of the almost shared fate displaces onto nature another crucial identity between detective and murderer. For the detective *is* a killer in an era of the death penalty for murder.

So it is suggestive how far detective fiction tries to mask the fundamental role of detectives whose final prisoners will face death. For example, Agatha Christie never deals with the aftermath of a trial. Here, in *The Hound of the Baskervilles*, Holmes and Watson, listening to the drowning Stapleton, are dodging the more likely fate of attending his hanging. Fascinatingly, the detectives, perched on the edge of the bog, avoid overtly revealing their responsibility for Stapleton's death. Effectively, their risk of sharing his end in the bog shows their ultimate kinship with him. The English author dealing most interestingly with detective-sponsored legal killing is Dorothy L. Sayers. Her detective, debonair Lord Peter Wimsey, also has a problem with a bog. Sayers makes no pretense that detectives can be wholly separated from criminals in both investigations and in dealing out death. In *Strong Poison* (1930), Lord Peter Wimsey falls in love with a woman on trial for murder and facing hanging. In *Clouds of Witness* (1926), he is at one point forced to choose between his brother or his sister as favorite suspects.

Contrary to the ethos of the Holmes stories, Sayers's detective makes use of what I have called elsewhere an 'erotics of detecting' (Rowland 2001). By exploiting the Gothic intimacy with wrongdoers, the violation of social and moral boundaries between detective and criminal (including finding an-Other within), the detective may create a 'solution'. Such a 'solving' is also a dissolving of boundaries in producing a more complex 'truth', one that includes identity with, as well as difference from, the criminal. For example, in *Clouds of Witness*, in what must be a tribute to *The Hound of the Baskervilles*, Lord Peter Wimsey and his faithful manservant, Bunter, traipse for hours over a lonely foggy moor. Here it is not the evil killer who falls into the bog but the detective himself:

> 'I tripped right into it,' said Wimsey's voice steadily, out of the blackness. 'One sinks very fast. You'd better not come near, or you'll go too. We'll yell a bit . . .' [. . .] For a few agonizing minutes two pairs of hands groped over the invisible slime. Then: 'Keep yours still,' said Bunter. He made a slow, circling movement. It was hard work keeping his face out of the mud. His hands slithered over the slobbery surface and suddenly closed on an arm.
>
> (Sayers 1926: 172–173)

Lord Peter is saved from drowning by his faithful manservant, Bunter. They are both saved from the bog by Mr Grimethorpe, a local farmer with a brutal temper. Here we notice how the body of the earth takes on a texture that we associate with the interior of the human body in its slime and liquid qualities. Later I will consider the cultural relationship between bogs, bodies cast into them, and the body in *House*, with its trope of penetrating the slimy, bloody interior.

Now shown to be mortal, detective Wimsey wakes the next day in the Grimethorpe farmhouse. Wedged in the window, he discovers a vital piece of evidence that will help to clear his brother from a murder charge: a lost letter. It proves to Wimsey what he ought to have suspected before, when Mrs Grimethorpe mistook him for his brother: that the married Duke of Denver has been having an affair with the sublimely beautiful Mrs Grimethorpe. At the end of the novel, Mr Grimethorpe dies while trying to kill his wife in London. Effectively, Wimsey, the detective, is saved by a future murderer from Stapleton's fate in the bog. At the same time, he discovers his familial and sexual proximity to the man currently accused of murder (for Wimsey too has been stirred into desire by Mrs Grimethorpe).

Unlike Holmes, Wimsey almost succumbed to the murderer's fate in the body of Mother Earth. Yet, through this vulnerability *in his body and to the body of nature*, he is able to locate the evidence he desperately needs. Also, this detective-hero's fate significantly repeats a seminal event, one which deflected him from the life of a wealthy gentleman to becoming a detective. Here Wimsey's rebirth from slimy liquid earth echoes his earlier rebirth, when he survived the muddy horrors of the First World War trenches.

Gothic, detectives and war

Another Gothic function fulfilled by the genre of detective fiction is as a displacement of, and ultimately non-realistic attempt to heal, the trauma of war. As Gill Plain has so effectively argued, Golden Age English detective fiction between the wars tried to 'tidy up' the lost bodies of the war dead (Plain 2001). My own argument has been that the very unreality of some detective fiction is an attempt to overcome death.

When the dead body belongs to a cipher and not to a character the readers care about, then the detective who pinpoints the killer and removes him/her, is essentially restoring the world (Rowland 2001). For such narratives, the detective banishes death itself, for it occurs only as an 'unnatural' crime and not as indigenous to either the human or the social body. Born in an age of increasingly mechanized death, in self-conscious fictionality, detective fiction effectively restores Eden, the Golden Age, and a world without death.

Hence, the mythical underpinning of detective fiction is a quest for the Holy Grail (Rowland 2010). The detective is the pure knight who is able *to ask the right questions* so he may heal the sick Fisher King, who is society itself, by finding the Grail, the sacred object or 'true solution' to crime and death. However, as I have been arguing so far, the fictional detective is *not* pure, in that he cannot epistemologically or morally be wholly separated from the criminal. In these terms, the Grail myth is the structure of desire underpinning the drives of detective fiction. The Grail myth operates *as a space* in which some detectives may aspire to the pure (and very self-consciously fictional) role of the Grail knight, such as Miss Marple and Hercule Poirot. At the same time, other detectives, at the Gothic end of detective fiction, find themselves implicated in the criminal and the Other within. These 'soiled' and morally flawed detectives in the processes of detection assume the role of the unhealed Fisher King.

Too often for comfort, the detective either fails to be pure enough, so not wholly separate from the criminal, or, the 'solution' is not the Grail itself but a metonym for it. Here the murder is solved, but what is revealed in the process is the depth of social and personal wrongdoing. So the detective, instead of healing the Fisher King, becomes him. In his own pain and guilt, the detective comes to stand for the suffering of society itself.

Fisher-King detectives abound in modern detective fiction, in the form of tormented and drunken male figures. One such example is Ian Rankin's Rebus in *Black and Blue* (1997). We are also, of course, getting closer to the unhappy House. Holmes's drug addiction, Wimsey's physical vulnerability to the bog, and even the battered bodies of hardboiled private eyes are also signs of the failure of the Grail myth to be completely embodied – *as yet*. Detective fiction incarnates the Grail myth as a trope of *desire* for social renewal. The rebirth of the detective from the earth in Holmes and Wimsey is another mythical trope that associates the genre with natural cycles and renewal.

Now it is time to consider Freud, Jung and bog bodies. For the bog is suggestively present at the birth of a cultural practice similarly anxious about the relationship of self/Other, observer and observed: psychoanalysis.

Freud, Jung and the bog bodies

In 1909, when Freud and Jung were about to embark for America, Jung made a tactless remark that enabled their suppressed conflicts to surface. Recalling that well-preserved bodies were being recovered from northern European bogs, Jung momentarily confused them with discoveries of mummies in lead-lined German cellars. Freud was shocked and faltered. Weakened in his body, he fainted and accused Jung of speaking through a partly conscious death wish towards him (Jung 1963/1983: 156).

It was Freud's diagnosis that an Oedipal narrative was being played out between the two men. In his idea of the Oedipus complex, the myth in Sophocles' play *Oedipus Rex* resonated down the centuries because it was an inner drama in the origins of every man. Jung did not disagree. However, their *interpretation* of the myth recounted in the play did differ. Within this crucial difference lie alternative paths for psychoanalysis, for detective fiction, and for the relationship of the detective/doctor to the body of the (m)Other. Indeed, Jung and Freud's quarrel over bodies in the bog echoes in the struggle of Holmes and Wimsey over bogs, and for the mythical paradigm that relates the detective/hero to Mother Earth.

To Freud, Oedipus's actions trace the archaic desires of the boy baby. The newborn child is entirely fixated on the mother as source of his being. Having discovered the contours of his body in the oral, anal and phallic stages, infant sexuality is mother-directed. As soon as the boy-child realizes that there is an unwelcome third in the family, the father, he experiences a murderous rage at the threat to his exclusive access to the mother. Then, in the hazy chaotic sense that the mother's body is different, having no penis, he fears the father's castrating rage.

So the only safe option is to renounce the sexual obsession with the all-embracing mother, and identify with the father's gender. Renouncing the love of the mother is a splitting off of forbidden desires that creates the unconscious. Founded upon sexual repression, the unconscious haunts masculine subjectivity as tabooed sexuality. Oedipus, who to Freud is the one person in history who does not suffer the Oedipus complex, because he *does what is forbidden*, remains the ur-myth of Freudian psychology.

In 1909, Freud believed that his body, in fainting, had taken on the role of Oedipus's unfortunate father, Laius. The younger Jung is the threatening aggressive Oedipus. Though neither admits it, it would appear from the context that the mother whose body, whose *matter* they both desire exclusively, is psychoanalysis itself. For they are both invited to lecture in America, with Jung implicitly challenging the primacy of the older man. Also, Freud's insistence on interpreting a death wish cuts through Jung's typical habit of analogy. Idly chatting, Jung finds himself moving from bog bodies to mummies in cellars. What links the two examples of the dead is preservation: deliberate in the case of the mummies, natural in bogs.

However, what separates these two examples of the long-dead is that the bog bodies were all murdered. Scholars assume that the bog victims were either executed criminals or ritual sacrifices to a fierce earth goddess. Bog bodies invite detectives, while mummies are archaic cultural practices. The Freudian psychoanalyst is a classical detective because he searches for a crime and a criminal. However, he challenges the Newtonian paradigm of objectivity because he knows that one would-be murderer is himself.

Needless to say, Jung's view of Oedipus, the hero, is a little different. He focuses on that aspect of the myth barely mentioned by Sophocles: the Sphinx. To Jung, Oedipus *fails* to conquer the Sphinx, and therein lies his disaster. True, Oedipus does give a clever answer to the Sphinx's riddle of what goes on four legs, then two legs, then three legs; answer: man. However, this easy intellectual triumph is no true answer to the Sphinx, who is part woman, part winged lion. For she, in her animal-human-divine chaos, is the true primal mother, the true archaic origin for whom a mere triumph of the intellect is nothing at all. Oedipus fails to realize, *fails to make real to himself*, the original chaos that the Sphinx represents. Hence, he will be horrifically defeated in the matter of origins and birth. To Jung, the Oedipus myth is one in which the hero fails in his true task of separating from the unconscious. Failing to discover familial boundaries, he falls into the unconscious by merging with his mother, and is finally forced to see that he is both son and lover. In effect, Oedipus thought himself to be like Holmes, secure from the bog-body of Mother Earth, only to find himself to be more like the hapless Stapleton.

Oedipus is also more Lord Peter Wimsey than Sherlock Holmes: he falls into the bog/body of the (m)Other Earth. What is integral to Jung's Oedipus myth is that it remains a myth in an embryonic state. The Sphinx in her chaotic multiplicity (animal, divine etc.) has the potential for myriad stories. There are many forms of the hero myth possible here, if only Oedipus would be a hero and truly separate from her. Indeed, the Sphinx as the primal great mother has not just the potential for annihilation, but also for rebirth from the mother, as Lord Peter Wimsey demonstrates.

Oedipus: Freud and Jung disagree about myth

In that harsh short exchange between Freud and Jung there are actually two possibilities for interpreting myth. Is it *one story*, so cleanly repeatable that it can generate an abstract concept such as the *Oedipus complex*? Or, is it a story possessed of such psychic energy (not always confined to a sexual interpretation) that it is the source of many stories? This is a question equally embedded in the series format of both Sherlock Holmes and *House*. In the repeating format of the series episode, do we have a structure as in Freudian psychoanalysis, in which one core narrative is detected time and time again to a similar interpretative end? For *House*, this might be the ever repeating triumph of House the diagnostician, even when he has to diagnose the physical and moral perishability of the human body.

In a more Jungian mood, the episodic narrative structure might offer more possibilities for re-investigating the relationship of self and other. *House*, as a detective fiction, is connected to both Oedipus as a fatally successful sleuth and the Grail myth paradigm of desire. In Grail myth terms, if House manages to ask the right question his diagnosis becomes gnosis, divine knowledge that restores sacred and social harmony. It is time to look at what kind of a detective House is, and whether he can assist Jung in his anxious debate with Freud.

House helps Jung

Jung is famous for his lifelong preoccupation with houses and homes. He built his own in the Bollingen Tower (Jung 1963/1983: 223–237). Also, in his late memoir, *Memories, Dreams, Reflections*, he records dreaming of *his* house while on that same 1909 trip with Freud.

> This was the dream. I was in a house I did not know, which had two stories. It was 'my house'. I found myself in the upper storey, where there was a kind of salon furnished with fine old pieces in rococo style . . . These [steps] too, I descended, and entered a low cave cut into the rock. Thick dust lay on the floor, and in the dust were scattered bones and broken pottery, like remains of a primitive culture. I discovered two human skulls, obviously very old and half disintegrated. Then I awoke.
>
> (ibid.: 158–159)

In his dream, as Jung descends from the highest storey to a cave below the building, he believes that each material layer represents a stage in human culture and consciousness. While Freud insists it is an Oedipal dream of repressed murderous desires, Jung interprets it as a portrayal of the psyche consisting of its collective existence in human cultural evolution (ibid.: 159–160). Freud thinks that he has found the murderer; Jung believes that he has discovered a space, or more specifically, the *home* of the psyche.

> The deeper I went, the more alien and darker the scene became. In the cave, I discovered remains of a primitive culture, that is, the world of the primitive man within myself – a world which can scarcely be reached or illuminated by consciousness. The primitive psyche of man borders on the life of the animal soul, just as the caves of prehistoric times were usually inhabited by animals before men laid claim to them.
>
> (ibid.: 160)

There are many striking features to this dream, but here I will mention only three. Jung's interpretation makes of the strange house of the dream a *home* for his, and ultimately everybody's, psyche. Second, the dream emphasizes cultures as layered on top of one another, implying a hierarchy of values. Ending up in the primitives' cave, Jung nevertheless suggests that the 'highest' culture is a superior civilization. Finally, what also seems to lurk here is Jung's recent, fateful, conversation with Freud about bodies in bogs and mummies in cellars (ibid.: 156). In penetrating the cave full of dust and bones and pottery, has Jung, too, fallen into the bog into which a 'primitive' culture casts those it has sacrificed or executed?

Crucially, Jung accepts this alien house as his own. His interpretation acknowledges that the house is not only built above, but also still connected to, a very primitive type of dwelling. The cave is carved out of rock and is full of earth or dust. In accepting the layered house as his home, Jung also accepts the cave and the earth. He is like Lord Peter Wimsey tumbling into the earth/bog and being reborn from it. Also like Lord Peter Wimsey, the experience enables Jung to *shift the story*. He wants an-Other story to Freud's Oedipus complex, just as Lord Peter falls into the bog when he despairs of finding another story to clear his brother of the charge of murder. Now, what about House and the bog? A repeated narrative motif of the *House* series is the journey into the body of the sick patient. Without cutting or further injuring the body, the camera takes the audience into the flesh. We see fragments of foreign matter, perhaps signifying disease, the wet stickiness and palpable plasticity of the body's interior. Slimy as a bog, which stands for the Other as the body of Mother Earth, this plunge into the human body actually tumbles the viewing audience into the bog. Moreover, this immersion into the *matter* (mater) of the human body is always done in relation to the detecting team of House and his subordinates.

As we are taken into the sick body when House or his sidekicks have a theory, were these stories simply dedicated to the triumph of a rational scientific detective, this expedition into the soma would either confirm or refute the doctor-detective's theory. In fact, it is never possible for the audience to tell if the diagnosis is correct from looking into the body's interior. On the other hand, the audience is not plunged into matter absolutely devoid of meaning. Rather, just as Jung can make meaning from discovering dust and skulls, so the camera's penetration seems to reflect the detecting team's effort of imagination.

They have a theory. The audience is outside that theory because the medical patois they use is alien. Yet the juxtaposition of theory and interior shots of the sick body begins to *relate* the immaterial idea, the diagnosis, to the dark matter. And the body is dark matter, because it is 'unknown' in its pathology, and therefore not yet enlightened by the detecting psyches of the doctors. Basically, can House turn the bog of the body mired in otherness into a home for the patient's psyche? Can House do what Jung does in turning a strange (here diseased) house into the psyche's home, one that integrates that aspect close to animal nature? So Jung is a possible prototype for House. Can House help Jung? In my view, House can aid Jung by being a trickster.

Gregory House: More than just a trickster?

As other essays in this volume demonstrate, Gregory House is a trickster figure. Like the trickster, House violates taboos and boundaries. Also like the trickster, House's taboo breaking is essentially social. By shocking, challenging and angering his colleagues, he forces them to come to terms with the Other in themselves and in the social order. House refuses to act as if there are rules. By so doing, he exposes contradictions in the practice of medicine and forces his colleagues to make psychic investments in the rules they fight to create or maintain. In effect, the trickster serves to individuate society; House serves to individuate his colleagues. He turns a house into a home, and offers some social lessons for Jung as well.

House causes his professional peers and subordinates to individuate by testing their social and psychic endurance to the limits and beyond. In a way, we can see House in his very impossibility, embodying what Jung would recognize as psychic stages. Too often House is the *nigredo* bringing a primal chaos into the cool white house that is the hospital. Or he is the trickster violating the conventions that medicine is a 'caring' profession. House does not want to care. He stays away from actually meeting patients, and would prefer to experiment on them rather than treat them.

Yet at times, House in his genius is a symbol of some 'higher unconscious potential' in his suffering colleagues. He can, if only momentarily, incarnate a self for Wilson, his 'best friend'. All this sounds a bit like Jung traversing the different psychic stages or 'layers' of his dream house. However, there is one vital difference: House himself does not individuate. Trickster-like, he provokes individuation in the collective. However, in himself, he suffers greatly and learns nothing.

House, *House*, and houses in psychoanalysis

The hospital is a material house that becomes a home through individuation in all the staff we see – except House. Here the suffering 'wounded healer' has something to offer Jung. For the advantage of House's psychic recalcitrance is that the downside of representing a hierarchy of cultural or psychic 'stages' is avoided. Like Jung, Gregory House goes up and down in the hospital. House getting into or out of an elevator is a frequent image. Also like Jung, House finds bones, bodies and dust in the basement, such as in his trips to the morgue or sojourns in the men's room. By having his team discover him in the toilet, a place where surely we are adjacent to our animal nature, House refuses to be inspired in the 'appropriate' spaces. Here the interior body sequence becomes an analogy to House shifting around the hospital, seeking its margins and unspeakable places in order to make this body a *home*.

In his house dream, Jung is stuck in layers, implying social stratification. Gregory House shows him how to become a trickster in the apparently stratified building. The result is that House could individuate Jung as well, were Jung to challenge his psychic house-home, rather than simply accept it. House plays tricks with the hospital; Jung, by contrast, seeks to wrest control of his building/dream away from Freud's detective narrative of Oedipus. Jung betrays an essential twist in his writing here. He is both a radical and a conservative. A conservative with revolutionary ideas, Jung here adopts the hierarchical appearance of the house and revolutionizes psychoanalysis by calling it 'home'. He is comforted by evoking the forward march of western civilization, while insisting that the 'primitive' dwells within it.

On the other hand, House will not let anyone in the hospital get away with the idea that any part of it securely rests upon the triumph of western values. Here, House's own lack of individuation is of real value as social criticism. For if House is not healed, he will remain a dangerous trickster. While the trickster remains, social values cannot stabilize. So House's lack of psychic development is on the one hand a cause of his immense suffering, while on the other hand it is the text insisting on an openness to its social criticism. Of course, a social openness itself has limitations because it means that the narrative weight of the show never endorses any particular social change, nor can it stabilize the meaning of a social evil. Yet, the absence of telling the audience what to think and do does have a very important function in connecting the viewers to the show.

Before considering the role of the viewers, there is a last note about the journey into the slimy, bog-like human body to take up. Combined with the flourishing of a theory, the journey into the body seems to represent the desire of House to enter the body, not as a fellow suffering creature, but as a Sherlock Holmes who keeps to the known path. He fails. What appears as a pathway into the body is later revealed as flopping into a bog. A bog is the body of the (m)Other that swallows cultures (we do not know if the bodies were sacrificed or executed), maps, and knowledge. Before anyone can be saved, House has to realize that he has fallen into the bog himself, and he must use his trickster powers on the house that is the hospital. Only when House has violated the hospital's coded space, and the coded space of public and private 'houses' by entering the patient's home, can he have accrued enough of a relationship with the other to extricate himself from the bog that is the Other.

Ultimately, House gets out of the bog by curing the patient. The patient's body is the bog. So is the hospital. So is the *matter* surrounding House in his own painful body, and the 'animal souls', as Jung puts it, of his weary colleagues. Each episode consists of House *getting bogged down* because he insists against all precedents that he can make a diagnosis at a distance from the patient. He insists that he is a scientist/detective, where the observer is wholly distinct from what is observed. He is wrong. Being wrong, he and the viewer have to fall into the bog that is the chaotic sick body (of the patient) and discover it to be also the sick body of House, and even of the hospital itself as a functioning organ of healing. Moreover, like the literary detective, House in his failure to learn how not to fall into bogs comes to incarnate a social and mythical meaning. Poor House, with a throbbing leg and a tormented mind, is the Fisher King himself. But what about the audience?

House not Holmes: The audience as a detective

Two psychoanalysts and two literary detectives meet at the bog, the open and dangerous body of Mother Earth. Freud detects a murderer; Jung detects the Sphinx, the possibility of many stories, and man's root cellar in the psychic earth of nature. Sherlock Holmes detects the death of the villain, and a disguised revelation of his own role in killing. Lord Peter Wimsey detects his own 'other' self: he is swallowed up by his bodily nature and weakness. He realizes at last that the suspect is his other self, his brother, which on a literal level he has known from page one of the novel. Here he discovers his Gothic kinship to his brother in *desire*. To put it another way, Holmes detects the other as also within, just as Irene Adler became also an image for part of himself. Wimsey detects a self after his rebirth from the body of the (m)Other. House detects the audience.

Perhaps in *House*, the television show, the real bog, the real body that needs to be in-spirited, inspired, is the audience. In the sequences of the juicy, slimy interiors of the patient, we see a metonym for the audience. In House's refusing to be hands on with the patients we see an ironic representation of our own distance from events on the screen. To reiterate the main tropes for implicating the audience: bringing the audience into the body *blindly*, as we do not know what we see; the language of the multiple diagnoses being foreign to most viewers; House as trickster making the soulless hospital into a home; House as agent of individuation; House in hell.

House plays to 'an' audience. The fiction is that it is the audience of his peers in the hospital. In fact, House implicates the 'external' audience in the narrative processes of each episode. We are with House in his imaginative penetration of the patient's body; yet we are differentiated from him by his over-confidence in his thread of narrative, while we sink into the bog of sloppy, undifferentiated matter. Like Wimsey and Bunter, House's early diagnostic threads save him from drowning while he finds the real way to save the patient. We witness him doing this by re-mapping physical space with tricksterish unconventionality. By violating hospital boundaries and social taboos of privacy in the patient's home, House stirs up enough psychic matter to reconfigure the body of the patient from being the bog to one reborn from it.

So a particular difference between House and Holmes is the extent that House stands as a creator, a re-maker of the (social) world by forcing individuation, thereby turning houses into homes. Hence, like Jung, he is finally able to offer the house of the patient's body as his or her home. In fact he does more than Jung, because Jung's assumption of homeliness in a stratified society suggests social stability decaying into stagnation. House, on the other hand, is unable to settle social questions; they are rather deflected onto the audience.

The narrative processes of the show make the audience into detectives. We cannot understand our journey into the bog-like body. We do not understand much of the dialogue in highly technical medical language. House's outrageous behavior challenges the audience as much as those around him. So the audience cannot sit back and enjoy a cerebral puzzle. Rather we are forcibly immersed in the messiness of the body, our help-lessness before experts, and our own inability to deal with people who do not acknowledge rules. Like House's colleagues, we fear and suffer. Yet also like House's colleagues, we have the chance to individuate.

After all, House is not the only character. His very impossibility displaces our desire to know, and for narrative resolution, onto other characters. Between the core group in the early series – House, Foreman, Chase, Cameron, Cuddy and Wilson – the initial attempt at diagnosis, which means seeking enlightenment by examining parts, becomes gnosis, a way of knowing that takes account of the whole. Of course, gnosis is a diagnosis that has forged a relationship with the body as other, as bog, as metonym for the (m)Other.

House: A hero who is not a hero

House is a hero in that he ultimately enables his patients to be reborn. He is trickster as hero who refuses to individuate; he refuses to structure a relationship with his Other, or otherwise the unconscious, which would enable him to live sanely. In psychological terms, House is terrified of his own unconscious. One more vital difference between himself and Sherlock Holmes is how he drives away his Dr Watson, Wilson. Holmes treats Watson as a friend. Episodes of *House* demonstrate House's dependence upon Wilson. Yet House repeatedly violates their friendship.

House is not Holmes because he is in a detecting framework that does not allow him to triumph over the Other, even if he has to admit some participation. Holmes ends 'A Scandal in Bohemia' and *The Hound of the Baskervilles* able to shake the dust or mud from the bog off his feet. Holmes is unchanged and almost untouched. Whereas House after treating a nine-year-old girl dying of cancer receives a hug from her on the way out of the hospital. She insists on her 'story' of goodness and bravery in the face of death over his despairing cynicism. Wilson tells House that the little girl, although dying, enjoys her life more than House does his. This is no triumph for more trickster than hero, House. He can get patients out of bogs, but is unable to clean the mud off him-self. As a figure muddied by drowning in the bog of the other, signified by his constant physical pain and drug addiction, he provokes individuation rather than embodying it.

So House is not Holmes in his 'relations'. He is not Holmes in his relations with his cases or patients, failing to make the clean break suitable for one of superior heroic talents. Holmes can pretend to uphold modernity's reductionism and 'objective' science; House wants similarly to pretend, but cannot. House is also not Holmes in his relations with other people. Holmes manages to keep some life in his friendship with Watson, whereas House messes up his relations with lovers, friends and colleagues. In the detecting myth paradigm, Holmes comes close to the 'pure' Grail knight who will learn how to ask the 'right' questions. House falls into the bog of the other, and so stands soiled as the sick Fisher King waiting for a miraculous healing.

To sum up, House is not Holmes in his relations to the other as unconscious, body, nature, other people etc. Holmes understands the dangers of the bog and knows how to stay on the path to avoid it. In this he is like Freud, who offers *one path only*, but a secure one, around the bog in the narrative thread of the Oedipus complex. House is close to Jung in immersing himself in the bog and trusting in its powers to enable rebirth. However, he only trusts in the powers of the bog to give rebirth for his patients, not for himself. He is ultimately not Holmes because he is terrified of his own powers of chaos, of him-self. House is so terrified of his unconscious self that he remains stuck in it. He is always drowning in the bog of his other. House's link to the body of the (m)Other, to nature as Mother Earth, is a terrible chaos that he refuses to try to individuate or heal.

Hence House is in hell. He is in hell because drowning in the bog of the (m)Other is for him a torment. He is in hell because each episode in the series is a terrible circling for him, without progress, while other characters describe a spiral movement. Each episode has had a similar narrative arc. The patients get closure in that their sickness is diagnosed. Rather than the diagnosis working as a single heroic narrative of progress, House's tricksterish interventions, the intractability of the body as bog, stretch psychic energy into a wider social movement.

In effect, the patient's final correct diagnosis comes to work as a metonym for a larger gnosis that is a partial individuation of the collective. Other characters make the repeating story formula a ritual because they individuate through its repeating patterns. For House the repetition is a circle that simply marks his psychic imprisonment. For him, the episodes are his incarceration in hell.

The audience puts House in hell

So what about the audience? In the end, it is we who have put House in hell. Only the audience can release him from his torment. Here at last, House is like Holmes. For Holmes died, perhaps as his only way to escape a similar narrative entrapment in stories that were beginning to stagnate into the psychic aridity of repetition. Holmes died and the audience brought him back. Conan Doyle could get away with his highly speculative rewriting of the disappearance of Holmes at the Reichenbach Falls only because the desire of the audience for the detective was greater than their need for plausibility (Doyle 1894).

House, similarly, can be saved only by the audience. By accepting House's end, either in the character's demise into insanity, or the simple cancellation of the series, he can be extracted from the (narrative) circles of hell. Or, another possibility is to work narratively on the bog in which he is drowning. So in the fifth series, House ends up in a mental hospital. Can anyone but he pluck a patient from the bog of the other into social and psychic rebirth? We shall see.

In the last analysis, there is no last analysis, for from the bog of Mother Earth come bodies whose marks can be interpreted in more than one way. Jung intuited that bogs and bodies were intimately related to the house of the human psyche. Gregory House is Jung but crazier and more tormented, a trickster who forces individuation onto others partly as a way of avoiding it himself. So House means chaos, which serves to productively stir up the social dialogues in the series and offer a space for the audience to imaginatively engage with them. On the other hand, House and *House* offer a very limited *diagnosis* and no *solutions* to social problems. While avoiding the conservative implications of Jung's house and psyche-home, *House* seeks to make the audience into the final detectives.

In the cave below the dream house, Jung perceived a society in which the bog, the matter/mater of earth and nature, was integrated into society. Ultimately, I suggest, Gregory House is one of our sacrifices to the bog, which is the unconscious, the body, earth and nature. We watch House in hell and hope to learn from him how not to go there. What his story seems to show, contrary to his loud protestations of adherence to rational science and desire to keep well away from messy patients, is that the bog sucks down those who deny her in fear and loathing. Patients are reborn from the bog by an openness to new narratives, new understandings of the 'other' as body.

House is really telling us how to be at home in our psychic house of the body. We can only be at home in the body when we understand it as metonymically connected to the bog of our primal mother, the earth. Our bodies fall into bogs, our bodies *are* bogs into which we fall. Rather than the detective myth of the search for the Holy Grail, *House* is built on the myth of rebirth from the earth. It implicates the audience so we may start to imagine our psychic house at home with nature. For then nature need not psychically engulf us like a bog. And more than the patient, society itself, may be reborn.

References

Botting, F. (1995) *Gothic: New Critical Idiom*. London and New York, NY: Routledge.

Doyle, A. C. (1892/1992) A Scandal in Bohemia. In *The Adventures of Sherlock Holmes*. Ware, Hertfordshire: Wordsworth Editions Ltd.

—— (1894) The Final Problem. *The Memoirs of Sherlock Holmes*. London: George Newnes.

—— (1902/2001) *The Hound of the Baskervilles*. London: Penguin.

Harrington, E. B. (2007) Nation, identity and the fascination with forensic science in Sherlock Holmes and *CSI*. *International Journal of Cultural Studies*, *10*(3), 365–382.

Jung, C. G. (1963/1983) *Memories, Dreams, Reflections*. London: Fontana.

Plain, G. (2001) *Twentieth-Century Crime Fiction: Gender, Sexuality and the Body*. Edinburgh: Edinburgh University Press.

Rankin, I. (1997) *Black and Blue*. London: Macmillan.

Rowland, S. (2001) *From Agatha Christie to Ruth Rendell*. London: Palgrave.

Rowland, S. (2010) The Wasteland and the Grail knight: Myth and cultural criticism in detective fiction. *CLUES: A Journal of Detection*, forthcoming.

Sayers, D. L. (1926) *Clouds of Witness*. London: Collins.

—— (1930) *Strong Poison*. London: Collins.

Sophocles (429 BCE, 1984) *Oedipus the King* (Trans. Robert Fagles). Harmondsworth: Penguin.

Shore, D. (2006) Developing the Concept. Retrieved from http://www.Hulu.com

Chapter 9

Gestures of excess

An exploratory analysis of melodrama as a collective archetype

Leslie Gardner

The central figure in *House* the TV medical series, Dr Gregory House (Hugh Laurie), is a type whose personality can be sourced in various cultures whether on a conscious or an unconscious level. He is a wounded healer, a hero, and a scapegoat. Jungian parlance would also place him as a trickster, or else as a *puer aeternus*, as is explored elsewhere in this volume. The actor playing a character constituted by these varieties of elemental cultural forms must dodge and swerve to fashion a presentable, plausible personality.

In this chapter, I propose to explore a model of analysis that uses the notion of the collective complex as it plays out in melodrama derived from Jung's discoveries of the individual complex. There has been much work in Jungian studies to delve into the notion of the 'cultural complex'. But this is an idea that has appeared before in history, or it would not have authority. Therefore, to substantiate these ideas further, reference will be made to the early discovery of collective cultural and pre-conceptual patterns as explored by the eighteenth-century rhetorician and philosopher of history, Giambattista Vico. In his revolutionary volume *The New Science* (1798/1968) he not only discovered and analyzed what he called 'universal imaginative figures' (heroes being his main focus), but also correlated style and genre with eras and cultures.

Following a discussion of collective cultural complexes – and, then, using Vico and Jungian commentators – and further exploration of melodramatic modes as they relate to this television series, the conclusion will be a pointer to a kind of critical analysis that depends on an understanding of how a genre relates to its culture, based on Jungian ideas of the complex. My proposal in this chapter is that melodrama is an elementary cultural complex and in its particular manifestation in *House* we might explore ways of articulating what the deep popular appeal of the series is. (Another assumption of this chapter is that melodrama has built-in popular appeal.)

The cultural complex

Singer and Kimbles (2004) distinguish the collective complex (which they refer to as the cultural complex – which I am not certain is a necessary designation, but I will not take this up here) from the general idea of culture. The notion of a complex accommodates an unconscious aspect associated with high-toned emotional fields. Kimbles and Singer compare the aspects of the complex:

> Cultural complexes structure emotional experience and operate in the personal and collective psyche in much the same way as individual complexes, although their content might be quite different. Like individual complexes, cultural complexes tend to be repetitive, autonomous, resist consciousness, and collect experience that confirms their historical point of view.
>
> (Singer and Kimbles 2004: 6)

What I would call collective complexes in Western cultures animate instinctive attitudes toward doctors or healers as saviors or else as ambulance-chasing charlatans. While cultural contingency associates a doctor with a white coat, or with charlatan leanings, the magical powers of the healer are ubiquitous. Cultural perceptions shift through the ages, but collective complexes are universal patterns.

The melodramatic complex

One of the assumptions of this chapter is that elements of melodrama conform to our inner hyperbolic imaginings of feeling, suffering, sacrifice and redemption. These elements participate at a deep level in the collective as complexes which seize us all.

My definition, apart from the sense of destiny, or the visitation of fate on its characters, concerns, in fact, all forms of drama, not only its birth in French and German medieval dramas with music attached. Melodrama has always been a streetwise, popular form evolving from earliest days in which the music (often choral) indicated a moral dimension and its associated affect. Patterns of sacrifice or redemption or heroism have strong impact on the cultural manifestations of television, visual art forms, fiction, dance and theater. Instinctively we share the reactions of our fellow audience members.

Eric Bentley points out that melodrama is 'the quintessentially dramatic' form. There are four dramatic types, he says: melodrama, farce, tragedy and comedy. But, for him – and broadly what I am proposing too – melodrama is the root impulse of drama: 'the primal need for dramatization, "acting out", is ubiquitous' (Bentley, in Brooks 1995: 1–2).

This hyperbolic or overly inflated affective impulse has collective and autonomous energy that defies personal psychological analysis: 'it refutes depth psychology [in analysis of the fictional characters] in order to stage a drama of emblems, constructing an architecture of significance' (Brooks 1995: 53). Characters appear just at the point of the intersection of 'primal ethical forces' and this 'confers on character enactments a charge of meaning referred to the clash of these forces' (ibid.: 8).

What we are left with is the 'interplay of metaphysical vehicles'. I would propose that while, in fact, depth psychology is the most effective form of analysis of what are essentially emblematic actions and characters, critical attention might better be focused on the material of primal archetypal themes rather than on individual fictional characters as if they were real people with interior psychological lives. Analytical psychology is, in fact, best placed to delve into this type of critical analysis. This is one of the assumptions to be explored further in this chapter. In looking back at Vico's ideas, we begin to see why.

Characters in melodrama have the ancient tracings of Vico's primal 'heroic characters' embedded in them, which Vico wrote about in nearly Jungian terms:

> The [poetic] characters of which we speak were certain imaginative genera (images for the most part of animate substances, of gods or heroes, formed by their imagination) to which they reduced all the species or all the particulars appertaining to each genus.
>
> (Vico 1798/1968: para. 412–427)

Vico's heroic imaginative figures are closely tied into the cultural forms of contemporary times: for example, it is he who proved by demonstrating the shifting mores of Homer's epics that there was not one Homer (c.f. Vico 1798/1968: Part 2). He did not arrive at this by analysis of the individual personality traits he may have gleaned reading Homer's work, i.e. by attempting to arrive at an individual or a real author implied by the storyteller's commentary. This reductive psychological trail did not interest him. He concluded that Homer was a collective imaginative figure by analyzing the ethos of the narrator, and discovering a *type* implied by the narration.

The wounded healer

To investigate further it is useful to focus on one aspect: House's characterization as a wounded healer. This depiction points to elements that comply with our cultural expectations of what a doctor should be, but also with other expectations of what they may not be. Much of House's portrayal satisfies different and deeper levels of what a healer is. We (secretly?)

expect a level of complicity with some outside force to enable healing. And, further, in line with this unconscious expectation, we feel, perhaps, that the doctor is a supernumerary figure who may aid this process by taking on the hurt and pain as a way to facilitate healing. To engage closely with a doctor is to sense the pain and illness in their life.

Complexes form cultural myths, parables or hero personalities which operate autonomously and unconsciously, passed on through the ages, creating significance which 'drive[s] at certain intentions which are contrary to the conscious intention' (Jung 1953: para. 1352). They substitute for the ego complex in the individual as conscious active agent.

> I conceive the complex to be a collection of imaginings, which, in consequence of this autonomy, is relatively independent of the central control of the consciousness, and at any moment liable to bend or cross the intentions of the individual.
>
> (ibid.: para. 1352)

In his discussion of the effective, traditional doctor who he characterizes as a 'wounded healer', Kirmayer highlights the shadow component which is part of the doctor's constitution: 'The gods do their work of healing; medicine [seen in this way] puts us in a position of wielding an active destructive power but also allows us the possibility of choosing to be passive before the natural forces of sickness, suffering and death' (Kirmayer 2003: 260, 262).

Both the positive and the negative elements we experience in this cantankerous figure on television comply with our real experience to a degree. This level of expectation is part of a cultural heritage.

In other instances in this medical series (as in others), the writers foist on their characters illnesses that work towards revelations of their psychic evilness: in one episode we find it appropriate that the game a dominatrix and her lover plays has nearly fatally exacerbated an abscess in his jaw (*Love Hurts*, 1: 20). In another episode a couple engaged in rough sex-play are revealed to be partners in what is an attempted murder (*Clueless*, 2: 15). Melodrama deals in disguise and revelation, the play of vice versus virtue, the innocence of children, repressed goodness, and hidden significance. These elements function as constraints along with other melodramatic elements.

Dr House is at the same time master and victim and as such, he participates fully in the melodramatic schema. He is self-appointed but also a figure who is designated a healer: a wounded healer, scapegoat and hero, which I investigate as a melodramatic type below.

What is House like?

Gregory House is tall, skillful, lame and irritable; he is also sexy and unmarried. He is possessed of a pragmatic wit and a sense of irony and humor that is sometimes cruel but which basically is deployed in service to his role as healer. Alongside this, however, he does *not* seem to have a consistent interior life. And even when he does refer to his inner life, he seems not to articulate it in a subjectivist way, which we ordinarily think is part of the experience of the human interior. There are often rationalist dialogues with an interior other self – but these dialogues play out as sophistical casuistry and are not reflections per se of a subjective interior of emotion, desires or fears (see Series Two, episode finale *No Reason*, 2: 24).

We could speculate that these psychic 'soft' elements are simply fully repressed in Gregory House, but even when he does seem to move into zones of personal dementia, the writers ascribe it to external factors, such as drug abuse. It is not his personal drug abuse, but drug abuse in general that impacts on him. (In the first episode of Season Six, *Broken* [6: 1], when House is held in the psychiatric ward of a hospital, we are told that House is beginning to perceive that his drug abuse is related to different personal problems that he ought to explore – he doesn't explore them, though.) The dementia House suffers appears fantastical and it is too neatly tied into the television series, narrative events, such as the figure of Amber (Anne Dudeck), who is presented as a hallucination. Would such a peripheral figure in his life take on such a central psychic role? The conclusion to arrive at is that these events do not seem to be *personal* psychic episodes.

His colleagues interpret and react to him with confusion too; I would propose that these attributes are aspects of strategies of the narrative drive. Since they are not able to see this as they are not outside the drama, the characters in the series also speculate about him.

Cameron (Jennifer Morrison) observes House watching Stacy (Sela Ward) and her new husband cuddle on a hospital bed. 'It is not,' Cameron says to House, 'that you cannot love, but that you could not love me'; she's just figured out that House's earlier deflection of her affections is not an indication of a flaw in him but that he feels no chemistry between them (*Honeymoon*, 1: 22). Earlier he'd told Cameron (plausibly enough) that she was attracted to wounded men (like her cancerous deceased husband). Therefore, he suggests that her affections are inauthentic (*Love Hurts*, 1: 20). That is as deep as he goes.

Not only does this open up doors to the further story of Cameron and Chase (Jesse Spencer)'s cold sexual relationship (full-blooded Australian Dr Chase is not 'wounded', after all, so she is improving in her choice of men!), but House reveals a new trait, i.e. that he can love and this will allow the story of Stacy, his ex, and House's past and present to spin out into a satisfying story of sacrifice. (The means to flesh out this sacrifice comprise the contingent story elements; the pattern of sacrifice is the elemental and melodramatic level of the story.) These are aspects of strategy to spin out his conflicts. In future episodes, House will renounce Stacy's love again, and she betrays him.

His close buddy, Dr Wilson (Robert Sean Leonard), speculates that House has turned Stacy down because he wants to maintain a level of misery that Wilson associates with his diagnostic skill; i.e. this unhappiness keeps House on edge and more effective (*Need to Know*, 2: 11). This idea is a strategic one that has to do with allowing the writers to use House's purported edgy self-pity to leave him an unattached and sexy loose cannon in the narrative for future exploits – with Cuddy (Lisa Edelstein)?; – with Amber?

In the later episode *One Day, One Room* (3: 12) where has his self-pity disappeared to when he speaks of his own abused past to a rape victim? The victim feels that if he admits his pain, or vulnerability, to her, it will open the gateway for her healing (a classic setting out of the theory underlying the wounded healer's technique); so she badgers him to tell all.

In his first story to her of the childhood abuse he suffered, he tells a lie – allowing more interplay between them about authenticity and what victim-hood is about; and then the truth emerges: it was his father who forced him to sleep in the freezing cold yard outside when he fell short of expectations (not his fictional grandmother). This revelation releases the rape victim to express her own pain. But House has not softened or shared any self-pity with her really. He mocks people's sentimentality. And he seems not to have any sentiment of his own except when called upon to raise some to fit narrative purpose (often in his relationship to his child patients as befits a melodrama where children are innocent beings).

Displays of his inner life are presented as a derangement of the rational – as discussed above – and take the form of hallucinations, including inappropriate people, and including himself. In the finale of Season Two, *No Reason* (2: 24), for example, the shooter who tried to kill him appears in his hallucinations while he is recovering, helping him to solve the dilemma of what is happening in the real world. How can he (or anyone) objectively assess that he is dreaming? This is a rational dilemma that is not explored emotionally or with dramatic consequence in *House* – as in Calderón's *Life is a Dream*, a drama of the same theme (or even as the skeptical Descartes explores in *Meditations*). In fact, when he wakes up on the gurney taking him to the operating theatre, he discovers it has all been a fanciful diversion (entertainment for us?). Somehow he has also decided that he should be given a particular drug that will temporarily change his life, and provide more self-pitying drama for us. But this suggestion is not a result of the events in his hallucination.

What makes the House character consistent is not the collection of traits that compose an integral human personality so much as the *topos* of a doctor figure who is a cipher for the melodrama. If the thrill of sacrifice by renunciation of love, or the display of a wound from the past as a way of reaching out, serves the way the story goes, Gregory House will come up with it. It is the actor's great comedic skill and presence that keeps this figure consistent episode after episode.

It will be useful now to set House into the world of the hospital and its surrounding environs where the drama is set – entirely a place of life-and-death decisions. If melodrama is about characters' motivations as they refer to transcendent moral themes, the *mise-en-scène* must provide them with an appropriate emblematic world they may combine this with.

Melodramatic character and *mis-en-scène*

In fact, this is the *mise-en-scène* of paranoia, as Brooks points out in *The Melodramatic Imagination* (1995): the scene of the probing melodrama, (deployed also in crime stories) and in such a story as House's where doctors are probing for the cause of an illness.

Certain stylistics of camera shoots and settings become signatures of the program and feed into the emblematic nature of the playing out that is characteristic of melodrama.

We follow House's obsessions and trains of thought in the action. The environment seems to respond to his ruminations, his sacrifices and wounds, reflecting the action of the plot. Many consultations are made, walking at top speed despite his cane and limp, with his associates as they go from operating room to office; House leads his assistants along the corridors of a well-funded hospital: followed close up by the camera. And, in fact, in some instances, House will suddenly turn and lead on in an entirely different direction when he's changed his mind about a medical idea. In one instance, while running in the rain, he comes up with a diagnosis and switches direction to run to Cuddy's house late one night to tell her (*Meaning*, 3: 1). Dressed in his running shorts, dripping from the rain outside, he taps on her bedroom window. This is inappropriate behavior but Cuddy and we forgive him since it is in the pursuit of his heroic aim to cure a patient.

In another instance, his cane splits under him as he walks with Wilson away from a problematic diagnosis toward the cafeteria where he always puts his lunch on Wilson's tab. To get back at House for drugging him to make a point, we understand that Wilson allowed his dog to chew through House's cane. And we see House topple onto the shiny corridor floor of the hospital. But this event also underscores that House is tolerating the foibles of living with Wilson. The writers use this incident to give us some insight into the physical fragility that is a constant presence in House's life (*Family*, 3: 21). But also, House immediately reckons he knows what has happened. He suspects Wilson knew all about it. The camera swoops in on Wilson's amused shrug, and House's smile as we contemplate their friendship – in preparation for the full support Wilson will give to House later: his sacrifice of his practice and finances to bolster House. In another episode, as a sign of his determined and hostile authority over the doctor, Tritter, the policeman with an obsession to catch House, pulls his cane out from under him (*Fools for Love*, 3: 5). The game is on.

A comic place specifically designed to play up the ironic competition of House and Stacy's wheelchair-bound husband is played out on a hidden set of back stairs in the hospital (*Spin*, 2: 6). These stairs are also often used as backdoor escapes for other plot events. Our sense of indecorous play between doctor and patient is engaged here, but also the sheer tact we all expect in interacting with disabled people is upset. In this case, House should not be treating a man in a wheelchair unfairly, yet their matching lameness might seem to cancel that sentiment out. But our instinctive sense of the unequal status of doctor and patient plays into this scene. House should know better. We are unsettled.

Using ironic technique in the hospital environs to play again on House's disability, in televisual terms (*The Greater Good*, 5: 14), Cuddy provokes House by making him climb stairs by disabling the elevator specifically when he wants to use it. The unfair, pitying play on his disability heightens the illicit frisson of pleasure an audience obtains in this scene. Hitting a wounded man when he's down is a secret image of foul play, experienced in our dreams and fantasies as happening to us. The power play between them sets the tone of the interface of boss and employee, making us aware of her fearless and playful status. These scenarios highlight the nature of a world where dramatic switches of direction mirror swiftly changing ideas, displayed failings, or commentary on disabilities which are part of the *mise-en-scène* proper.

What kind of drama is melodrama?

Theatrical or television or film audiences are prepared to witness conflict, the substance of what drama is, including in *House*. Conflict generates heightened emotion; this is one of the appeals of drama. Hyperbolic emotion and situation reflect a sense of a time of catastrophe. And alongside this expectation, the catastrophe is also 'homely'; it is expected that there will be a shift in the story but this must also depend on a shared sense of what the common experience is.

Working in both film and theatre, Sam Shepherd sets out how crucial the recognition of this change is as a technical device. This sense of 'shift' derives from a sense of life around us which the writer seeks to replicate:

> You begin to hear an underlying rhythmic sense in which things are shifting all the time. These shifts create the possibility for an audience to attach their attention. That sounds like a mechanical process, but in a way it's inherent in dialogue. There's a kind of dialogue that's continually shifting and moving, and each time it moves it creates something new. [There's] a knack for marking the spot where something shifted.
>
> (Shepherd 1997: 219)

A dramatic insight can shift an audience into a new position and into a radically new perspective but it must also be familiar.

As fellow human sufferers along with the patients in television medical melodramas, we feel we share their travails. It is also our experience to be ill, and our experience also to be at the mercy of the disease's constant companion, the doctor. We project our experiences and fears onto these fictional figures, these blank slates who are markers in the melodramatic scheme of things. There is a particularity to any character, however.

And this Doctor House is definitely unusual. But we also note similarities: he shares our human plight in being biologically fragile; like we are, he too can be ill and in pain. His double bind as both being ill and a healer is exploited by the writers and directors of the series in unsettling its world, in creating a distinctly ironic atmosphere that also makes up the *mise-en-scène*. This irony is about just who the wounded healer figure is, a doctor. He is literally wounded.

In this context, the doctor seems to display appropriate dramatic characteristics. The writers consciously use style as meaning: the highly illustrated and discussed symptoms and the way they ravage the body are set out for us in diagrams as logical evidence and proof that House has made the right diagnosis in nearly every episode. But we don't know if these clues make sense – the biology of the body is not rational and, besides, we have no way of judging whether the medical conclusions are correct; they seem all neatly tied up. And that's pleasing. Our expectations are fulfilled. Being satisfied by the denouement in a television episode is familiar to us and we expect it.

Primarily we want to be 'entertained before anything else' (Lehman 1999: 41); we enjoy it *before* we understand it and, in fact, the longer we remain in the dark, the greater our pleasure: 'The culmination of our pleasure will also mark its demise; [the] paradox prevails' (ibid.: 42).

In melodrama, constrained by its form, phenomena are 'not so much given in a primordial language as in a primordial form of perception, in which words [in my discussion, however, "forms"] possess their own nobility as names, unimpaired by cognitive meaning' (Benjamin 1969: 36). In other words, our *perceptions* of the forms resonate with the primal reality of hyperbole and drama we experience psychically; these perceptions come before the construction of the drama itself and so are the basis of our cognitive formation of meanings and patterns. The fictional forms of melodrama as expressed in *House* are shaped by pre-cognitive impulses such as the collective complexes mentioned above. These pre-cognitive impulses are also manifest and attach to other elements in the formula of a television series.

Familiar central protagonists take the studio floor each week, and the writers adhere to their profiles in each story. Actors contribute continuity between episodes with their appearances – the actors' physiques and any personal events (i.e. their escapades external to the series, in the press outside the show. For example, in real life we are told on various internet sites that the actors playing Chase and Cameron, junior doctors in the series, who begin a romance and marry in the series, were also personally involved). New figures weave in and out to highlight the purposes of the melodramatic plots.

When old-time rocker Meat Loaf appears as a devoted husband, members of the audience will remember his early wild days of hard drinking and womanizing in real life. They will find it ironic and the situation untrustworthy when he plays a monogamous and moderate man. But we learn in this episode that in fact his fictional devoted wife had gone travelling with a lover friend when he kept putting it off (*Simple Explanation*, 5: 20). Irony intended!

Melodrama is often dismissed as a 'lower' form of drama. Is that because it appeals to us viscerally? And in this medical television series, where death is often wielded by House as a kind of parody of threat, its dangers seem trivialized, i.e. 'melodramatic', in this regard. Nevertheless, this dramatic mode focuses the plot line, the dialogue and the producers' sense of decorum.

In fact, in *House* death is one of the panoply of weapons Dr House has at his fingertips. Death is used as an ironic weapon for manipulation, sometimes as a release, and/or as a gateway to healing. And death in melodrama is traditionally a means of reward or punishment too. Fate will conform in melodrama to the impulses of good or evil in its transcendent world by wielding this final threat.

In one episode, House tells a young woman who secretly attempted suicide by swallowing a cleansing tablet, thinking she could hide this even from him, that unless she tells him what she's swallowed, she will die. And the reality of what that means hits home to us and to her (*Resignation*, 3: 22); she is punished for attempting suicide, which is evil, by what will now be her permanent disability. In another, the threat of death inspires a patient to reveal that his beloved dog has attacked him, and the lethal poison, the bacteria in the dog's mouth that is killing him, is revealed (*Three Stories*, 1: 21). Because in melodrama the innocent are good, and animals are innocents, the patient is healed and is seen sporting a new dog, albeit with an artificial leg – the price he willingly paid.

Melodramatic themes

What themes do television medical series audiences (and producers) expect? As referred to earlier, there is a problematic administrator, Dr Cuddy in this case; she is sexy and demanding, expecting clinic hours from Dr House, which he dreads. There are younger medical colleagues who challenge the senior, central doctor: as mentioned, Drs Cameron, Chase, and Foreman etc.; there are patients' personal stories running parallel to their treatments (and often, as in true melodrama, commenting on their illness in its ethical dimension) and the personal stories of the doctors, which have an impact on their illnesses; and there is exploration of the personal lives of the doctors in a hospital that is a luxurious and affluent site of healing (Turow 1989).

Does the sense of communal instinctive fair play extend to allowing someone to reject treatment, or to insist on treatment? Should demands of profit impact on pharmaceutical treatment? (In the extended program schedule in Series Three, businessman Vogler makes costs at the hospital paramount, and when House defies him, his job and others' jobs are put on the line [*Control*, 1: 14].) These are deeply contested moral issues, engaging a deep sense of purity of purpose for doctors.

The medical genre lends itself specifically well to melodrama because of its location at the nexus of life and death. Production strategies are primarily aimed at issues that reveal the scientific, sometimes cruel and cold, moral center of medicine that Gregory House, the central figure, represents in the show. House's core is a 'cold' moral center because it is in the final analysis not a personal moral center at all. In these series of stories, melodramatic or overblown and sharp ironic dialogue and the signature gestures of excess refer to primal moral issues, as the team decipher clues in hidden places, literally on the bodies and in the homes of their mostly emblematic patients, assessing lies and disguised identities. Latent meanings play out among them. Their choices are referred to the tenets of melodrama where virtue is tested, and vice is defeated. That is what they discover along with specific medical conditions.

In *The Softer Side* (5: 16) House treats a young girl/boy whose multiple physiological genders are making her very ill; we have already witnessed that Thirteen (Olivia Wilde) is a bisexual who picked up a new girl nightly as a way to keep away her own demons (*Lucky Thirteen*, 5: 5). By this point in the series, she is heavily committed romantically, however, to a male associate, Foreman (Omar Epps). We've been educated by previous episodes in which Thirteen appeared, and now we bring our knowledge to bear, as Thirteen sits at the patient's side, sharing life's experience.

When House lectures a class on diagnostics, he uses multiple patient stories, all of good versus evil, mostly concerning the pros and cons of lying, including his own story, to explore the pitfalls of being a good diagnostician (*Three Stories*, 1: 21). The writers and characters sustain this multiple level of everyday story and moral tale, the backdrop of which seems to offer deeper meanings. They resonate with us in our dreams, in our imaginings and fantasies.

Positioning melodrama: Contexts

Audience assessment of melodrama is pervasive and it is incorporated into the shapes of the drama. Narrative is melodramatic form at its inception with archaic underpinnings.

Dershowitz (whose commentary on the O J Simpson trial is a classic analysis) refers to an argument he used in court, based on Chekhov's tips. If a character in a drama carries a gun, the audience will expect it to go off, and the writer had better write a plot line including that gunshot. But this is not what happens in real life:

> On TV, when they show a businessman or a wife buying life insurance on someone, every viewer knows there's going to be a murder, and they know who the murderer will be. It's a set-up . . . Everything is relevant to the drama . . . scholars live by a rule of teleology that has little resonance in 'real life' – namely, that every event, character and word has a purpose. Freud, whose forebears came from that tradition, similarly believed that all words, even those dreamed or spoken in error, have meaning.
>
> (Dershowitz 1996: 99–100)

This juridical tactic is *narratio*: the proposition that the deliberate and calculated arrangement of events works to shape an argument. It is necessarily a procedure that every dramatist and television writer uses. It partakes of a very basic human instinct about narrative. We are aware of the calculated nature of events in a television drama. And we hope we can trust the writers to hold the story together. We do a fair amount of interpretation as an audience. In *House*, for example, fast switches from patients' homes to parts of the hospital are techniques of narrative we have learned from watching TV narratives for years. A naive viewer might not comprehend what's happening. The drama is opening out into the world outside what might seem the claustrophobic location of the hospital. Our judgment about the storyline's veracity or authenticity is engaged in these ways, and depends very much on our feeling for the connectedness of a storyline or a character's motivations as they are given to us. Our emotions and feelings are engaged in order to draw us in.

Jung finds meaning when it is marked in the evidence of the intensity of that feeling-tone or affect. And the stylized affect of melodrama plays out here in marking the pity and fear that are the traditional Aristotelian emotions of drama. Melodrama draws on the most certain moral notions of the collectivity, indicated in the feelings attached to events. The action in the drama is emblematic of the interactions of good and evil; and narrative is the means of engaging with this common moral pool of feeling. It is a representation that mediates as well as manifests the truth, particularly in melodrama.

In addition, I would suggest, in corroboration with Jungian principles, the hyperbolic form of melodrama is a fulfilling and fundamental form playing out our inner symbolic meanings (dreams, hallucinations and fantasies).

What follows are a series of incidents that attempt to characterize the nature of this genre as it plays out in *House*.

In one instance a generally, almost abstractly, empathetic Cameron in *House* interacts with a dying man who refuses pain-killing medicine so that 'he will be remembered'. There is no psychological consistency or (perhaps) veracity to their interplay involved – except that the actors must try to make it persuasive – but a 'discussion' of the moral plight of invisible and homeless persons is set out (*Sleeping Dogs Lie*, 2: 18). In effect, here the dramatic conventions constitute a kind of 'alienating mask rather than a medium of expression' (Brooks 1995: 67). I would contend that this extends to the central character of the series, Dr House. It is partly what makes him so fascinating a figure.

Upon investigation, further melodramatic elements include the most basic: abduction, discovery of hidden identities, innocence winning through, the purity of children upheld, etc.

Take, for example, the justifiable kidnap of Wilson's girlfriend and House's student, Amber, from the emergency room of the hospital she has been taken to after a horrific bus crash (*House's Head*, 4: 15): kidnapping is meat and drink for melodrama and it plays over the last quarter of Series Four; or a neurotic patient, kidnapped for his own good, with Cameron's unease at going against his wishes (*Sleeping Dogs Lie*, 2: 18); or sibling identities being revealed and a strange affinity confirmed (i.e. classically siblings are attracted to each other in melodramas without knowing they are related [*Fools for Love*, 3: 5]). Mostly people walk away healed by almost any practical means, legal or illegal.

The discourse and scenarios are appropriate to the theme of moral and physical catastrophe. In Elsaesser's judgment, 'melodrama has a myth-making function, insofar as its significance lies in the structure and articulation of the action, not in any psychologically motivated correspondence with individual experience' (Elsaesser, in Landy 1991: 69).

What Jungian theory brings to the table is an extension of this primal pattern of myth-making and a mix with psychological truth: deeply underlying the patterns of melodrama is the inborn model of interior hyperbolic emotion and meaning. Finding this deeper level is the analytical psychologist's access to understanding what the appeal of *House* is, in this instance.

Dr House and melodrama

Dr Gregory House, the central figure in *House*, is actually a fictional product, and reflects cultural complexes shared by audience, producer, writer and actor. His inexplicable behavior infects the entire drama – its setting, style and pace, and its storyline.

In these concluding remarks, I will attend to the elements of the scape-goat and the wounded healer, i.e. 'folds' – to use Deleuze's word (1993: 5) –

in the archetype of the hero. We find these elements in the character of House. The kind of hero House is, however, reflects the nature of the times. Unabashed heroism in the first decade of the twenty-first century won't play, however. And, in this case, the tone of the comedy is irony: and irony helps negotiate the meanings and judgments of the series. In his book on the categories of forms, *Anatomy of Criticism* (2000), Northrop Frye includes 'comic ironical form' as a classic deep pattern of literary and dramatic form, sourcing its beginnings in Aristophanes, and Menander's Greek plays.

Ironic comedic form is the fourth division in his scheme. There is the comedic timing of the lead actor, Hugh Laurie, playing Dr House, who is a former comedian. Along with his deftness as a performer, there is witty, sharp dialogue which alleviates the black-and-white emotional sentimentality of melodrama which modern audiences would inappropriately laugh at. The comic edge helps us absorb the life-and-death stakes involved. Additionally, often beautiful men and women represent good while ugly, fat or older figures represent evil; catastrophes abound, as do last-minute escapes, or solutions – one patient's skin starts falling off but not before the team come up with a cure (*Under My Skin*, 5: 23); mostly events are visited upon their victims, and these events proliferate.

In *House* the melodramatic mode takes the ironic aspect of the stricken warrior who fights disease in a worthy battle on the battlefield of a modern teaching hospital. In melodrama, physiological flaws reflect inner vice as the patients, as in these cases, and they are emblems of evil. This plays out in many ways as I have proposed.

One of the keynotes of the series is that many patients, including House in the long episode *Three Stories* (1: 21) mentioned above, lie to protect some aspect of their lives that has an impact on their physical condition. He must battle this 'evil' in paradoxical style and it is a constant pressure in the series.

His diagnoses – musings – are deployed to arrive at an irrational 'eureka' moment, the 'peripeteia' of melodrama that reveals all. His common sense acts as a lie detector seeking out deceptions. He uncovers falseness which normally implies moral weakness. For example, a woman pretends she is being treated for fertility to have a child with her new husband secretly also takes birth control pills. It is killing her but House finds it a reasonable, loving action. Her deceptions are discussed among the team who cannot decide if she is good or bad (*Need to Know*, 2: 11).

To amplify here further on the *topos* of the wounded healer, who takes on suffering, is the figure of the scapegoat, another 'fold' of the hero. The scapegoat is an innocent outsider who takes on evil and is punished for it. It is one of the most significant 'folds' in the figure of House. He absorbs medical, technical errors even as he deploys those techniques. The cost of his mostly always being right is that he has had it go wrong for him. His bravura in the face of this downside is necessary in the overwhelmingly crushing atmosphere of dire illness in this hospital scenario, where his patients are those at the end of the line. In one episode, the husband of a drowned and ill refugee, having secreted himself and his wife on a boat, insists that despite all – in fact, she technically dies – House can cure her and even after House has insisted that they have the choice of God's solution, achieved by prayer, or his, achieved by science. In the end, a miracle occurs and she lives in a cosmic analogy to House's own 'eureka' moment (*Human Error*, 3: 24).

Of course his offering to have his head penetrated with strong doses of electricity to recover a memory (*House's Head*, 4: 15) is a clear example of House's willingness to sacrifice himself to recover a patient, Wilson's girlfriend in this case.

We feel abashed satisfaction when his scapegoat role is confirmed in several other episodes, for example, when, after seeming to be cured of the pain in his leg after an operation to remove a bullet after he was shot by the disgruntled husband of a former patient, the pain begins to re-emerge. And then, it is enjoyable that his status as our suffering surrogate is confirmed again when he fails to overcome his addiction to Vicodin across Season Five, as well as his struggles on the psychiatric ward in *Broken* (6: 1). He remains the wounded healer and scapegoat and this is most satisfying. We are moved by pity and by a most comforting form of *Schadenfreude*. He is an innocent, for the most part, sent to suffer for us.

We excuse his inhumane behavior in the same way that his colleagues do: he is innocent because his transgressions are in a good cause, but he is punished for those transgressions by his constant pain and the physical and mental abuse he suffers in return.

And as part of the combination of scapegoat and hero, there are many instances of House's dangerous behavior. When he seems to know all too quickly what Tritter's problem is – a rash caused by the nicotine substitute gum he chews – Tritter demands corroboration by scientific testing, and retaliates for the humiliating lesson he suffers when House leaves him indefinitely with a temperature monitor stuck up his rectum; and further, House openly consumes the drug we know enables him to function in Tritter's presence (*Fools for Love*, 3: 5). We know that his talent raises alarms even as it accurately pinpoints problems. Tritter is a state and legal authority and House is finally forced to accommodate him. In the court-room, at the end of this sequence, his other-worldly diagnostic skills are both condemned and protected; he is made the scapegoat of the magic of his medicine. Courtroom sequences where truth is subverted are always places where things go wrong in melodrama. Judgments are mistaken; in this case, House goes off to jail for a night (*Words and Deeds*, 3: 11).

Other elements of melodrama permeate the series: children are emblems of innocence, and the wrongs done to children get restitution. The *House* writers play with this theme in many ways; there is an autistic child who reaches out to House, giving Wilson the chance to speculate on House's personality – is it that House, too, has a form of autism which would explain his style? (*Lines in the Sand*, 3: 4). In another story about a child, an adolescent has become inordinately rude and aggressive and indulges in an acerbic form of wit that House appreciates and thinks must be retained. House discovers the problem, and matches him barb for barb, enjoying the encounter (*The Jerk*, 3: 23). In another, a young athlete has been guarding the secret of her pregnancy to rebel against the overwhelming constraints in her life (*Kids*, 1: 19). And in another House protects a child's sacred relationship to his mother when he conceals that it was her decision to send him temporarily to a children's home while she recovered (*Socratic Method*, 1: 6). These are stories that show us the essential innocence of children and House's compliance in engineering their continued isolation from the anomalies and evilness of adult life.

There are formulae for drama, especially television drama, which instantiate deeper patterns in the culture, and not simply cultural or sociological patterns. The closer these formulae resonate with the deeper complexes of the common culture, I suggest, a deeper engagement with an audience will ensue. In *House* it is my contention that producer, actors, writers and directors have managed to draw up those depths into the series to make it the compelling entertainment that it is. But far more investigation is required to establish this model and to explore how melodrama functions as a manifestation of cultural value.

Bibliography

Beebe, J. (2004) A clinical encounter with a cultural complex. In T. Singer and S. L. Kimbles (eds), *The Cultural Complex*. Hove and New York, NY: Brunner-Routledge (pp. 223–236).

Benjamin, W. (1969) *Illuminations* (Trans. Hannah Arendt). New York, NY: Shocken.

Benjamin, W. (1998) *The Origin of German Tragic Drama*. London: Verso.

Bentley, E. (1966) Melodrama. In *The Life of the Drama*. London: Methuen (pp. 192–218).

Bishop, P. (2010) Social (collective) unconsciousness and mythic scapegoating: C.G. Jung and René Girard. In M. Stein and R. Jones (eds), *Cultures and Identities in Transition: Jungian Perspectives*. Hove: Routledge.

Brooks, P. and Gewirtz, P. (eds) (1996) *Law's Stories: Narrative and Rhetoric in the Law*. New Haven, CT: Yale University Press.

Brooks, P. (1995) *The Melodramatic Imagination* New Haven, CT: Yale University Press.

Corrigan, R. W. (ed.) (1972) Melodrama and the common man. In *The Forms of Drama*. Boston, MA: Houghton Mifflin (pp. 187–196).

Cumberbatch, G. and Negrine, R. (1992) *Images of Disability on Television*. Hove and New York, NY: Routledge.

Deleuze, G. (1993) *The Fold: Leibnitz and the Baroque* (Trans. Tom Conley). Minneapolis, MN: University of Minnesota Press.

Dershowitz, A. M. (1996) Life is not a dramatic narrative. In P. Brooks and P. Gewirtz (eds), *Law's Stories*. New Haven, CT: Yale University Press.

Frye, N. (1961) Myth, fiction and displacement. *Daedalus*, *90*(3), 587–605.

Frye, N. (2000) Comic fictional modes. In *Anatomy of Criticism*. Princeton, NJ: Princeton University Press.

Heilman, R. (1960) Tragedy and melodrama: speculations on a generic form. *Texas Quarterly*, *3*(2), 136–149.

Henderson, J. L. (1984) *Cultural Attitudes in Psychological Perspective*. Toronto: Inner City Books.

Jacoby, H. (2009) *House and Philosophy: Everybody Lies*. Hoboken, NJ: Blackwell.

Jung, C. G (1953) *Experimental Researches* CW 2. London: Routledge & Kegan Paul.

Jung, C. G (1968) *Analytical Psychology: Its Theory and Practice*. New York, NY: Vintage Books.

Kalsched, D. E. (2000) Jung's contribution to psychoanalytic thought. *Psychoanalytic Dialogues*, *10*(3), 473.

Kimbles, S. L. (2004) A cultural complex operating in the overlap of clinical and cultural space. In T. Singer and S. L. Kimbles (eds), *The Cultural Complex*. Hove and New York, NY: Brunner-Routledge (pp. 199–211).

Kirmayer, L. J. (2003) Asklepian dreams: the ethos of the wounded healer in the clinical encounter. *Transcultural Psychiatry*, *40*(2), 240–277.

Landy, M. (ed.) (1991) *Imitations of Life, a Reader on Film and TV Melodrama*. Wayne State University, Detroit, Michigan.

Lehman, D. (1999) *The Perfect Murder*. New York, NY: Free Press.

Podrazik, W. and Castleman, H. (1982) *Watching TV: Four Decades of American Television*. New York, NY: McGraw Hill.

Sedgwick, D. (1994) *The Wounded Healer*. London: Routledge.

Shale, R. (1990) Images of the medical profession in popular film. In *Beyond the Stars: Studies in American Popular Film, Volume 1*. Madison, WI: Popular Press/ University of Wisconsin Press.

Shepherd, S. (1997) The art of theater no 12. *The Paris Review*, *39*(142), 205–225.

Singer, T. (2004) The cultural complex and archetypal defenses of the group spirit: Baby Zeus, Elian Gonzales, Constantine. In T. Singer and S. L. Kimbles (eds), *The Cultural Complex*. Hove and New York, NY: Brunner-Routledge.

Singer, T. and Kimbles, S. L. (2004) *The Cultural Complex*. Hove and New York, NY: Brunner-Routledge.

Turow, J. (1989) *Playing Doctor: TV, Storytelling and Medical Power*. New York, NY: Oxford University Press.

Vico, G. (1798/1968) *The New Science* (Trans. Thomas Bergin and Max Fisch). Ithaca, NY: Cornell University Press.

Chapter 10

Not as a stranger

John Beebe

At the heart of *House*, a television series that dramatizes the unmasking of medical mysteries[1], is a recurrent image of the crippledness of its master sleuth, Dr Gregory House. This diagnostician in a teaching hospital suffers from damaged muscles in his thigh[2] that will not stop hurting. His own wound is instructive. Seeking an injection of morphine to ease his pain in *Skin Deep* (2: 13), he exposes his scarred, atrophied thigh muscles to the Dean of Medicine. The shocked viewer can see that he bears what Jungian analysts who have studied the Grail Legend[3] have learned to call an 'Amfortas' wound,' (Haule 1992[4]) – after one of the names of the suffering Grail King, who is sometimes shown as crippled and staff-bearing, not unlike House with his cane. In the Grail story, the King had been wounded while fishing or boarding a ship, and his wound was around the hips or through the thighs, that is, in the sexual region (E. Jung and von Franz 1970).

It has become axiomatic in Jungian psychology that this mysterious, archetypally wounded figure of the Grail King epitomizes the distortion of *eros* in the Judeo-Christian culture, and the presence of a nearly identical wound to his in the central character of *House* suggests that the doctor is not a stranger to the archetypal level of the suffering he is called upon to diagnose. He takes it upon himself to challenge the subterfuges in the way his patients relate to others and themselves. In so doing he demonstrates to his colleagues what integrity might demand to correct the perverse ways which all of us sometimes manage our relationships. House's antidote to the relational toxicity he regularly identifies in his patients' families is to get us to swallow salutary weekly doses of his own acerbity. His treatment plan for what is killing us as people begins with the recognition that the empathy we usually accord to our own and each other's failures to relate has become in the face of so crippling a syndrome only an enabler of it.

In a Jungian volume, it would be easy to dismiss this abrasive wounded healer as just one more one-sided masculine maverick on television, deficient in anima and pushed to perform heroic rescues to buttress his flagging self-esteem. The other characters on the show keep trying to tell him as much. As played by Hugh Laurie, an actor whose sly, sensitive, mobile face credibly animates House's grins and even his grizzled two-day beard, House is connected to others even though he is perceived by the other characters as being antisocial. We need to linger on the character of this outrageous healer in an effort to establish more precisely where the virtue of his personality resides.

House is a cynic in the true, classical sense. He is reminiscent of the philosopher Diogenes, who looked up from the Athenian gutter in which he was sunning himself to ask Alexander the Great to stand less between the sun and him, an expression of his Cynic belief that 'surrender to any external influence is beneath human dignity' (*Webster's College Dictionary* 1992: 339). In our day, the appellation cynic has come to mean 'a person who believes that only selfishness motivates human actions and who disbelieves or minimizes selfless acts or disinterested points of view' (ibid.) – in other words, Ayn Rand. However, it once referred to 'one of a sect of Greek philosophers, 4th Century BC', who would not kowtow to the power of the persona that rules everyone else because they 'advocated the doctrine that virtue is the only good and that the essence of virtue is self-control', not surrender to authority. The oppositional shadow of the founder of this school, Diogenes, has been cast across the centuries to create the image of the refuser of the authority of others, like House, as 'a person who shows or expresses a bitterly or sneering cynical attitude' (ibid.).

Cynis, which in Greek literally means 'dog', referred to the habit of the Cynics in Athens and elsewhere to live in the street, like dogs, so that they would not have to make the compromises other humans have to make to afford their housing. Interestingly, the dog is the animal House most resembles, with his constant need for attention, his unembarrassed openness about his bodily functions, and his willingness to bark at what bothers him. He shows, however, little of the sweetness of a dog, or even the virtue. He embodies, rather, another archetype, the Latin name of which sounds like cynis but is not etymologically related to it. *Senex*, meaning 'old man', is a decidedly human addition to our animal nature. The word is generally used by Jungian analysts with a negative connotation to denote the cold, contemptuous shadow of the father archetype. The senex, like a condescending father, is an eternal enemy of the illusions of naive youth and thus of all idealistic sentiments. James Hillman, who has made the definitive delineation of this archetype for analytical psychology, begins by quoting (from Seznec's classic *The Survival of the Pagan Gods*) a medieval prayer to Saturn. It could almost be a prayer a viewer of the series could imagine someone making silently to House himself, before supplicating the wounding and wounded healer for his diagnostic acumen:

> O Master of sublime name and great power, supreme Master; O Master Saturn: Thou, the Cold, the Sterile, the Mournful, the Pernicious; Thou, whose life is sincere and whose word sure; Thou, the Sage and

Solitary, the Impenetrable; Thou, whose promises are kept; Thou who art weak and weary; Thou who hast cares greater than any other, who knowest neither pleasure nor joy; Thou, the old and cunning, master of all artifice, deceitful, wise, and judicious; Thou who bringest prosperity or ruin and makest men to be happy or unhappy! I conjure Thee, O Supreme Father, by thy great benevolence and Thy generous bounty, to do for me what I ask . . .

(Seznec 1961: 53, cited in Hillman 1979: 15)

What is most Saturnine in Gregory House may be understood to reflect an ideology urged by the archetype: people, though they may wish to, do not change. As Hillman puts it, amplifying Saturn as senex:

But the pessimism of Saturn has deeper implications. Although the virtues and vices of character may be modified, they do not ultimately disappear through cure because they belong to one's nature as the original gift of sin. Congenital structure is karma, character is fate. Thus personality descriptions of the senex . . . will be . . . a self-description of the bound and fettered condition of human nature set within the privation of its characterological limits whose wisdom comes through suffering these limits.

(Hillman 1979: 16–17)

In the case of House, the 'old man' would refer to everything that seems old about the character in contrast to the youth of the doctors he is training. The cane he carries might as well be Saturn's sickle, for it is as much a signifier of his status as an elder as it is of the infarction that caused his right thigh muscles to die and made his gait unsteady. Using it to point and prod as often as to walk, he deploys it also like a senex wand, to cut at the puerile conceptions of his colleagues.

No one archetype, however, can circumscribe House. His lined face, even if aged by pain, is as impishly boyish as it is avuncular,[5] and the trickster is at least as important to his character as the senex. Both are archetypes of the shadow (Beebe 2004), that part of personality that is normally repressed in public situations by most of us, the face of our character we don't usually show in public, because we have signed the social contract and accepted the collective standards that govern social intercourse – at work, in dating, with friends. House, perversely, ignores such taboos and shows his shadow openly. His character is written so that the play of trickster and senex define the honesty on which he prefers to situate his medical persona. He eschews the usual *persona medici*, the dialectic between wise father and idealistic lifelong student that a doctor in a teaching hospital normally exhibits before his patients. The usual professor of medicine conceives himself to be learner and teacher in one, and the pure-hearted stiffness with which he attempts to maintain this paradox is symbolized by the white coat he wears. In contrast, House has chosen to vest himself in grungier costume – sneakers, jeans and five o'clock shadow – that freely admits to the world that medicine can be dirty and sneaky. For all that, he remains competitive and committed to excellence. Indeed, he is bent on offering an incisive alternative to the everyday medical mind.

The persona House himself brings to work spans, in Jungian typological terms (Beebe 2004), thinking that is introverted and cynical and feeling that in an offensively extraverted way is jokey and manipulative. Introverted thinking concerns itself with defining situations freshly so that their true meaning may be clarified, and House is so bent on diagnosing for himself what goes on with patients (since he feels he cannot trust anyone else to do so) that he will simply dismiss what other physicians think may be trans-piring. He will also, at first, avoid contact with a patient in favor of an algorithmic network of diagnostic associations that he keeps within his own mind. Extraverted feeling is directed toward, and concerns itself with, the feelings of others, but House does this in a dismissive way that puts the person who opens up to him in the double bind of wanting to get some validation from House but not knowing whether to go on trusting him. This is the confusing effect of a manipulative trickster (Beebe 1981). House's uses of senex introverted thinking and trickster extraverted feeling to deal with patients and colleagues are intended to provoke the medical estab-lishment. They constitute his angry rebuttal to the safe extraverted thinking/ introverted feeling dance most doctors have learned to do.

With his own abrasive and intrusive medical performance style, which signals from first contact with a patient or family of a patient his unwill-ingness to respect their fictions or to hide his own impatience to get at what is really going on, House challenges the idea that the best bedside manner is a quietly empathic respectful feeling that constrains the doctor from putting his or her own needs first. That kind of fatherly medicine is safely lodged in the protective emotional style of House's best friend, the oncologist Wilson. Even when scolding House, Wilson (Robert Sean Leonard) exudes the kind of equanimity the nineteenth-century 'Father of Modern Medicine', Sir William Osler, had in mind when he advised other doctors to 'Live neither in the past nor in the future, but let each day absorb all your interest, energy and enthusiasm' (Braude 1962: 575).

As Chief of Diagnostic Medicine at Princeton-Plainsboro Teaching Hospital, Dr Gregory House is constantly bringing up the patient's past and future, and that of his colleagues as well. This strategy keeps all their wounds open. He seems to feel that the healing of patients will mostly come from that openness and its gaping rawness. Disease, for him, is what hides behind what is withheld. The other members of his team, however, make a strenuous effort to stay unexposed and they resent House's frequent needling of them to open the wounds they are concealing. This offers comedic possibilities, because when he is not embarrassing them by bringing up what they are trying to hide, he draws exaggerated attention to himself, often calling attention to the body in ways that are shocking to others. He may be the only leading character on television to joke about the smell he makes when defecating in a men's room stall. It is pretty clear from the script that he does not always wash up before he comes to work. House's body exhibits the raunchiness that Jungian psychology associates with the trickster archetype,[6] but there is a sexy vitality to his efforts to draw the attention of others to what his body is doing, even in moments that most people would consider private. When Wilson lets House stay in his apartment and comes upon him masturbating on the living room couch, House tells him, 'I was picking the lint from my navel . . .' and a few minutes later, 'I wasn't picking the lint from my navel' (*Brave Heart*, 6: 6). His tricksterish extraverted feeling regularly puts the tolerance of others in a double bind. His way of communicating his wide-roaming sexuality to others often shocks the staid Wilson, who, though House's best friend and privy to most of his deepest secrets, is so much more private in the way he approaches women. House, under a cover of homophobic rhetoric and without any apparent sexual intent, even flirts with men, for instance the detective he hires to check up on his staff, Lucas Douglas (Michael Weston, a grandson of Artur Rubinstein, whose playful charm he seems to have inherited), who is quickly becoming his rival for the affections of Dean of Medicine Lisa Cuddy (Lisa Edelstein).

House's uses of his mind are similarly edgy, as when he rushes through an algorithm to a tentative diagnosis and then insists that it defines the patient's situation, ignoring the warnings of his staff that this sort of elimination-match thinking is a dangerous game to play at a patient's expense. Undaunted, House frequently takes the patient to the brink of a wrong treatment to prove or disprove a transient hypothesis.

We have to linger on the question of why this particular combination of archetypes – senex and trickster – is so satisfying for viewers to watch House enact as he goes about healing. One answer is the opportunity it gives Hugh Laurie to portray opposed character styles at the same time. The conjunction of contraries makes his House an outsize character, a Don Quixote and Sancho Panza rolled up into one, too much the fool to be a doctor, and too much the healer to be a fool. In English, we would have to go back to the Renaissance to Ben Jonson's *Volpone* to find such a character in the role of doctor. The principle that seems to guide House was in fact enunciated by an actual physician in the Renaissance: Paracelsus, the father of homeopathy, who taught that 'Like cures like'.[7] That dictum means that if a disease is a trickster (with protean manifestations) and a senex (tending toward chronicity and death), the doctor must find it in him to be both of these too. He has to train himself to use methods that are paradoxical, both inviting and threatening to the status quo of an illness, to provoke it to reveal itself so that the health of the patient can be restored.

American culture, fearful of decline, had at precisely the time *House* was first envisioned overused the senex and the trickster to prop up the failing heroism of the country (Beebe 2007: 275–296). A character who could summon the very same archetypes, this time in the service of healing, nearly convinces us that America can still be healed. House's value to viewers sympathetic to American culture is that, though sharing in the common narcissism, he refuses in his therapeutic role to collude with it and yet does not judge others for trying to take care of themselves. It is all he expects. His very cynicism puts us, therefore, in a therapeutic double bind. In his view, we are all self-serving, and everybody lies to cover this up. Our only way to get better is to do better. Seeing this is our path to recovery.

One way House himself uses the trickster and senex archetypes to get us on this path is to puncture the inflated presumptions of the Victim, the other side of the Hero (Mitchell 1996). The Victim is a role Americans particularly embraced after September 11, 2001, and House's sarcasm, aimed at the sympathy his patients would like to elicit from him, cuts into the masochism of our collective stance as well. His own tricksterish resilience in the face of pain makes him understand that traumatized people tend to embrace the Victim role as a strategy to survive. His deployment of senex is similarly trenchant, because it is so much in the service of eros.[8] Redeeming the misanthropy we usually associate with the senex, House wields the archetype like a bowie knife to hack away at the fictions that make communication between people impossible. A number of his interventions succeed because they are also psychotherapeutic: by removing a tissue of lies, they allow authentic communication to emerge.

A typical *House* episode unfolds with House riding roughshod over a patient's illness with tests and interventions, bent on getting at the truth of the matter and not knowing when to stop. He is relentless because he is trying to test the limits of the physical system he is investigating. At some point, often because the patient continues to 'crash' medically, he figures out that ruthless attempts to define the patient's reality (what a Jungian might call senex introverted thinking) and manipulative efforts to get the patient and family to disclose personal secrets (in Jungian terms trickster extraverted feeling) are not going to conquer the illness his team is trying to treat. House then moves away from the project of imposing rational order on the unruly illness. Pragmatically, he begins to employ a more empirical dialectic to get his answer. He tries harder to balance his hunches with verifying observations. The intelligences informing this new approach are Jung's perceptive functions of mind (sensation and intuition), cognitive modes that prefer to deal directly with what is presented and to rely far less on what can be deduced by reason.

We are shown that adopting them involves a move within House from a less masculine to a more feminine way of working. The main archetype leading the way in this reorientation of perspective is the part of him that a

Jungian viewer can recognize as his creative and dissatisfied anima. House's anima, the feminine pole of his psychological bisexuality and the prime imprinter of his most vital emotional interests, does not serve him well in love relationships, where he is intense, needy, and demanding, but it comes into its own when he is intensely gripped by the mystery of disease and willing to receive its message. In marked contrast to the self-preoccupation occasioned by his thigh pain while he is trying to think, when his anima-led intuition suggests to him what is going on, he becomes passionately other-directed and loses himself in merger with the patient as an object of interest. The effect is contagious for the viewer of the series, who comes to engage with illness as something other than a frightening disruption of the patient's life, something more integral to the pattern of that life as a whole. We are led by House to an unexpected empathy for the patient's overall condition.

It may be hard for some viewers to see House as having an anima that can stir this kind of compassion, since his usual presentation of self is so one-sidedly 'masculine' in tone. The feminine, if present in him, would have to be operating unconsciously. And so it is: House is strongly galvanized by what he can do with, find out, or get from the other person. Moreover, even when he is most passionately driven to find out what is really wrong with the patient, he is not trying to connect with the person, but rather to engage possibilities in the person, whether it is the person's advance into worsening illness or their potential return to health. But rather than these being signs that House does not have an anima, they indicate that House's anima is expressing itself out of the unconscious in an inventive, extraverted intuitive way.

To explore possibilities is to be extraverted intuitive, and House's anima keeps generating creative hypotheses, even if on the basis of limited evidence. In the service of an anima-driven intuition, House is forever jumping over the feelings, both extraverted and introverted, of others (their pride, their secrets, the conventions, which govern their relations with others and their values); their thinking (the way they have defined their situation and the plans they have made around it); and even the sensation of others (House breaches their bodily integrity, risks their comfort). Playing hunches, the classic penchant of extraverted intuition, is not all of what House is about when he lets this anima have its way with him. House's anima is hypomanic and intrusive, and it leads him to insist on having the standpoints of others to engage with, if only to establish how few possibilities they can offer him. The emotional force of the anima archetype driving House is distracting to his colleagues, at least until House's introverted sensation (his ability to verify on the basis of everything experienced so far) surfaces. Then, in its Sherlock Holmesian way, it can more coolly review what has actually been observed and find the detail that leads to the diagnosis.

It is at this point in each episode that House steps out of the shadowy role he has assumed *vis-à-vis* the patient, hearing about the case second-hand, and reveals himself as the super perceiver that he is. Even if he has convinced us up to now that his greatest discoveries occur in the privacy of his own mind, now he goes back on that promise and is willing to break his rule of never wanting to see the patient if he can help it. Thrillingly, he goes by himself to the bedside to look first-hand for the signs, or interrogate for the crucial (and usually embarrassing) history that will reveal the fundamental disease. If this process is anima-driven, we have to accept that House's anima, though creative, is essentially unconscious, and that he deploys it in this characteristic way because he must. Another way of saying this is that the character cannot escape his role in the series, which has the quality, as does an unconscious anima in an actual person, of shaping his fate. House is thus frequently a tragic figure, whose freedom is curtailed by his destiny to behave like a series character.

Nevertheless, insofar as he can take existential freedom in such a situation, House does so by choosing to define what is going on around him, a freedom rarely granted any character in a television series. House is forever challenging the thinking of others, and even at times seems to step beyond the formula given to him by the series creators and reinforced by the viewers' expectations. The individuation of Gregory House, to which Hugh Laurie's extraordinary range as an actor lends credibility, seems to develop the plan of the show itself along lines that seem to belong entirely to how this differentiating character wants to define it. As someone constantly differentiating the way he wants to use his mind, Gregory House can be said to be exercising his faculties not just to evince a philosophy[9] but to develop one for the viewer to witness. Yet we can also name this philosophy that evolves by engaging with the varieties of lived experience. Even if House's final aim as a diagnostician is truth, and his method Socratic, as a therapeutic philosopher what he embraces is American pragmatism, which carries the value of thinking about life in ways that support the living of it.

Looking at the series through the lens of analytical psychology's similarly pragmatic view of mind, it is not so hard to see the different characters as functions of consciousness driven by archetypes, trying to differentiate themselves along lines specific to each individual character (Beebe 2004). For instance, I see two main ways House deploys his mind in the service of finding the truth. They define a pair of opposites. His first way can be described as the *skeptical*. It draws upon the cynicism of the senex archetype, but the formal operations in House depend on his introverted sensation, which is constantly asking if what he is being shown and told is real. As Jung, the first to describe this faculty of mind so precisely, puts it, 'What will make an impression and what will not can never be seen in advance, and from outside' (Jung 1921: 395). To use his introverted sensation in a disciplined way, House must be determined to mistrust what the patient says and what the other doctors have managed to learn with their hypotheses and their tests. He has to notice what is going on inside him, 'the intensity of the subjective sensation excited by the objective stimulus' (ibid.). House can't really explain the nature of that process to anybody else, but it is how he knows whether something he has noticed about a case jogs any sense he might have of its participation in a larger reality, what Jung describes as 'the background of the physical world rather than its surface' (ibid.: 395).

The second way House deploys his mind might be described as the *emergent*.[10] It involves making himself fully open to the emergence of new information that will unlock the case. This he does by distracting himself as much as possible, so that his mind cannot know in advance what the important information coming in really is. Then he will be open to the chance remarks of others, and the hunches that pop up from within. This is the cognitive process Jung defined as extraverted intuition.

> The intuitive function is represented in consciousness by an attitude of expectancy, by vision and penetration; but only from the subsequent result can it be established how much of what was 'seen' was actually in the object and how much was 'read into' it . . . The primary function of intuition . . . is simply to transmit images, or perceptions of relations between things, which could not be transmitted by the other functions [thinking, feeling or sensation] or only in a very roundabout way. These images have the value of specific insights which have a decisive influence on action whenever intuition is given priority.
>
> (Jung 1921: 366)

One sees such a moment of insight in just about every *House* episode, and it usually comes after the rational leads Gregory House has been following have led him down a number of blind alleys. It is then that a chance perception of some apparently trivial sort leads him to a new insight as to what is actually going on in the patient.

House's intuition is extraverted because it is centered on what is happening in the object, and it employs introverted sensation, that is 'simple and immediate sense impression understood as a clearly defined physiological and psychic datum', as the starting point 'for . . . perceptions' (ibid.: 367). The intuitive 'selects' such sensations 'by unconscious predilection. It is not the strongest sensation, in the physiological sense, that is accorded the chief value, but any sensation whatsoever whose value is enhanced by the intuitive's unconscious attitude' (ibid.).

It is this combination of sensation and intuition that Foreman (his very name suggesting a person whose superior function has come to the fore) cannot make sense of. It informs a creativity in House that Foreman, whose introverted sensation is cut off from his extraverted intuition, simply does not have. Foreman, not House, is the doctor in the series who is most out of touch with his anima.

The anima is the energy in House that delivers his intuitions to him in an unconscious but creative way, and which drives him to act on them impulsively. Foreman, in team meetings, stands up against this hypomanic, out of control extraverted intuition, insisting on the normal ego processes and medical procedures that House refuses to allow to confine him. Yet even in the area of his own greatest strength, a cautious introverted sensation (which we recognize from the way his often immobile poker face is always quietly checking on House[11]), Foreman is no match for House. Despite the fact that Foreman and House have a similar conscious standpoint – this is underlined in *Poison* (1: 8), where they discover, after entering an elevator, that they are wearing the same kind of shoes – House's powers of observation are greater: he picks up details and recalls precedents for their relevance to disease with uncanny powers of observation and recall. When House uses introverted sensation, which I read as his superior function, the one he employs when he is not dipping into his shadow for theatrical effect, he does so far more imaginatively than Foreman, and with greater depth of focus. This may be because the entire axis of irrational consciousness on which introverted sensation and extraverted intuition reside[12] is alive in House (a sign of his basic integrity as a character[13]). It also suggests a superior function that is more free to function heroically (by going outside the box to deploy its introverted sensation) than is the case for the inhibited Foreman, who is limited by his insistence on 'toeing the line', a reaction against his early forays into sociopathy.

House also uses his ego more idiosyncratically than other characters. His superior introverted sensation, though ever observant, really comes into its own only when it is led by his anima, his extraverted intuition, to make an original but definitive diagnostic formulation, one that 'nails' what is going on. The effect is uncanny, because House then slips into hero mode. At such times, he is quite unlike the way he is at other times: no longer depressed and sometimes not even in pain – something that hospital administrator Dr Cuddy points out to him in *Skin Deep* (2: 13). He seems most essentially himself at such moments. The rest of the time he almost refuses to use his introverted sensation in the way most people would, to make things more convenient, tidy, or efficient, to the despair of Cuddy, who with her abundant extraverted sensation (comically illustrated by her ample bosom and behind and her sexy clothes) becomes House's foil.

House is such a post-heroic character that he puts no particular emphasis on his own heroism when he does use it. Narcissistic as he is, in this one regard he comes across as appealingly modest. He is so rooted in his anima and his inferior function – the extraverted intuition that fuels his creativity – that it is possible to take him for an extraverted intuitive type. But such a conclusion would be a mistake: it is always finally his introverted sensation ego that surfaces at the end of a show, and causes him to abandon his medical snap judgments and heroically manages to establish the actual disease process he is dealing with by matching details to their precedents in his experience. Introverted sensation's greatest gift, moreover, is its ability to figure out any process as a sequence of causes and effects, verifiable by close observation of the process from inside – hence House's insistence on getting inside the patient's home, inside the patient's family, and inside the patient's body to discover where those causes and effects reside. Watching House deploy his skill at getting at this level of information and putting it all together, we can easily associate House with a physician-detective at the top of his form, but this normalization of the character's genius always has the force of a surprise. His mastery of detail appears only after a series of maverick, wildly intuitive stabs at diagnosis have almost convinced us (along with Foreman) that when he does manage to identify the patient's condition, it will only be because he got lucky.

The key to House's success as a doctor, which the more conservative Foreman finally cannot fathom, is the degree to which he relies on what he does not know. For instance, he frequently initiates treatment not knowing whether it will work, in order to eliminate those conditions that would disappear if it did. He also is never sure just what will stress the patient's body into getting sick enough to reveal its weakest spot, so he provokes every area of potential vulnerability. Only when he finds the patient's Achilles heel does he start to use what might be called a rational procedure to establish what can actually be done about it. And even then, the measures he comes up with will be improvised and risky. It is as if he knows that when a patient is really sick the appearance of health is a trick, one that he must find a way to see through. With the clinic patients he is forced by Dr Cuddy to see, the situation is reversed: their complaints, he realizes, are almost always tricks to convince others that they are really ill when they are not.

On a show like this, the serious illnesses that do emerge as a consequence of House's intense and invasive attempts to make what is undermining a person's body show its true face will have to be different with every episode, but I have found that all of them share certain psychological characteristics. An illness on *House* will (1) be initially imaged in a sinister way for the viewer, (2) turn out to be surprisingly life threatening, (3) be hard to diagnose, and (4) occur in the context of a love relationship whose integrity is being tested and may have serious dysfunctional aspects, even if these are not at first obvious.

A typical illness in this regard is the one in *Adverse Effects* (5: 3). In the opening scene of this episode, a beefy married man who is somewhat testy about being middle-aged is watching with possessive pride as his wife is being painted, nude, by an artist who is still a young man. 'I still can't believe you talked me into this,' the woman says to her husband. Finally, the painter tells them that the picture is finished, and the couple join hands to look at it. The portrait, however, is grotesque: it looks like a bad imitation of a late Picasso, with surreal and cubist distortions of the woman's face and figure. The shocked husband protests that this is not his wife. When the painter replies, 'You asked me to paint her exactly the way she looks; that's exactly what I did,' he slugs him. The painter's girlfriend verifies that the painting is distorted, even though the painter still cannot see it, and she brings him to the hospital to have the basis for the distortion of his visual perspective examined. Called in to help, House dispatches various members of his staff to investigate the painter's storage space and learns that there are many unsold paintings there, some with the same kind of perspective distortions, and some without. The latter are rather conventional and indicate that he does not have a great deal of talent. It quickly becomes obvious that he cannot be earning a living from the sales of his paintings. House surmises that the patient must be supplementing his money somehow and tumbles onto the fact that he is a 'guinea pig' volunteer paid to test experimental drugs in their first medical trials. This explains the origin of the distortion in his perception, since this is a not uncommon side-effect of some new drugs.

The painter, however, does not want his girlfriend to know that he has been supporting himself through the income he gets from these risky clinical trials. He has been concealing from her the fact that he is not a success as an artist because he imagines she will not respect him if she finds out. In a side plot during the same episode, one of the other doctors on House's team, Taub (Peter Jacobson), learns through a private investigator hired by House that his wife has been making deposits into a private bank account. House's surmise is that she may be planning to leave her marriage with Taub because she is having an affair with someone else. Instead, she has been saving up for the really expensive gift of a sports car, a gift Taub does not feel entitled to receive because he himself had had an affair. Taub, a rather Adlerian character, a strong introverted feeler who does love his wife, has a very hard time believing that a good marriage could be based on anything but fictions. As a further complication in the realm of eros, the private investigator House has hired turns out to be drawn to House's boss, Dr Cuddy, the hospital administrator, the one woman to whom House has not been able to admit the extent of his own erotic interest. Therefore, in a single episode, the wife talked into posing for a nude portrait by her husband; the painter and his girlfriend; Taub and his wife; House and Cuddy; and the private investigator are all shown to be involved in love relationships in which a great deal is being left unsaid.

The painting of the wife in this episode, though distorted, gives thus a true picture of the anima common to all these arrangements, an image of eros that has lost its integrity. The twisted image of the wife in the painting echoes the figures in Picasso's *Les Demoiselles D'Avignon*, a painting that testifies to the great twentieth-century artist's introverted intuition. It reveals that the feminine image, an archetype that is commonly used to symbolize relational integrity, has somehow become warped. The same demonic intuition informs other images we get of patients' illnesses in *House*. Its images play with archetypal or religious motifs which have become dislocated and, in the process, distorted. For instance, in *Damned If You Do* (1: 5) House tries to treat a nun for a contact dermatitis he believes is an allergy to the soap she uses to wash dishes at the convent. In the course of trying to understand the untoward response the Sister has had to an antihistamine, House pays a visit to the convent and learns from the Mother Superior that the nun had self-aborted an unwanted pregnancy in years past. This plot development is taken into an even deeper erotic problem at the religious level. It turns out that the nun still has a copper intra-uterine device inside her from a long-ago effort to introduce birth control. Copper, a naturally occurring metal that is sacred to Aphrodite, signifies that the problem of erotic love has somehow remained in the nun's pelvic organs even though she imagines that she has the Christian God in her, and that He wants to take her.

Repeatedly through the series, House uncovers examples of disturbed erotic connection or trust, though there are also examples of intense and honest connection that challenge his own cynicism and force him to look at the status of his own relationships, which are often dismal, even if intensely felt. We get the best sense of disturbance of eros, however, in the subplots that swirl around the various members of his team, which so far has consisted of two overlapping sets of characters. Each of these characters mirrors some aspect of House's personality.

Though all of the members of the team are ambivalent about House, respecting him as a doctor but sure that he is an 'ass', each of these characters has his or her own wound in the area of relatedness. Not one of them, for instance, sensed that their likeable Indian-American colleague Kutner (Kal Penn) was insecure or depressed enough to kill himself, which he does in *Simple Explanation* (5: 20), and that his brave extraverted feeling was no more than a skillfully constructed facade concealing a sensitive, lost boy. At the level of his introverted feeling, he was so much more wounded by the traumatic loss of his parents (they were shot in front of him when he was four) than anyone realized. He could not articulate it in part because his adoptive parents had been so nice and he had tried so far to fit into their world, even taking their name rather than his birth parents' Indian name, Choudhari. The ambivalence about his life, hidden behind his use of a likeable, tricksterish facade, serves the series as a gloss for the reason that House has decided to investigate the possibility of psychiatric treatment for himself – a fact uncovered by Wilson in the previous episode of Season Five, *Locked In* (5: 17).

A character on the show who is much less ambivalent about covering his tracks with extraverted feeling is Dr Robert Chase (played by the young Australian actor Jesse Spencer), who has the opposite problem to Kutner.

Chase has trouble letting people experience his sincerity, which others often fail to appreciate when he uses his extraverted feeling to placate them. His dilemma in this regard becomes urgent in the aftermath of his arranging, in *The Tyrant* (6: 4), for the genocidal African dictator Dibala to get the wrong treatment and die after he confides to Chase that he plans to kill off the remaining members of his country's ethnic minority. Chase has just married the idealistic Dr Cameron (Jennifer Morrison), who has been urging him not to treat Dibala at all. She represents almost too pure an integrity, one that cannot admit an ambiguous, tricksterish moral imagination into her naively sincere way of holding ethical issues. As a consequence, she cannot empathize with her new husband's ethical dilemma and after offering the solution that they both give notice at the hospital and try to make a new start somewhere else, a plan he is reluctant to follow, she leaves him.

Foreman's problem, on the other hand, is that he cannot allow himself to be vulnerable to anyone else. He is simply too proud to do so, and he keeps the lion's share of his suffering to himself, as in *Simple Explanation* (5: 18). Taub is similarly afraid to let his much-loved wife really know him. She eventually has to learn that in the early years of the marriage he often turned to other women for sexual reassurance.

The moon-faced 'Thirteen' (Olivia Wilde), also referred to as Dr Remy Hadley, is bisexual. She tries, in relations with both men and women, to avoid becoming truly intimate with anyone because she is afraid of burdening someone else once the neurological illness she is carrying – Huntington's Disease – starts to progress. The extraverted intuition she brings to medical diagnosis, on display in *Remorse* (6: 12), suggests what House's own anima might be like if it were more focused and conscious. Thirteen's eros, however, echoes something that operates more unconsciously in House, as a man sexually drawn to women but clearly loving no one in the world more than his best friend Wilson. Conversely, Thirteen's on-and-off partner Foreman (Omar Epps) is more overtly an introverted sensation type than House but also more ego-bound and persona-oriented. Foreman shows us what House could have become if he had ever allowed himself to function like an ordinary doctor: hemmed in by the rules at hand, afraid to let any of his shadow show, and always longing for more prestige.

All these characters, in fact, reflect sides of House himself. He knows this, and consciously uses them to dialogue with himself in order to make a diagnosis. Their presence on his team, however, has another meaning as well. It encourages him to try to live the different sides of himself as fully as possible, and to develop an integrity that can contain them all. There are some signs, as the series progresses, that this is happening. House, even in his woundedness, is not fragmented. Rather, with all these facets, he is a much more complete figure than we usually find on television. In the episodes of the Sixth Season when House actually surrenders to inpatient psychiatric treatment and psychotherapy for the control issues behind his addiction to painkillers (*Broken* 6: 1–2), everyone can begin to see the potential for individuation in him.

One of the signifiers of House's unusual inner potential, exquisitely conveyed by Hugh Laurie in mostly unspoken ways even though the script gives hints, is his bedrock bisexuality, which a psychoanalyst might describe as expressing his need to bring his parents into a loving intercourse through their connection to him. This was never possible with House's actual parents, for reasons that the series clearly spells out in *Birthmarks* (5: 4). But in current time, he loves both the fatherly Wilson and the maternal Cuddy, who sometimes huddle to discuss his needs. Wilson, to whom House said directly in *97 Seconds* (4: 3) 'I love you', stands for the containing father that House has a great deal of trouble being for others because he has not experienced it in his own life. Cuddy, a watchful mother where House is concerned, is able to convince Wilson, at the time of House's actual father's death, to kidnap House and take him to the funeral home where his actual mother is waiting for him 'to do her proud' at the funeral that House would otherwise have boycotted (*Birthmarks* 5: 4).

Connecting to Wilson as surrogate father has been an essential step in the development of House's ability to make conscious contact with the anima. Wilson, with his extraverted thinking, is systematic in his planning, but he is also animated, deliberate in feeling matters and protective of others, where House is brusque and typically clueless as to how to lend moral support to people who are hurting.

Anima is not a role that Cuddy, with her voluptuous extraverted sensation, is suited to play for him typologically. Perennially, she confines herself to being a would-be mother-figure to House, and she is charming in the maternal way she tries to compensate for his deficits and still protect his creativity. Archetypally, though, she takes up the role of Opposing Personality (Beebe 2004), the one whose job it is to neutralize the excesses of his aggressive drive. She has to be the heavy, the adult who forces him to observe at least some of the boundaries and rules that like all trickster heroes he prefers to flaunt. With her great body and tight, exposing clothes, she does, however, seem to promise an erotic wholeness that the hobbled House lacks. He longs for her, and for a time she him, but she turns out to be more signpost than destination. As the administrator of his development, her role is to mirror his lack of relatedness when it affects his work and get him to see that he must strive to resolve the same illness in his own person that he finds again and again in his patients.

What is exciting in the series is the sense that House is actually doing this work of connecting to himself and not just projecting his own woundedness onto others. House's stay in a psychiatric hospital, shown in *Broken* (6: 1–2), reveals his ability to work through his early resistance to treatment and finally to admit that he actually needs a psychiatrist's help to get better, not just to get him out of the hospital. The breakthrough is accompanied by his first mature love affair, with a married woman who cannot bring herself to leave her husband and children for House, even though she loves him back. He does, however, extend himself to help her sister become released from a catatonic spell, with the parallel implication that the worst inhibition of his own eros is at an end.

But House's potential for becoming more loving is not why the staff in the diagnostic department return to him, even after they have quit. Nor is it why Cuddy and Wilson risk their own medical licences to protect him. Colleagues find it hard to abandon House because he is in touch with a truth they need to take on board – that, in taking care of another, empathy by itself is usually insufficient. To meet the deepest needs of the other person, there must always be integrity as well. House is the one character on the show who consistently seeks truth, whomever he has to hurt to get to it. Hard as it can be to believe that House's ruthlessness is called for to achieve the results he does, we cannot watch the series without celebrating the integrity of the central character. Participating in his struggles to find out the truth about his patients, his colleagues, his parents and himself, it is almost like getting a call from a worried friend. As she pours her heart out to us, we feel as if our ability to care and be cared for are unexpectedly rendered vulnerable.

References

Beebe, J. (1981) The trickster in the arts. *San Francisco Jung Institute Library Journal*, 2(2), 22–54.

Beebe, J. (1992) *Integrity in Depth*. College Station, TX: Texas A&M University Press.

Beebe, J. (2000) *The Wizard of Oz*: A vision of development in the American political psyche. In T. Singer (ed.), *The Vision Thing: Myth, Politics and Psyche in the World*. London and New York, NY: Routledge (pp. 62–83).

Beebe, J. (2004) Understanding consciousness through the theory of psychological types. In J. Cambray and L. Carter (eds), *Analytical Psychology: Contemporary Perspectives in Jungian Analysis*. Hove and New York, NY: Brunner-Routledge (pp. 83–115).

Beebe, J. (2007) The memory of the hero and the emergence of the post-heroic attitude. *Spring*, 78, 275–296.

Braude, J. M. (1962) *Lifetime Speaker's Encyclopedia*. Englewood Cliffs, NJ: Prentice-Hall (p 575).

Cambray, J. (2005) Towards the feeling of emergence. *Journal of Analytical Psychology*, 51(1), 1–20.

Haule, J. (1992) Jung's 'Amfortas' wound: Psychological types revisited. *Spring*, 53, 95–112.

Hillman, J. (1967) Senex and Puer. In J. Hillman (ed.), *Puer Papers*. Dallas, TX: Spring Publications (pp. 3–53).

Jacoby, H. (2009) (ed.) *House and Philosophy*. Hoboken, NJ: Wiley.

Jung, C. G. (1921) *Psychological Types, Collected Works 6*. London: Routledge & Kegan Paul.

Jung, C. G. (1963) *Memories, Dreams, Reflections* (A. Jaffé, Rec. and Ed.; R. and C. Winston, Trans). New York, NY: Pantheon.

Jung, C. G. (1976) *The Symbolic Life, Collected Works 18*. London: Routledge & Kegan Paul.

Jung, E. and von Franz, M.-L. (1970) *The Grail Legend*. New York, NY: G. P. Putnam.

Kazan, E. (2009) *Kazan on Directing* (R. Cornfield, Ed). New York, NY: Alfred A. Knopf.

Mitchell, M. B. (1996) *Hero or Victim?* Los Angeles, CA: M. B. Mitchell.

Paracelsus, Theophrastus (1988) *Paracelsus: Selected Writings* (J. Jacobi, Ed.; N. Guterman, Trans). Princeton, NY: Princeton University Press.

Radin, P. (1972) *The Trickster: A Study in American Indian Mythology*. New York, NY: Shocken Books.

Seznec, J. (1961) *The Survival of the Pagan Gods*. New York, NY: Harper Torchbooks.

von Franz, M.-L. (1971) The inferior function. In M.-L. von Franz and J. Hillman, *Lectures on Jung's Typology*. New York, NY: Spring Publications (pp. 1–72).

von Franz, M.-L. (1975) *C. G. Jung: His Myth in Our Time* (W. H. Kennedy, Trans). Boston, MA: Little, Brown.

von Franz, M.-L. (2008) Jung's rehabilitation of the feeling function in our civilization (Lecture given in Küsnacht, November 25, 1986). *Jung Journal, 2*(2), 8–20.

Webster's College Dictionary (1992). New York, NY: Random House.

Notes

1 The conception is based in part on the *New Yorker*'s 'Annals of Medicines' articles by Berton Roueché, which became a regular feature of the magazine between 1946 and 1994.

2 In the episode *Three Stories* (1: 21), via a flashback, House is shown to have suffered a blockage of the blood supply to the quadriceps muscle of his thigh and narrowly to have avoided amputation of his leg by the removal of the most damaged muscle groups.

3 The attempt to make sense of this cycle of stories from the standpoint of analytical psychology was itself a Grail Quest, started by Emma Jung and carried forward to publication by Marie-Louise von Franz. For an amplification of the imagery in the legend that parallels House's wound, see especially Chapter XI of their study, 'The Suffering Grail King' (E. Jung and von Franz, 1970: 187–212).

4 Haule (1992) traces the term to *Psychological Types*, in which Jung (1921: 70) relies exclusively on the telling of the story in Wagner's opera *Parsifal*, where Amfortas's wound is to the thighs. He notes that Jung himself sees the wound as not about sexuality or even eros, but rather a disturbance in the balance of psychic functions (Jung 1921: 70), which he believes reflects the influence of religious attitudes that have forced animal sexuality and power into the unconscious, leading these animal instincts to surface in primitive and perverse ways

(Jung 1921: 219–220). In *Memories, Dreams, Reflections*, Jung says that his memory of his father was 'of a sufferer stricken with an Amfortas wound, a "fisher king" whose wound would not heal – that Christian suffering for which the alchemists sought the panacea' (Jung 1963: 215). In her biography of Jung's work, von Franz says that Amfortas's 'wound is in the thigh, or the genital region, undoubtedly an allusion to the problem of sexuality, unsolved in Christendom' (von Franz 1975: 274). In Jungian psychology sexuality is understood symbolically as the body of eros, meaning our very relatedness to each other, and that it has been repressed and resurfaces in perverse ways is revealed by the often brutal ways human beings treat each other. Such behavior has created an ever-deepening cultural wound that can only be healed through an acceptance of the realistic need for a more conscious feeling in our relations with each other (von Franz 2008). House's interest, however, lies not in the lack of empathy, but in the lack of integrity that compromises those relations.

5 Hugh Laurie, who plays House, and turned 50 in March 2009, effectively uses his own look, which is both juvenile and mature, to span these opposites.

6 In the Winnebago Trickster Cycle that Paul Radin used to introduce the archetype, Trickster, coming upon a lovely land belonging to another tribe, puts his penis in a box and instructs it to lodge itself in the chief's daughter, which it proceeds to do. Earlier he has burned his anus and eaten his own intestines. (Radin 1972: 17–20).

7 'Similia similibus curantur.' This principle, cited by Jung (1976: 6) at the beginning of his 1935 Tavistock Lectures, is expressed by Paracelsus as follows: "Is not a mystery of nature concealed even in poison? . . . He who despises poison does not know what is hidden in it; for the arcanum that is contained in the poison is so blessed that the poison can neither detract from it nor harm it . . . when hot is applied against hot, and cold against cold, all this accords with the arcanum. For in administering medicine we must always set entity against entity, so that each becomes in a sense the wife or husband of the other" (Paracelsus 1988: 95–96).

8 Eros here is used in the Jungian sense of 'capacity to relate' (Jung 1963: 170, par. 224).

9 This is the theme of the book edited by Henry Jacoby (2009), in which professional philosophers examine House's views on life, logic and method, ethical principles, virtues and character, and the contrasting philosophies of the characters around him.

10 See Cambray (2005) for a discussion of this concept from complexity theory and its application to the process of healing in psychotherapy.

11 'In describing herself,' Emma Jung 'said that the introverted sensation type was like a highly sensitized photographic plate. When somebody comes into the room, such a type notices the way the person comes in, the hair, the expression on the face, the clothes, and the way the person walks. All this makes a very precise impression on the introverted sensation type; every detail is absorbed . . . Outwardly, the introverted sensation type looks utterly stupid. He just sits and stares, and you do not know what is going on within him. He looks like a piece of wood with no reaction at all – unless he reacts with one of his auxiliary functions, thinking or feeling. But inwardly the impression is being absorbed . . . This type is very often misjudged and misunderstood by others because one does not realize what goes on within' (von Franz 1971: 27). I feel this passage by von Franz well describes Foreman.

12 Jung postulates that the different functions of consciousness outlined by his typology are arranged in pairs that define axes, i.e. extraverted feeling and

introverted thinking; introverted feeling and extraverted thinking; introverted intuition and extraverted sensation; and introverted sensation and extraverted intuition. When one member of a pair is the superior function and the other the inferior function, I speak of that axis as the 'spine' of the individual's personality, drawing upon a term Elia Kazan (2009) took from Stanislavsky to guide his preparation of actors, to help them understand the characters they were playing. We can identify such a spine readily in a character like House, and I am exploring it typologically here building on work I have developed through the study of film (Beebe 2000, 2004).

13 See Beebe 1992: 106–107.

Chapter 11

'I feel like a failure' – in-*House* feminism

Catriona Miller

The popular television drama *House* was first broadcast in 2004 and it reached its hundredth episode in February 2009. A sixth season began in late 2009. In the intervening period it won numerous awards and tremendous critical success. According to one ratings agency, in 2008 *House* had more than 81.8 million viewers (Eurodata TV Worldwide, 2009), making it the most popular drama series in the world that year. It is more than just a popular drama; it is a *globally* popular drama.

To quote from the Fox Network's website, 'House, an innovative take on the medical drama, solves mysteries where the villain is a medical malady and the hero is an irreverent, controversial doctor who trusts no one, least of all his patients' (Fox Network, 2009). The central character of the show is, of course, Dr Gregory House (Hugh Laurie), the 'controversial doctor' whose damaged leg leaves him in constant pain and taking serious pain killers. He is misanthropic, manipulative, a player of games, lazy, and a drug addict, but he always solves the puzzle of the symptoms and usually saves the life of the patient as well.

Fox makes much of *House*'s 'innovative' nature, but historically hospital and medical dramas have constituted a significant proportion of drama on television in both Britain and America and *House* is only the latest in a long line of medical dramas, albeit one of the most successful ever. In the 1950s and 1960s, in shows such as *Dr Kildare* (1961–1966) or *Ben Casey* (1961–1966), it was the usual practice to construct a narrative structure around the hub of a dominant central character and in these early programs, the emphasis was on the 'good work' of healing performed by the white male doctor.

The 1970s and 1980s however, saw new medical shows such as *M*A*S*H** (1972–1983) and *St Elsewhere* (1982–1988) which were much more critical of authority figures and began to suggest that (white, male) doctors were neither above reproach, nor infallible. These shows also began to discuss contentious social issues, such as homosexuality, rape, abortion and drug addiction. It became less a question of the heroic (male) doctor versus disease, but under-pressure medical *teams* doing their best to deal with society's blind spots and failures, often at great personal cost, a trend that continued into the 1990s and beyond with dramas such as *ER* (1994–2009) and *Grey's Anatomy* (2005–ongoing).

So hospital dramas have been the staple fare of television's scheduling since it became a mass medium in the 1950s, and, despite Fox's insistence on innovation, *House* rather seems to regress to an earlier model of medical drama, in which the central character, a brilliant male doctor, battles the specter of disease. *House* is not a drama particularly interested in social or political issues, and it is very tempting to link the reactionary return to the character of the heroic, white, male doctor with the Fox Network's widely reported right-wing bias and its owner Rupert Murdoch's own well publicized conservative values.

However, where *House* does differ significantly from the dramas of the 1950s and 1960s is in the character of House's boss, Dr Lisa Cuddy (Lisa Edelstein), a new type of character which is becoming increasingly common in US television drama – the foxy, professional female. (See, for example, *The Closer* [2005–present] starring Kyra Sedgewick, a police drama, which, after soap opera and hospital drama has been the other staple of the television drama schedules.) Cuddy, as she is known in the show, is, on first acquaintance, a competent, ambitious, professional woman. She is the Dean of Medicine, the hospital administrator, and the woman who hired Gregory House in the first place. She is the female boss of a maverick male doctor, and this *is* an innovation in the medical drama.

This chapter will focus on Lisa Cuddy, to draw attention to a character who is not centre stage, but who none the less raises some profound questions about the role of women in positions of authority. The fundamental aspects of leadership will be discussed in the light of the Jungian idea of the cultural complex in order to better understand the conflicts and apparent difficulties that arise when a woman performs a leadership role. This type of analysis represents a kind of 'scribbling in the margins' of the drama, in the manner of a *scholium* or a gloss, or perhaps Derrida's *supplement* (Derrida 1974: 145) rather than suggesting a definitive reading of such an extensive text.

Under pressure? – Dr Lisa Cuddy

Cuddy is represented on the surface as a smart, sassy woman, exercising power over an (in)subordinate male character. Surely this is the kind of image feminists have been encouraging networks to deploy for many years now and it is appreciated by many fans of the show. As one fan says: 'I love Lisa Cuddy because she's smart, funny, beautiful, and can take what House throws at her and dish it right back! Not to mention she's the only one who can come close to keeping the reins on House. Plus, she just oozes Girl Power!' (lisacuddy.com 2009).

The use of the phrase 'girl power' in this context should tip us off to the fact that we are wandering into the contested territory of third-wave feminism and/or post-feminism. Both terms are difficult to define with any measure of agreement, though perhaps third-wave feminism maintains a connection with the politically activist second wave, while post-feminism suggests a greater concern with lifestyle choices rather than activism *per se* (for further discussion see Gamble 2001: 293, Lotz 2001). This complexity and confusion over the meaning of these terms illustrates the complexity and confusion that surrounds women in the twenty-first century. Cuddy can be taken as a representative of the intricacies of negotiating the 'gender jungle' of our era.

Cuddy is presented to the audience as a strong professional woman, in a position of some authority and performing a leadership role. In *Control* (1: 14), Cuddy tells new chairman of the Board Edward Vogler (Chi McBride) that she is one of only three female Chiefs of Medicine in the US. In *Humpty Dumpty* (2: 3), she tells a friend and colleague: 'I graduated medical school at 25, pissed off because I was second in my class. Chief of Medicine at 32, second youngest ever, first woman.' She handles House with a mixture of threat and bribery, prepared to argue the odds with him; she is as articulate and crafty as he is smart and manipulative. Indeed, they do seem intellectually well matched in many respects, which leads perhaps to the inevitable question of romance explored further in Season Five and no doubt beyond.

Cuddy is a high achiever, or, to borrow a phrase from Marion Woodman, she might equally be described as a handmaiden of patriarchy. The handmaiden of patriarchy (the father's daughter, or daughter of the mother's animus): 'Having been immersed in patriarchal standards, she values logic, order, mind, spirit, goals' (Woodman 1990: 111). Jung's rather gender essentialist concept of the anima/animus archetype suggests that:

> The anima gives relationship and relatedness to a man's consciousness, the animus gives to woman's consciousness a capacity for reflection, deliberation and self knowledge.
>
> (Jung 1959: para. 33)

Post-Jungian writers have, however, insisted that social and cultural factors are taken more seriously and a less gender essentialist approach is adopted and have suggested that for many women the animus is a negative experience representing an 'internalized psychic reception of patriarchy' (Rowland 2002: 50).

The character of Cuddy has internalized the dominant ideology of patriarchy, pursuing attributes which are admired by the external world, and has achieved power and influence. She has authority, competency, and ambition matched with capability. There is, however, a price.

Initially, then, the audience is presented with Cuddy as the successful professional woman in a key leadership role. She runs the hospital, she is on the Board, she sits on other important committees such as the transplant committee, she controls budgets and hires and fires staff (including House and his team at various times). However, the continuing narrative of the show then seems to set about dismantling this apparent power and confidence and Cuddy is *re*-presented to the audience in a more subtle way that puts her into a different light.

In terms of Cuddy's narrative arc, the most overt challenge to her authority in the hospital and over House comes in Season One in the form of billionaire businessman Edward Vogler, who makes a donation of $100 million dollars to the hospital which instantly buys him tremendous power and influence. Predictably, perhaps, Vogler does not take to the maverick House and immediately begins pressuring Cuddy to get rid of him. He is a confrontational and belligerent character, asking Cuddy in an aggressively blunt fashion if she is sleeping with House, suggesting that her judgment about him is compromised by a current (or prior) relationship. In the subsequent episode Vogler announces that he will not leave Cuddy's office until she can show him 'one good reason for keeping House', telling her that she is soft and wants people to like her.

Often the ways in which his power is demonstrated are non verbal. In *Mob Rules* (1: 15), for example, Vogler snatches a letter House is holding out to Cuddy, thus pre-empting any decision she might make. His power is also made evident through the production design and framing. In the same episode, as Cuddy argues with Vogler over House, she is surrounded by files and piles of paper, suggesting chaos and a certain desperation as she searches for a reason that Vogler will accept to keep House. In the subsequent episode, *Heavy* (1: 16), there are shots of Cuddy trailing along hospital corridors in the wake of Vogler, seemingly helpless to do anything to stop him, literally or metaphorically.

Eventually, Cuddy stops attempting to accommodate and persuade Vogler, but not before she actually voted *with* him to get rid of House, and Wilson (Robert Sean Leonard), House's best friend, has been voted off the Board. Although Cuddy eventually persuades the Board not to cave in to Vogler she is not really the hero of the hour and in the final scene where House toasts her victory she seems far from pleased. Vogler's offensive is an overt attack which Cuddy eventually counters, but far more insidious seems to be Cuddy's own sense of deficiency which is gradually revealed as the character's narrative continues.

The speech from the episode *Humpty Dumpty* (2: 3), mentioned above, in which Cuddy lists her achievements – 'I graduated medical school at 25, pissed off because I was second in my class. Chief of medicine at 32, second youngest ever, first woman,' actually ends with, 'House is right. I've been so anxious to get ahead, I haven't been a doctor in years.' The writers have Cuddy's character undermine herself.

When the audience is given insight into Cuddy's personal life, or when Cuddy lets slip her professional persona, viewers are often shown her own sense of inadequacy. In *No More Mr Nice Guy* (4: 13), House, always the diagnostician, writes a performance appraisal for her where he tells her 'What you want, you run away from. What you need, you don't have a clue. What you've accomplished makes you proud, but you're still miserable.' It is as if House, as is his wont, says out loud what Cuddy secretly fears. He confirms her inner voice, which has been called 'Internalised Oppression' (Wehr 1987: 18) or the Self-Hater – a voice which always says 'try harder', 'do more', 'not good enough' (Ulanov and Ulanov 1994: 197). Young-Eisendrath (1986) once commented, 'I have yet to encounter an adult woman who did not evaluate herself in some highly convincing way as uniquely deficient or inadequate' (in Wehr 1987: 17). Cuddy has internalized the values of patriarchy and the voice that tells her she can never measure up. This is the negative animus that Rowland calls the 'internalized psychic reception of patriarchy' (Rowland 2002: 50). When House speaks, he only confirms what Cuddy already fears about herself.

However, the writers often go further and depict Cuddy as prone to hysteria. In *Humpty Dumpty* (2: 3), when her handyman falls off her roof and is seriously ill, Cuddy is thrown into confusion, demanding radical treatments even before House does, racked by guilt, and unable to make a decision. In *Airborne* (3: 18), hysteria is more explicitly invoked when Cuddy and House are on an intercontinental flight with increasingly ill passengers. Cuddy thinks it is meningitis, but eventually House diagnoses 'conversion disorder', better known as mass hysteria, but not until Cuddy has joined in with the vomiting, and developed a rash and photophobia.

There is a final aspect of Cuddy's character the writers use to make her an increasingly fragile and sometimes even tragic figure. Cuddy is a woman living alone, but desperate for a child and unable to conceive. In *Finding Judas* (3: 9), which revolves around the case of a dying child, Cuddy is reduced to tears and hiding in her office after House tells her, 'It's a good job you failed to become a mother because you suck at it.' She later tells Wilson that she had several rounds of IVF treatment, two of which did not take, and she lost the third pregnancy. Once again, she seems to take House's assessment of her seriously: 'Maybe my wanting to be a mother is like a tone deaf person wanting to sing opera.' In *Joy* (5: 6), Cuddy has the child she has been approved to adopt in her arms, only for the birth mother to change her mind. Later, in *Big Baby* (5: 13), she is given another chance to adopt, but once again struggles to believe in her own fitness to be a mother, and seems to take House's suggestion of giving the baby back seriously, at least for a while.

Over the course of five seasons, Cuddy's persona of the powerful, competent authority figure seems to become weaker and more friable. Naturally, this can be viewed simply as character development by the writers, trying to make Cuddy more human and conflicted, and by extension a more interesting and dramatic character. At some level this is likely to be true, however, it is noticeable that House's persona of the brilliant misanthrope remains resolutely unchanged after five seasons and he very rarely seems to suffer from any lack of confidence in his own abilities – his stint in rehab and apparent contrition for past mistakes in *Words and Deeds* (3: 11) is a fake. Season Five's cliffhanger ending, which sees House check himself into a mental health institution, is interesting, but his self-esteem is not in question, even if his sanity is.

So, despite over a century of feminism, Cuddy seems to represent a contemporary woman still struggling with patriarchal notions of what women should be and, in this particular instance, it seems that what women should be is *not* in a position of leadership. As the show progresses, Cuddy is increasingly shown out of office attire in her dressing gown at home (usually alone) in the middle of the night. Her failure to become pregnant is also seen as a motivating factor in her becoming a little more hysterical: shown crying in her office, trying last ditch, risky attempts to save sick babies, getting psychosomatically sick and suchlike. One could argue that the split between persona and self (between public 'work' self and private 'home' self) has become harder to reconcile for the character.

Cuddy is in a clear position of leadership in the hospital, but the personal price of that leadership is rather high for the character and the question arises as to why Cuddy's authority should be undermined by the writers in this way. In order to delve deeper into the difficulties and contradictions of Lisa Cuddy's role in this television drama, it is necessary to look more closely at this idea of 'leadership', a concept that appears at first glance transparently obvious, but contains its own difficulties and contradictions. As will be argued below, it is a term that is both culturally and psychologically deeply embedded in patriarchal notions of manhood.

Leadership

Since Classical times at least, the issue of leadership has been written about, while in modern times it seems to single-handedly sustain a section of the publishing industry as parts of the business world appear to believe that the key to success lies in the unraveling of the Gordian Knot of leadership. In his book surveying writings on leadership (beginning with Plato), Grint suggests that 'much of our knowledge and many of our models of leadership are . . . drawn from the military' (Grint 1997: 10). Much of the traditional literature on the subject starts with the 'knight on a white charger' style of command-and-control leadership and tends to assume that a leader must have certain qualities to succeed.

Chester Barnard, for example, writing in the 1940s, was very clear that leadership was something that could be identified (or achieved) through certain character traits. Leaders must have certain 'active personal qualities', such as vitality and endurance (i.e. energy, alertness, spring, vigilance); decisiveness; persuasiveness; responsibility; and intellectual capacity, which he intentionally leaves in last place (Barnard 1948: 98).

The literature seems to agree that leaders need to be tough, displaying physical stamina and endurance, but also emotionally tough, not showing weakness or flinching from what needs to be done; self-reliant, not dependent or vulnerable; and assertive or even dominating, able to get their point of view heard and accepted. Studies have indicated that corporate rituals are designed to foster this, rituals such as working long hours/weekends; rarely taking sick leave or even annual leave; sacrifice of family or personal time: and capacity to travel at short notice and be available for the job which must come first (Sinclair 1998: 38). Not to conform to these 'norms' is to suggest that one may not be 'tough enough' for the job, one might not be 'up to it'.

Many of the qualities, character traits, or 'active personal qualities' of this command-and-control style of leadership are connected to traditional ideas about masculinity and heroism. There is a clear correspondence in terms of the language and concepts employed that clearly links leadership to the mythology of the hero often in quite direct ways. As Grint suggests, 'perhaps the most significant role model derived from the military is that of the superhero – the charismatic knight on a white charger' (Grint 1997: 12).

It is not coincidental that there is this relationship between leadership and heroic masculinity but it often remains taken for granted in discussions. Joseph Campbell, for example, has been particularly influential in disseminating the idea of the monomyth of the hero's journey, which has been keenly read by scriptwriters in Hollywood and beyond. In Campbell's schema, the hero, having gone alive into the kingdom of the dark, then 're-emerges from the kingdom of dread . . . The boon he brings restores the world' (Campbell 1993: 246).

Woodman, however, puts a slightly different slant on this type of story, pointing out that often 'the hero is the descendent of the sun god, that symbol of absolute authority upon which all life depends. The sun god continuously reasserts his absolute authority by the conquest of the forces of darkness that challenge his reign' (Woodman 1990: 19). This kind of heroic masculinity, where the hero descends to some dark realm to bring light, Woodman has labeled the 'founding myth of patriarchy'. It is a mythology that continues to infuse most contemporary mainstream dramas and underpins the dominant ideology of patriarchy. The performance of hegemonic masculinity is the key to being accepted by other men, and the values championed are those of toughness, rationality and lack of emotion, epitomized again and again in the heroes of Hollywood. The laconic, tough, impassive hero of mythology becomes the laconic, tough, impassive leader of the boardroom.

More recently discussion has shifted away from the 'active personal qualities' of a leader, towards the idea of a 'leadership function' – a socially constructed role created as much by followers as leaders. As Sinclair notes:

> Leadership is always the product of some *collusion*, whereby a band of supporters agrees that an individual, their leader, has what they need to lead them at a particular time . . . leadership and authority are constructed by audiences, by subordinates and superiors, by followers and peers.
>
> (Sinclair 1998: 16, emphasis as original)

This has the benefit of immediately appearing to be more gender-neutral, as if it were a role that could be inhabited by anyone who happened to fit the bill. However, it fails to address the issue of the same patterns of leadership reasserting themselves time and again.

> While it seems organizational research and theory keep on asking for new approaches and innovation and that re-conceptualizing leadership has been a focal point of these endeavors. . . it also seems that the more things change, the more they remain the same.
>
> (Calás and Smircich 1991: 339)

The issue of leadership seems to resist attempts to change because the basic power relations have not changed and the discourses in which leadership are embedded – masculinity, the myth of the hero and patriarchy – are still very strongly represented in the dominant ideology of the day, feminism notwithstanding. As one writer puts it, 'anyone who believes that a few decades of feminist thought and action is about to overturn centuries of ingrained prejudice, stereotype and discrimination against women is not living in the real world' (Whitehead 2002: 3). Simply consciously recognizing the attributes that go in to making the role of leader has done little to change the intrinsic masculinity of leadership. However, the relatively recently developed concept of the cultural complex arising from Jungian theory may be able to shed some further light on this resistance to change.

The cultural complex

The concept of the cultural complex arises from Jung's notion of the 'personal complex', an idea central to Jungian theory to the extent that Thomas Singer has suggested that even now it 'forms the foundation of the day-to-day clinical work of analytical psychology' (Singer and Kimbles 2004a: 13).

The personal complex is

> a collection of images and ideas, clustered round a core derived from one or more archetypes, and characterized by a common emotional tone. When they come into play (become 'constellated') complexes contribute to behavior and are marked by affect, whether a person is aware of them or not.
>
> (Samuels, Shorter and Plaut 1986: 34)

Following on from Joseph Henderson's introduction of the cultural unconscious (Henderson 1990), Singer and Kimbles have elaborated on the idea of the personal complex and developed the concept of the *cultural* complex:

> We define a complex as an emotionally charged group of ideas and images that cluster around an archetypal core. The basic premise . . . is that another level of complexes exists within the psyche of the group (and within the individual at the group level of their psyche). We call these group complexes "cultural complexes" and they, too, can be defined as an emotionally charged aggregate of ideas and images that cluster around an archetypal core.
>
> (Singer and Kimbles 2004b: 176)

They further elaborate that cultural complexes arise from 'repetitive, historical group experiences which have taken root in the cultural unconscious of the group' and that they can 'seize the imagination, the behavior and the emotions of the collective psyche and unleash tremendously irrational forces in the name of their "logic"' (ibid.: 187).

So leadership can be considered a cultural complex because it seems to consist of a long-standing and entrenched collection of images of the hero (an active, dynamic, charismatic figure, the slayer of the dragon, bringer of light, the knight on a white charger) clustered around the archetypal core of the Father. It is interesting that going back to the third millennium BCE, the Sumerian word for king was *lugal* meaning literally 'man, big' (Postgate 1994: 28). It may seem too absurdly archaic to mention but recent research has suggested that in more difficult times, American voters prefer taller candidates for the office of President (Pettijohn 2009).

A characteristic of the cultural complex which chimes with the socially constructed theory of leadership is that the complex tends to be bipolar or consist of two parts. Singer and Kimbles suggest that most often, 'when a complex is activated, one part of the bipolar complex attaches itself to the ego and the other part is projected onto a suitable other' (Singer and Kimbles 2004b: 179). This fits well with the idea that followers essentially create the role of the leader by projecting certain attributes onto a suitable candidate. Gemmill and Oakley suggest that 'disempowered and helpless people strive to take control of their surroundings by attributing another individual with powers of control that diminish their own anxiety . . . once the leader has been recognized, all responsibility is projected onto him or her' (Gemmill and Oakley 1992: 228).

To return to *House*, Cuddy is the ultimate arbiter and the authority that House's team appeal to (including House himself). Although she often disagrees with tactics and diagnoses, Cuddy is still the one who must be convinced to give her permission for many procedures. In Season Three in particular, Cuddy seems to perform this function for House and his entire team. In the episode *Foetal Position* (3: 17), a pregnant photographer discovers that her unborn child is killing her. House decides quite quickly that termination is the only option but Cuddy, on discovering that the woman is 42 and has several failed pregnancies behind her, takes over the case and with only hours before the mother is likely to die, still refuses to terminate the pregnancy. This discomfits House's team enormously. Cuddy storms out of her own office leaving Chase, Cameron and Foreman standing around nonplussed. Cameron asks if anyone is going to stop her, leading Chase to reply, 'Stopping the madness is her job!' and Foreman to comment, 'Someone's gotta be Cuddy's Cuddy.' When Cuddy steps out of her normal role of the responsible authority figure, it leaves House's team in some disarray. Complexes can be recognized by 'the simplistic certainty of a world view and one's place in it that they offer, in the face of the conflicting and not easily reconcilable opposites' (Singer and Kimbles 2004b: 20).

It is also Cuddy who saves the day for House when he enrages a patient, Tritter (David Morse), who turns out to be a policeman, every bit as intelligent and manipulative as House. Tritter then launches a vendetta against him. Eventually, in *Words and Deeds* (3: 11), Cuddy lies for House in court, thus protecting him from the consequences of his own actions.

The idea that leadership might be thought of as a cultural complex also helps to explain the inflated sense of optimism that attaches itself to a new leader, to be followed almost inevitably by deflation and disappointment as they fail to live up to expectations. Andrew Samuels points out that in the heroic model of leadership supporters will first passively follow and then seek out feet of clay in quite a predictable pattern (Samuels 2009: 287). Singer and Kimbles suggest that the 'bipolarity of the complex leads to an endless round of repetitive skirmishes with the illusory other – who may or may not fit the bill perfectly' (Singer and Kimbles 2004b: 179). This goes some way not only to explaining the pattern of optimism followed by disappointment around leaders but also the repetition of ideas in the literature surrounding leadership.

Consideration of leadership as a cultural complex takes account of the connection between leader and follower but recognizes that the followers are responsible for creating the image of the leader. It is as much unconscious as it is conscious and relies on established historical and cultural patterns. It is emotional rather than rational and such an ingrained cultural complex is unlikely to be easily refashioned, even if there is a wish to break the connection between heroic masculinity and leadership.

Leadership and women

The hero's journey, as mentioned above, is a familiar cultural trope. However, the heroine or female hero's journey is far less well described. As Covington points out, the 'archetypal image of the hero is familiar and has been described extensively in analytical psychology . . . There is, however, no reference in these works to "heroine" nor any description as to who she might be or what characterizes her' (Covington 1989: 243). Although she wrote this over 20 years ago, there is still far from widespread agreement on how the female hero's journey might play out. The real problem with applying the monomyth to a female hero's journey is that her 'return' is particularly problematic. There is no leadership role for her to step into. There is no kingdom (queendom) waiting for her to rule over. As Pratt pointed out, 'when a rebirth journey is attempted, the reward of personal power makes the conquering [female] hero a cultural deviant' (Pratt 1981: 169).

For a long time to prove oneself as a leader meant to prove oneself as a man and vice versa. For men, 'encultured images of . . . leadership offer opportunities to combine aspects of self in such a way that a man may assume authority for a relatively coherent self and project himself as a leader, this is not the case for women' (Höpfl and Matilal 2007: 203). Women in positions of leadership are trying to perform a role that is socially constructed to be inhabited by a male, and as such they try to reconcile the dissonance of their gender and the attributes of the role they must perform. 'Consequently women's opportunity to assemble a construction of self is more difficult because of a fundamental ambivalence in the imagery. In order to succeed and become accepted as an 'equal', women must subsume the feminine' (ibid.: 203).

In suggesting that leadership is a cultural complex associated with imagery of the hero and the father archetype, the reasons why women seem left in an eccentric position, at least when it comes to leadership of the traditional style, become clearer. However, writing in 1995, Rosener argued that women and men were exhibiting different forms of leadership. Previously the only women who successfully made it to the top were

> those who modeled themselves on men and led using command-and-control methods . . . However, a second generation of women leaders were now emerging who adopted forms of leadership conventionally

regarded as 'feminine' and subsequently relabeled as 'transformational leadership'.

(in Grint 1997: 153)

It has also been described as a sibling model of leadership (Samuels 2009) or a post-heroic model of leadership (Crevani, Lindgren and Packendorff 2007).

This appears to be a promising reconsideration of leadership, recognizing the role of the follower and recasting the leader into a more collaborative and enabling role within a group. However, there are still problems for women enacting this style of leadership. If, on the one hand, women perform leadership in the traditional command-and-control heroic style, then, as suggested above, to be successful they must take on the attributes of a man and tend to be congratulated for being 'tough enough', 'having balls' or showing their mettle. If, on the other hand, women choose to enact the more collaborative, post-heroic, transformational, sibling style of leadership, it tends not to be recognized as leadership at all (Fletcher 2004: 654). Women behaving in a consultative, empathic, collaborative way are not recognized as leading because that is how women are supposed to behave.

The issues for women in leadership become even clearer in an article by Calás and Smircich which deconstructs several key texts on leadership, suggesting that leadership is a theoretical construct set up in binary opposition to 'seduction'. 'Deconstructing "leadership" helps to analyze the dependency of supposedly opposite concepts on one another and shows how rhetoric and cultural conditions work together to conceal this dependency' (Calás and Smircich 1991: 340).

The etymology of the words leadership and seduction points up the binary opposites embedded in both terms – lead/seduce; guide/lure; correct/false; good/bad; male/female. Seduction, suggest Calás and Smircich, is considered to be 'leadership gone wrong', but the elements of attraction and stimulation necessary to leadership itself are ignored, and it is interesting that while 'seductress' remains current in English, the male equivalent 'seductor' is now obsolete (Calás and Smircich 1991: 344). (See Jones and Munro 2005 for further consideration of Calás and Smircich's work.)

This seems to suggest that a woman attempting to lead is likely to be perceived in one of three ways. If she is successful at the heroic command-and-control style of leadership she will be accorded honorary male status. If she enacts a command-and-control style but attempts to retain her female identity she will be considered a seductress, using her sexuality to get what she wants done. Or, perhaps, if she attempts to perform the more contemporary post-heroic/transformational/sibling style of leadership, there is a reasonable chance that she will not be recognized as a leader at all.

The character of Cuddy falls under the aegis of the first two categories. Rather than considering more examples from the *narrative* of the show – in recognition of the multimodal nature of a television text where, through design, viewers are offered an 'unstable, capricious, mobile spectacle' (Britton and Barker 2003: 207) – some consideration of Cuddy's visual styling seems appropriate as a way to demonstrate the intricacies of Cuddy's situation.

Cuddy's costumes certainly emphasise her femininity. Typically she seems to wear figure-hugging power suits, pencil skirts, heels, a choker or pearls, with open-necked shirts or V-necked cardigans, often displaying a daring décolletage. It is very sexy, in a professional context. Additionally, Cuddy's appearance is normally perfectly groomed, flawless and impeccable. This female display does not go unnoticed by House, who enjoys looking at her. However, he also uses it as ammunition to attack her, making an endless series of comments about her breasts and bottom. For example, in *Love Hurts* (1: 20) House taunts Cuddy: 'If only I was as open as you . . . actually it was your blouse I was talking about!' He also suggests on a fairly regular basis that that she has put on weight. House's imagination, in fact, seems to take Cuddy's perceived sexiness to almost degrading levels when, in *House's Head* (4: 15), during a drug-induced hallucination, House imagines Cuddy appearing in order to help him with a differential diagnosis; however, in his head he has her dressed as a schoolgirl and performing a pole dance for him.

So, Cuddy's femininity, as displayed by her appearance, is commented on, bringing her professionalism into question. However, sometimes the professional aspects of her look are then deployed to bring her femininity into question. For example, in *Joy* (5: 6), House doubts her ability to handle the mess and fuss that a baby will bring to her life and consequently her ability to remain professional-looking – he throws a cup of baby sick on her and dares her not to change the sweater.

However, House is also not above passing remark upon Cuddy's supposed masculine qualities. For example, in *Babies and Bathwater* (1: 18), after she has successfully got rid of Vogler, House toasts, 'Dr Cuddy! The man of the hour!' as he raises a glass to her. In *Frozen* (4: 11), while trying to guess who Wilson's new girlfriend is, he says, 'Can't be Cuddy, cos you're straight,' implying of course that Cuddy is a man.

So Cuddy seems to dress in an ultra-feminine way, but it leaves her open to comments about her body and appearance, and it fails to stop jibes about her perceived masculinity and sexuality. Her performance of a leadership role in the context of the drama is depicted as being complex and confusing. Leadership for Cuddy contains contradictions between her leadership role and her position as a woman.

Despite the increasing rhetoric of gender neutrality in business writings about leadership, leadership is a role that remains resolutely masculine. What society recognizes as leadership traits are in fact traits thoroughly embedded with hegemonic masculinity. Leaders should be heroic, rejecting weakness, valuing displays of courage, dominant and tough. To be a leader is to be a man and vice versa and when the cultural complex of 'leader' is constellated it seems that, however unconsciously, society expects the '*lugal*' or 'big man' to step into the role.

Women may attempt to perform the role but are likely to sacrifice some measure of their perceived femaleness in order to do so successfully. Cuddy is an adroit and accomplished character, trying to perform the role of leader at some personal cost, as the gap between persona and self becomes more painful and difficult to negotiate. She is a good handmaiden of patriarchy, but the price can be high. Occasionally the writers acknowledge this: in *Big Baby* (5: 13) Cuddy may feel like a failure, but Wilson, often a voice of compassion, reminds her to get help and not hold herself to some ridiculous notion of perfection. When she relinquishes power to Cameron in order to spend time with her newly adopted daughter, Cuddy eventually chooses to take up the burden once more and returns to work.

As discussed at the beginning of this chapter, *House* appears to be reactionary, putting the heroic (white, male) doctor at the forefront of the fight against disease, but the situation is not as straightforward as a restoration of old-time values. Dr House seems to embody what Woodman (1990) might call the 'ravaged masculine', the wounded king, or the crippled hero, far from the dashing young Dr Kildare (Richard Chamberlain) of times past, for example. House himself is not a leader. He is not a hero, and the dynamics between the two characters of House and Cuddy are constantly shifting. It is a contested terrain of boss/employee; mother/child (in the sense that House often acts childishly); woman/man. In fact, the two characters together seem to represent an 'under pressure' form of gender performance: a cripple and a hysteric, with neither, ultimately, in a position of permanent dominance and victories only ever being temporary and contingent. Cuddy may feel like a failure but the story is far from over. The narrative of *House* is still evolving, albeit at a snail's pace, and it may be that the drama will develop the character of Cuddy in less conflicted directions and allow the character to reconcile some aspects of persona and self.

References

Barnard, C. (1948) *Organisation and Management*. Cambridge, MA: Harvard University.

Britton, P. and Barker, S. (2003) *Reading Between Designs*. Austin, TX: University of Texas Press.

Calás, M. and Smircich, L. (1991) Voicing seduction to silence leadership. *Organization Studies*, *12*(4), 567–602. In K. Grint (ed.) *Leadership: Classical, Contemporary and Critical Approaches*. Oxford: Oxford University Press.

Campbell, J. (1993) *The Hero with a Thousand Faces*. London: Fontana Press.

Covington, C. (1989) In search of the heroine. *Journal of Analytical Psychology*, *34*, 243–254.

Crevani, L., Lindgren, M. and Packendorff, J. (2007) Shared leadership: A post-heroic perspective on leadership as a collective construction. *International Journal of Leadership Studies, 3*(1), 40–67.

Derrida, J. (1974) *Of Grammatology* (Trans. Gayatri Chakravorty Spivak). Baltimore, MD: JHU.

Fletcher, J. (2004) The paradox of postheroic leadership: An essay on gender, power, and transformational change. *The Leadership Quarterly, 15,* 647–661.

Gamble, S. (ed.) (2001) *The Routledge Companion to Feminism and Postfeminism.* London: Routledge.

Gemmill, G. and Oakley, J. (1992) Leadership: An alienating social myth. *Human Relations, 45*(2), 113–129. In K. Grint (ed.) *Leadership: Classical, Contemporary and Critical Approaches.* Oxford: Oxford University Press.

Grint, K. (ed.) (1997) *Leadership: Classical, Contemporary and Critical Approaches.* Oxford: Oxford University Press.

Henderson, J. (1990) *Shadow and Self,* Wilmette, IL: Chiron.

Höpfl, H. and Matilal, S. (2007) The lady vanishes: Some thoughts on women and leadership. *Journal of Organisational Change Management, 20*(2), 198–208.

Jones, C. and Munro, R. (eds) (2005) *Contemporary Organization Theory.* Oxford: Blackwell Publishing Ltd.

Jung, C. G. (1959) *Aion: Researches into the Phenomenology of the Self,* Collected Works 9(ii). London: Routledge & Kegan Paul.

Lotz, A. D. (2001) Postfeminist television criticism: Rehabilitating critical terms and identifying postfeminist attributes. *Feminist Media Studies, 1*(1), 105–121.

Pettijohn, T. (2009, August) Tough times call for taller presidents. *New Scientist, 2721,* 5.

Postgate, J. (1994) *Early Mesopotamia.* London: Routledge.

Pratt, A. (1981) *Archetypal Patterns in Women's Fiction.* Bloomington, IN: Indiana University Press.

Rosener, J. (1992) Sexual Static in K. Grint (ed.) (1997) *Leadership: Classical, Contemporary and Critical Approaches.* Oxford: Oxford University Press.

Rosener, J. (1995) *America's Competitive Secret: Women Managers.* Oxford: Oxford University Press (pp. 67–83).

Rowland, S. (2002) *Jung: A Feminist Revision.* London: Routledge.

Samuels, A. (2009) Transforming aggressive conflict in political and personal contexts. *International Journal of Applied Psychoanalytic Studies, 6*(4), 283–299.

Samuels, A., Shorter, B. and Plaut, F. (eds) (1986) *A Critical Dictionary of Jungian Analysis.* London: Routledge.

Sinclair, A. (1998) *Doing Leadership Differently.* Carlton South: Melbourne University Press.

Singer, T. and Kimbles, S. (eds) (2004a) *The Cultural Complex.* Hove: Routledge.

—— (2004b) The emerging theory of cultural complexes. In J. Cambray and L. Carter (eds), *Analytical Psychology: Contemporary Perspectives in Jungian Analysis.* Hove: Brunner-Routledge.

Ulanov, A. and Ulanov, B. (1994) *Transforming Sexuality,* Boston, MA: Shambhala.

Wehr, D. (1987) *Jung and Feminism: Liberating Archetypes.* London: Routledge.

Whitehead, S. (2002) *Men and Masculinities: Key Themes and New Directions.* Oxford: Wiley-Blackwell.

Woodman, M. (1990) *The Ravaged Bridegroom*. Toronto: Inner City Books.
Young-Eisendrath, P. (1986) New Contexts and Conversations for Female Authority. In D. Wehr (1987) *Jung and Feminism: Liberating Archetypes*. London: Routledge.

Internet sources

Statistics from Eurodata TV Worldwide (2009). Retrieved from http://www.google.com/hostednews/afp/article/ALeqM5gGRhjVWTeAVMws-iEDRJOY3IDH7g
Fox Network (2009) *House* show info, http://www.fox.com/house
Lisa Cuddy blog (2009), http://www.lisacuddy.com/new_page_131.htm

Glossary

Affect This is associated with emotions and feelings. The **Affect** is so strong that, unlike feelings, it can only be repressed with difficulty.

Amplification The rational associations brought to an image by the analyst – normally within the analytical context.

Anima/animus The feminine dimension of the male unconscious and vice versa. **Anima** and **Animus** may appear as personified figures, but it is more accurate to think of them as representing archetypal patterns. Modern Analytical Psychology tends not to like these and other psychological characteristics applied to gender, but regards them as alternative modes of behaviour, perception and evaluation. They may also be regarded as forming a bridge between the **Ego** and the **Objective psyche**.

Archetype An innate structuring potential which is inherent in the **Objective psyche**. The archetype is a pattern which is inherited and structures the development of the **Psyche**, and is not the image it assumes. It is the **Archetypes** which govern the **Individuation process**.

Association The connection of ideas or perceptions that can occur because of similarity, coexistence or opposition.

Collective unconscious See **Objective psyche** below.

Compensation This involves the balancing and regulating of the **Psyche.** Jung regarded the compensatory activity of the unconscious as balancing any 'defects' in consciousness. Many commentators regard this as a self-regulatory process of the Psyche.

Complex A collection of interrelated ideas and feelings which have impact on conscious behaviour and experience. The innovative concept of the complex is central in the development of analytical psychology and has entered general awareness.

Ego This process is at the centre of consciousness. The **Ego** both contains personal identity and responds to the **Objective psyche** by moving the **Psyche** towards **Individuation** and the **Self**.

Extravert An attitude of personality where energies are primarily directed towards the external world of people and events, rather than the inner world of ideas and feelings.

Identification To put it succinctly, identification is often an unconscious **Projection** of parts of the personality onto a place or person, thereby justifying the projecting person's behaviour patterns to him/herself.

Individuation This is the life process governed by the archetypal patterns, whereby a person becomes totally him/herself. It involves integration of the conscious and unconscious parts of the **Psyche**. Individuation is a lifelong process.

Introvert An attitude of personality where a person is more concerned with their own inner world. Ideas and feelings tend to be of more importance than places and events.

Mandala A magic circle, often divided into four. As a symbol of psychological unity it represents a phase in the development of the **Individuation** process. This may represent the completion of any of its stages and the **Mandala** marks the point at which the transition occurs.

Mythology This system is both the language and the images that a myth assumes. For example the Arthurian **Mythology** and the detective **Mythology** share the same **Mythologem**: that of the quest.

Numinosum The **Numinosum** is experienced as a powerful force beyond the control of the will. It can be a quality belonging to a visible object or experienced as an invisible presence causing a peculiar alternation of consciousness. Jung also regarded experience of the **Numinosum** as part of all religious experience.

Objective psyche A term used by Jung to indicate that the **Psyche** is an objective source of insight and knowledge. It also indicates that some of the **Psyche** is objective or, you might say, 'impersonal', as opposed to subjective and personal, in nature.

Persona The literal meaning of this word is 'mask'. Metaphorically, this mask is worn by the individual and is the way in which he or she approaches the world. It is the worldly aspect of the personality. As an **Archetype** it has the function of mediating between the **Ego** and the exterior world.

Primordial image This is a term that Jung originally used in place of **Archetype**.

Projection Difficult, or alternatively, positive, emotions or parts of the personality are transferred onto another person or place often by a process of identification. It is also a way in which the contents of the **Objective psyche** are made available to consciousness. However, to be of real use to ego-consciousness those projections must eventually be dissolved, by their being recognised by the individual. **Projection** most frequently happens with the **Archetypes** of **Shadow**, **Anima** and **Animus**.

Psyche Is the totality of all conscious and unconscious psychic processes. It can be symbolised by the **Mandala**, square, circle, etc.

Psychosis A state in which something 'unknown' takes possession of the **Psyche.** This is, further, an invasion by the objective **Psyche** in which it takes control of ego-consciousness.

Self The Self is the central unifying principle of the **Psyche**, and is the archetype of man's fullest potential and unity of personality.

Shadow At first glance, this seems to be the negative or inferior part of the **Psyche**. In fact it is just a part of the **Psyche** which has not been developed and integrated with ego-consciousness. **Shadow** is also the destructive element of the **psyche**, not just the inferior or non-integrated bits.

Spontaneous image creation A creation of the unconscious, often a dream but may also include paintings, poems, films, etc.

Symbol A **Numinous** representation produced by and of the **Objective psyche**, which seeks to unify and overcome opposition.

Transcendent function This function mediates between opposites of the **Psyche** and uses the **Symbol** to transcend the contradiction inherent in such opposition. It enables compensatory balances.

Typology This is a personality system developed by Jung to show different modes of psychological functioning in terms of personality types. There are two key categories, or attitudes – **Introvert** and **Extravert** – which combine with the four functions – sensation, thinking, feeling and intuition – to determine an individual's personality **Type**.

Index

101 Dalmations 45

Aceso 61
addiction (*see also* House, Gregory: use
    of drugs): pain and the cycle of
    70–2; to the status quo 70–2
alchemy 67, 113
aleatory objects 91, 94–5
Amber (character in *House*) 18, 37, 86,
    89, 119, 156, 164
American Medical Association 64
Amfortas wound 169, 185–6n4
Analytical Psychology *see* Jung's
    psychology
Ananse 70
Angels 2
anima 18, 39, 119, 127, 190; *anima-*
    driven intuition 175–6, 178; and
    move to more feminine way of
    working 174–6, 177–8
animus 190
Apollo 61, 106, 109
archetypal energy 63 (*see also* libido);
    caduceus/walking stick as fusion of
    Asclepian and Hermetic energy 64,
    65; trickster energy 59, 63, 70–1
archetypes: archetypal trickster *see*
    trickster; archetypal view of health
    16; childlike fantasy with archetypal
    appeal 21; contrasexual 15, 18 (see
    also *anima*; animus); feminine *see*
    feminine archetype; the hero *see* the
    hero; House's thinking and 16;
    individuation and 14–16;
    individuation and archetypal
    interplay of House and his team
    169–84; Jung 15–16; masculine *see*
    masculine archetype; medical TV

dramas and archetypal
    representation of the doctor 3;
    melodrama as a collective archetype
    see melodrama; mother archetype
    127–8; persona as archetype of
    social adaptation 15; senex
    archetype *see* senex; warped 180–1;
    wounded healer archetype *see*
    wounded healer
Aristophanes 165
Asclepian staff 61, 64–5, 70, 72 (*see also*
    walking stick)
Asclepius/Asklepios 34, 59, 60–2, 109,
    111; fused with Hermes 65, 66–8;
    Homeric hymn, 'To Asclepius' 60
association: associative thinking 79, 85,
    88, 89–90, 91 (*see also* non-directed
    thinking); mechanisms 84 (*see also*
    condensation; displacement);
    patterns 89
Atkinson, Rowan 47, 48
audience: global popularity of *House*
    188; and House's popularity 11–12,
    117, 119; puts House in hell 150–1;
    and the satisfying combination of
    senex and trickster 173–4
authority 48–52; personal authority of
    Laurie 54–6; two kinds of 52–4
autism 166–7
'Awi' (blogger) 39

Bainbridge, J. 2
Baker, V. 46
banality 76–8, 82, 89, 90, 91;
    constructing genius through banal
    conversation 92–4
Barnard, Chester 194
Bates, Alan 47

Beatty, Warren 43, 44
Beebe, J. 35
Ben Casey 121, 188
Bentley, E. 153–4
Bergson, Henri 122, 123, 125
bisexuality 162, 175, 182, 183
black humor 120–4
Blackadder 11, 43, 47, 49
body: bog bodies *see* bog bodies; crime
    as the corruption of the body 19;
    link with the unconscious in
    individuation 12–13; special effect
    incursions into the body 23, 27–8;
    the unconscious and disease 14–16
body-image 65–6, 70
bog bodies: bog as the body of the
    (m)Other 142, 146, 148, 149; Freud,
    Jung and 141–2; Holmes, Wimsey
    and the bog 137–9; House and the
    bog 144–5, 146–7, 151
Bolen, J. S. 40
Bollas, C. 83, 85–6, 91, 92, 94–5,
    99nn9–10
boredom/the boring 77–8; banality of
    boring people 76 (*see also* banality);
    the genius's need for boring people
    94–5; inspiration through boredom
    95–7
Bos, M. W. *et al.* 81
Braude, J. M. 172
Brecht, Berthold 121
British people, class and comedy 46–8
Britton, P. and Barker, S. 200
Brolin, James 1
Brooks, P. 153–4, 158, 164

caduceus 59–67 (*see also* walking stick)
Calás, M. and Smircich, L. 195, 199
Calderón de la Barca, Pedro 157
Cameron, Allison (character in *House*)
    18, 31–2, 39–40, 41, 50, 51, 60, 69,
    70, 79, 119, 127–8, 156, 164, 182,
    197
Campbell, Joseph 194
Campbell, Mrs (character in *House*) 31
cane *see* walking stick
Capaneus 62
Casualty 2
Challen, P. 43, 44, 55
Chamberlain, Richard 201
Chase, Robert (character in *House*) 36,
    38–40, 41, 60, 69, 126–7, 156, 181–2

Chicago Hope 2
children 103, 157, 166–7; *puer* see *puer*
Chiron 61, 111
Christie, Agatha 138
Churchill, John 64
class, and the British 46–8
Claxton, G 80–1
Cleese, John 47–8
Coleridge, Samuel Taylor 121
collective complex *see* cultural/collective
    complex
collective unconscious 64
comedy: black humor 120–4; and the
    British 46–8
compassion 40, 69, 108, 126, 175, 201;
    lack of 116, 117
complexes: complex theory 37–8, 155;
    cultural/collective complex 153,
    195–8; forming cultural myths 155;
    melodramatic complex 153–4;
    Oedipus complex 141, 149
condensation 83, 87–90, 93
contrasexuality 15, 18; *anima* see *anima*;
    animus 190
Cook, Peter 47
Coronis 61, 109
Covington, C. 198
CSI 133–4
Cuddy, Lisa (character in *House*) 17, 18,
    28, 36, 49, 50, 52, 60, 69, 70, 72,
    76–7, 90, 94, 97, 99–100n14, 120,
    127, 159, 161, 173, 178, 180, 183,
    197, 199–201; as handmaiden of
    patriarchy 190–1, 192, 201; her
    character and the feminine
    archetype in authority 189–93,
    199–201; persona 193, 201
cultural/collective complex 153;
    leadership, feminism and 195–8
Currie, B. 62
Curtis, Richard 48
Cynics/cynicism 37, 47, 149, 170, 172,
    174, 176

Danny (character in *House*) 93
death, as an ironic weapon of
    melodrama 161
Dershowitz, A. M. 163
Descartes, René 157
detectives: the audience as a detective
    147–8; the bog, Sherlock Holmes
    and Lord Peter Wimsey 137–9;

Freudian psychoanalyst as a
classical detective 142; and the
Gothic 136–7, 139–40; House as the
disease detective 16–20; *Oedipus
Rex* 135; parallels and differences of
Holmes and House *see* Holmes,
Sherlock; and war 139–40
Dijksterhuis, A. and Meurs, T. 85
Diogenes 170
directed attention 78–9, 82
disease: as the criminal 19; House as the
disease detective 16–20; the
unconscious and 14–16
dismemberment 23
displacement 83, 87–8
doctors, medical TV dramas and
archetypal representation of the
doctor 3
double bind 160, 172, 173, 174
Douglas, Lucas (character in *House*) 173
Doyle, Sir Arthur Conan, Holmes *see*
Holmes, Sherlock
Dr Kildare 121, 188, 201
dream thinking *see* non-directed
thinking
dreams 87, 88
dualism 103
Dudeck, Anne 156 (*see also* Amber)

Edelstein, Lisa 17, 60, 173, 189–93 (*see
also* Cuddy, Lisa)
Edwards. D. 35
ego-inflation 59, 68
Ehrenberg, K. 53
Elise (character in *House*) 31
Elsaesser, T. 164
Emergency Ward 10 1
enantiodromia 20; enantiodromic
movement 7
Epione 61
epiphanies 76–7, 79–80; through banal
conversation 92–4; through
boredom 95–7; through condensed
thinking 87–90, 93; how to have an
epiphany 82–4; incubation periods
and 80–6
Epps, Omar 60, 162, 182 (*see also*
Foreman, Eric)
ER 2, 121, 189
eros 169, 174, 180, 181, 182, 184, 186n4,
186n8
evidence-based practice 103–4, 111–12

evocative objects 91–2
extraverted feeling 172, 173, 174, 181–2,
186n12
extraverted intuition 175, 177–8, 182,
187n12
extraverted sensation 178, 183, 187n12
extraverted thinking 172, 183, 187n12

fantasy: childlike, with archetypal
appeal 21; sexual 17, 200
feeling (*see also* sensation): extraverted
172, 173, 174, 181–2, 186n12;
introverted 172, 181, 187n12
feminine archetype: *anima* see *anima*;
Cuddy's character and the feminine
archetype in authority 189–93,
199–201; and the female hero's
journey 198; feminine image 180–1
feminism: Cuddy's character and the
feminine archetype in authority
189–93, 199–201; and the cultural
complex 195–8; and leadership
193–201; third wave 190
film noir 17, 19, 30
Fisher King 103, 111, 140, 147, 149, 169
The Flight of the Phoenix 44
Foreman, Eric (character in *House*)
40–1, 53, 60, 69, 89, 162, 177–8,
182, 197
Fortysomething 44
Forward, W. H. 64
Four Weddings and a Funeral 48
Fox 1, 29, 44, 60, 188, 189
Freud, S. 12, 79, 89, 93; and the bog
bodies 141–2; disagreement with
Jung about myth 141–3; dreams 87,
88; Oedipus complex 141, 149;
relationship with Jung 141
Friedlander, W. J. 64
Froben, Johann 64
Frum, L. 30
Fry, Stephen 45, 46, 47, 48, 49
Frye, N. 165

Gabriel (character in *House*) 33
Gemmill, G. and Oakley, J. 197
gender (*see also* sexuality): feminine
archetype *see* feminine archetype;
feminism *see* feminism; identity 15;
leadership and *see* leadership;
masculine archetype *see* masculine
archetype; patriarchy *see* patriarchy

genius: anatomy of 75–97; constructed
    through banal conversation 92–4;
    epiphanies of *see* epiphanies; House
    as master of condensation 87–90,
    93; House's rapid incubation period
    84–7; House's thinking 76–90;
    inspiration through boredom 95–7;
    and the need for boring people 94–5
Gilmer, J. 51
Glaucus 62
gods 61–4, 106, 116 (see also *specific
    gods*)
Goldman, William 46
the Gothic 120, 136–7, 139–40
Grail *see* Fisher King; Holy Grail legend
Green, Martyn 123
Grey's Anatomy 2, 121, 189
Grint, K. 193, 194, 198–9
Grosz, E. 65–6
Guggenbuhl-Craig, A. 105

Hades (Greek god) 62
Hadley, Remy (character in *House*) 60,
    69, 182 (*see also* Thirteen)
Hall, Jennifer 18
Harrington, E. B. 133
Haule, J. 185–6n4
health (*see also* disease): archetypal view
    of 16; the bewildering search for
    health and clarity within 28
healthcare: the biomedical model and
    the curing-caring divide 103–4;
    breaking bad news 107–9; evidence-
    based practice 103–4, 111–12;
    nursing *see* nursing; workers as
    wounded healers *see* wounded
    healer
Heidegger, M. 95
hell: the audience puts House in hell
    150–1; Heaven–Hell dichotomy and
    House's reactions to the trivial 99n5;
    'Hell-house' of House's shadow 95;
    and House's clinic 77, 95, 99n5;
    House's life in 135
Henderson, J. 196
Hephaestus 40
Hermes 40, 59, 60, 61, 62–4, 69; fused
    with Asclepius 65, 66–8; Homeric
    hymn, 'To Hermes' 62–3, 69
the hero: crippled hero 201; hero myth
    142; hero's journey 194, 198; House
    as a post-heroic character 178;

House as hero who is not a hero
    148–50; leadership and the heroic
    masculine 193–5; wounded healer,
    scapegoat and the archetype of the
    hero 164–7
Hesiod 61, 67
Higgins, C. and Cannan, D. 123
Hillman, J. 61, 170–1
Hippocrates 61
Hippocratic Oath 61, 68
Hippolytus 62
Holby City 2
Holmes, Sherlock: dissimilarities with
    House 133–5, 147–50; and Dr
    Watson 134, 135–6, 137, 138, 148;
    the fallible infallible detective 135–7;
    Lord Peter Wimsey, the bog and
    137–9; parallels with House 17, 133,
    150
Holy Grail legend 111, 140, 143, 169;
    Fisher King *see* Fisher King
Homer 62, 154
Höpfl, H. and Matilal, S. 198
hospital dramas 1–3, 188–9
House, Gregory 183; aleatory objects
    and 91, 94–5; *anima* and move to
    more feminine way of working
    174–6, 177–8; archetypal
    dimensions of character and virtue
    of personality 170–84; audience
    popularity 11–12, 117, 119; and the
    bog 146–7, 149, 151; and breaking
    bad news 108, 109; and the
    combination of trickster and senex
    171–4; and compassion *see*
    compassion; as cynic 37, 47, 149,
    170, 172, 174, 176; as the disease
    detective 16–20 (*see also* Holmes,
    Sherlock); as doctor or shaman
    20–4; dysfunctional *puer*-like quality
    21, 116–17, 124–5, 127; ego-
    inflation 59, 68; as embodiment of
    contradictions 11, 18, 33, 155,
    173–4; evocative objects and 91–2;
    extraverted intuition 175, 177–8;
    feminine side of 174–6, 177–8; as
    Fisher King 111, 147, 149; genius of
    see genius; as heartthrob 11, 24; and
    hell *see* hell; as hero who is not a
    hero 148–50; Holmes and *see*
    Holmes, Sherlock; inspiration
    through boredom and banality

76–8, 82, 89, 90, 91, 92–7 (*see also* genius); integrity 169, 178, 184; introverted sensation 175, 176–9; intuition 17, 21, 33, 34–5; and Jung's debate with Freud 143–7; Laurie's portrayal of *see* Laurie, Hugh; liminality 19–20, 72; main features of character and behavior 1, 33, 37, 68, 155–8, 188; melancholia 32–7; melodrama and 158–9, 164–7 (*see also* melodrama); melodramatic character and mis-en-scène 158–9; narcissism 68, 117, 119; need for others to think for him 90–2; need of his demons 25; as *nigredo* 145; non-problematic keeping people at a distance 75–6; pain *see* pain; persona 22–3, 171–2, 193; as a post-heroic character 178; psychoanalysis, House and *House* 145–7; quasi-shamanistic practices 20–4, 35, 36; relationships with women 17–18, 39–40, 69–70, 90, 120, 156–7, 200; as saviour figure 67; as scapegoat 165–6; search for the truth 176–7, 184; and the senex archetype 170–4, 176; sexuality *see* sexuality; and the shadow 23, 77, 124–5, 127 (*see also* the shadow); and Sherlock Holmes *see* Holmes, Sherlock; support for Jung's interpretation of myth 143–7; as surrogate father 38–9; the team as presentations of his sub-personalities 38–41; thought processes 76–90, 176–9 (*see also* thinking); and the trickster 37, 59, 63, 66–70, 125, 126–9, 134, 145, 150, 171–4 (*see also* trickster); use of drugs 17, 34, 35, 53, 55, 59, 70–2, 156; walking stick *see* walking stick; and the work of individuation *see* individuation; 'work smart not hard' philosophy 80–2; as wounded healer 11, 22, 25, 34, 65, 113–14, 147, 154–5, 166 (*see also* wounded healer)

House (MD): audience *see* audience; black humor 120–4; as character-driven television 19; children in 103, 157, 166–7; complex armature 28–9; entertainment versus facts 29–31; feminism and *see* feminism; as a globally popular drama 188; hospital micro-world 31–2; melancholia *see* melancholia; and melodrama *see* melodrama; place in the television medical drama genre 1–3, 188–9; production techniques *see* production techniques; psychoanalysis, House and *House* 145–7; the team as presentations of House's sub-personalities 38–41

humor: black 120–4; the British and comedy 46–8

Hygieia 61

Iaso 61
The Ik 123
illumination 83, 84 (*see also* epiphanies)
incubation periods in thinking 80–6
individuation: and archetypal interplay of House and his team 169–84; archetypes and 14–16; and engagement with the shadow 77; and House's psyche and experience of life 12, 13, 14, 15, 21, 22–4, 25, 176; and the interconnectedness of our being 24–5; and the interweaving of the personal and the social 13; Jung on 12–13; meaning of 12–14, 24–5; not equated to psychological health 24, 25; provoked by House 149; and the quasi-shamanistic practices of House 21–4

Inktumni 70
innocence 155, 157, 161, 164, 165–7
integrity 169, 178, 182, 184; loss/lack of 180–1, 186n4
Internalized Oppression 192
introverted feeling 172, 181, 187n12
introverted intuition 180, 187n12
introverted sensation 175, 176–9, 186n11, 187n12
introverted thinking 172, 174
intuition 17, 21, 33, 34–5; *anima*-driven 175–6, 178; extraverted 175, 177–8, 182, 187n12; introverted 180, 187n12
irony 36, 48, 60, 95, 108, 147, 155–6, 159, 160, 161; ironic comedic form 165
Ischys 61

Jacobs, J. 1–2
Jacobson, Peter 60, 180 (*see also* Taub)
Jacoby, H. 186n9
James, William 79, 88
Jeeves and Wooster 11, 45, 46
'John' (blogger) 35
Johnson, Ben 173
Johnson, R. 111
Jung, C. G.: and the bog bodies 141–2; disagreement with Freud about myth 141–3; dream and preoccupation with houses and homes 143–4, 146; House's support in debate with Freud 143–7; letters between Dr S and 24–5; on Mercurius 63–4; on the novel 24; psychology of *see* Jung's psychology; relationship with Freud 141; on shamanistic psychology 23; on therapy and the man's need for difficulties 25; on the trickster 37, 41, 67
Jung's psychology: Amfortas wound 185–6n4; *anima/animus* 190; archetypes *see* archetypes; complex theory 37–8, 155; condensation 87 (*see also* condensation); cultural complex *see* cultural/collective complex; directed and undirected thinking 78–80; enantiodromia 20; extraverted intuition 177; and the healer who heals through their wounds 113; individuation *see* individuation; introverted sensation 176–7; mana personality 21–2; personality type theory 186–7n12; psyche *see* psyche; sexuality 186n4; transference 113; typological pairs of functions of consciousness 186–7n12; the unconscious *see* the unconscious
Jung, Emma 185n3, 186n11

Karpf, A. 2
Kazan, E. 187n12
Kekulé, August 81
Kelley, John (character in House) 36
Kerényi, Karl 63
Kidel, M. 103
Kiley, D. 118–19
King, M. and Watson, K. 2

Kirmayer, L. J. 155
Kutner, (character in *House*) 60, 69, 181

Laius 141
Laurie, Hugh 11, 61, 72; authority 48–56; and the British, class and comedy 46–8; casting as House 22, 43–56; portrayal of House 169–70, 173, 176, 183, 186n5
leadership 193–5; and the cultural complex 195–8; deconstructing leadership 199; and feminism 193–201; and the heroic masculine 193–5; and the myth of patriarchy 194–5 (*see also* patriarchy); and seduction 199; and women 198–201
Lehman, D. 160
Lenye, Lotte 121–2
Leonard, Robert Sean 60, 157, 172, 191 (*see also* Wilson, J.)
libido 16, 66
Life is a Dream 157
Life with Judy Garland: Me and My Shadows 45
liminality 19–20, 34, 72
Loewi, Otto 81
Lycurgus 62

McBride, Chi 190 (*see also* Vogler, Edward)
Machaon 62
McMahon, J. L. 99n4
Maguire, A. 16
mana personality 21–2
Marcus Welby MD 1
Mark (character in *House*) 33
masculine archetype: *animus* 190; leadership and the heroic masculine 193–5; and the myth of patriarchy 194–5 (*see also* patriarchy); the ravaged masculine 201
*M*A*S*H* 2, 188
'McDee' (blogger) 41
Meat Loaf 161
Medic 1
melancholia 27–41; of Gregory House 32–7; and *House*'s complex armature 28–9; and House's team 38–41; 'melancholy without hope' 77
Melanie (character in *House*) 18

melodrama: as a collective archetype 152–67; contexts and positioning of 162–4; House and 158–9, 164–7; House's melodramatic character and mis-en-scène 158–9; melodramatic themes of *House* 161–2; place in the drama genre 159–61
Menander 165
Mercurius 63–4, 67–8
Mercury 62, 64
Miles, S. H. 61
Milicevic, Ivana 18
modernity 134
Moore, Dudley 47
Moore, Mike 65
Morrison, Jennifer 18, 60, 156, 182 (*see also* Cameron, Allison)
Morse, David 197 (*see also* Tritter, Michael)
mother archetype 127–8
Mother Courage 121–2
Mother Earth 139, 141, 142, 144
Murdoch, Rupert 189
myth: cultural myths formed by complexes 155; 'founding myth of patriarchy' 194–5; Freud and Jung's disagreement about 141–3; hero myth 142; Holy Grail myth 111, 140, 143, 169 (*see also* Fisher King); House's support for Jung's interpretation of 143–7; mythological gods *see* gods; Oedipus myth 135, 141, 142–3; of rebirth 109, 150–1

narcissism 68, 117, 119
narratio 163
naturalism 28, 30
Neville, B. 63
Newtonian paradigm 134
Nietzsche, F. 50
nigredo 145
Nolan, Dr (character in House) 113–14
non-directed thinking 79–80, 83, 84 (*see also* incubation periods in thinking); condensed thinking 87–90, 93; displacement in dream thinking 87–8; and the need for other people's thinking 90–2; object-relations perspective on 91–2, 94–5
Notting Hill 48

nursing 103–5; impact on nurses of wounding others 106–7

object-relations, evocative and aleatory objects 91–2, 94–5
Odysseus 116
Oedipus 135, 141, 142; and Jung's disagreement with Freud about myth 141–3
Oedipus complex 141, 149
Olson, S. R. 2–3
Osler, Sir William 172
the Other 140, 144, 145, 146, 148; (m)Other 141, 142, 146, 147, 148, 149

pain: acceptance of 51; and body-image 66; and the cycle of addiction 70–2; leg pain 17, 33–4, 59, 99n6; mental 32, 33; as part of House's woundedness 55; of the shadow 23
Panacea 61
Paracelsus 173, 186n7
paranoia 158
Patients Association 104
Patients Not Numbers, People Not Statistics 104
patriarchy 136, 190, 192, 194–5, 201
Pausanias 62
Penn, Kal 60, 181 (*see also* Kutner)
Persephone 40
persona 15; clash of trickster-persona and trickster-energy 70–1; Cuddy's 193, 201; House's 22–3, 171–2, 193; quasi-shamanistic aspects of House's 22–3
Peter Pan syndrome 118–20 (see also *puer*)
Philoctetes 116, 119
Picasso, Pablo 180–1
Podalirius 61, 62
Poincaré, Henri 81, 83, 84
Polite Dissent website 20, 29, 30
post-feminism 190
Pratt, A. 198
problem solving: incubation periods 80–6; inspiration through boredom 95–7; thought processes *see* thinking
production techniques: melodramatic character and mis-en-scène 158–9; *narratio* 163; single-camera shooting 18–19; special effects 23, 27–8

projection 11, 20, 85, 91
projective identification 91–2
psyche: adolescent see *puer*; Jung's
    model 12, 14, 24–5; psychic rebirth
    see rebirth; psychosomatic nature of
    14, 24–5; shadow side see the
    shadow
Psyche myth 40
psychic energy: caduceus/walking stick
    as fusion of Asclepian and Hermetic
    energy 64, 65; distraction and the
    release of 81 (*see also* incubation
    periods in thinking); gods and the
    energy of the unconscious 61–4;
    libido see libido; trickster energy 59,
    63, 70–1
psychopomp 66–7
puer 38, 116–24; *aeternus* 118–19;
    dysfunctional *puer*-like quality of
    House 21, 116–17, 124–5, 127;
    represented by Chase 38; and the
    shadow 124–5; and the trickster 69,
    124–9

Radin, Paul 186n6
Ramos, D. G. 16
Rand, Ayn 170
Rankin, Ian 140
rebirth 109, 139, 140, 142, 149, 150–1
Reynolds, Frederick 64
ritual 22
Rosener, J. 198–9
Rowland, S. 190, 192

'Saint Nate' (blogger) 30
Samuels, A. 197; *et al.* 21–2, 118,
    196
Sanford, J. 109
'Sara' (blogger) 29
Saturn 171
Sayers, Dorothy 138–9
scapegoat 165–6
Schilder, P 65–6
science: Newtonian paradigm 134;
    quantum paradigm 135
'Scott' (blogger) 20, 29, 34–5
Scrubs 2
Se7ven 79
seduction, leadership and 199
self-absorption 60, 119 (*see also*
    narcissism)
Self-Hater 192

senex 170–4, 176; introverted thinking
    172, 174
sensation (*see also* feeling): extraverted
    178, 183, 187n12; introverted 175,
    176–9, 186n11, 187n12
sexuality (*see also* eros): *anima* see
    anima; bisexuality 162, 175, 182,
    183; contrasexuality see
    contrasexuality; of House 17, 173,
    183, 200; House's relationships with
    women 17–18, 39–40, 69–70, 90,
    120, 156–7; infantile (Freud) 141;
    Jungian psychology 186n4; sexual
    fantasy 17, 200; tabood 141
Seznec, J. 170–1
the shadow: attempts to distance oneself
    from 77; enlightenment through
    engagement with 95; House's
    shadow 23, 124–5, 127; House's
    shadow-clinic 77; individuation and
    engagement with 77; *puer* and
    124–5; trickster and senex as
    archetypes of 171 (*see also* senex;
    trickster); and use of an object
    91–2, 94–5; and the wounded healer
    155
shamanism 35, 36; dismemberment 23;
    and the healer who heals through
    their wounds 112–13; Jung on
    shamanistic psychology 23; quasi-
    shamanistic practices of House
    21–4, 35, 36; and the shadow side 23
    (*see also* the shadow); use of drugs
    35; and the wounded healer 22
Shepherd, S. 159
Shore, David 29–30, 43, 44, 45, 61,
    133
Sicko, Moore documentary 65
Sinclair, A. 195
Singer, Bryan 43, 45
Singer, T. and Kimbles, S. L. 153,
    195–6, 197
single-camera work 18–19
Sitconski 70
'snakes on a cane' campaign 60
Socratic Method 33
Sophocles 135, 141
special effects 23, 27–8
Spencer, Jesse 60, 156, 181 (*see also*
    Chase, Robert)
Sphinx 142
St Elsewhere 2, 188

Stacy (character in *House*) 33, 34, 53, 70, 76, 156–7
Steptoe and Son 47
Sternberg, G. W. 64
Steve 'Freedom Master' (character in *House*) 113
Stuart Little 45
Stuart Little 2 45

Tartini, Giuseppe 81
Taub (character in *House*) 60, 69, 180
Telesphorous 61
television medical drama genre 1–3, 188–9
thinking: associative 79, 85, 88, 89–90, 91 (*see also* non-directed thinking); condensed 87–90, 93; cynical 172; directed 78–9, 82; and dormant/ incubation periods 80–6; dream thinking *see* non-directed thinking; epiphanies in *see* epiphanies; extraverted 172, 183, 187n12; four-stage developmental model of creative thinking (Wallas) 82–3; House's need for others to think for him 90–2; House's thinking processes 76–90, 176–9; intuitive 35 (*see also* intuition); non-directed *see* non-directed thinking; props 78–9; and right and left brain functions 101–2, 103; senex (introverted) 172, 174; visual stimulus to 89
Thirteen (character in House) 22, 162, 182 (*see also* Hadley, Remy)
Thompson, Emma 47
Thoth 62
Threepenny Opera 121
trickster 37, 38, 40, 41; clash of trickster-persona and trickster-energy 70–1; combined with senex 171–4; embodiment and disavowal 66–70; energy 59, 63, 70–1; Hermes 40, 59, 60, 61, 62–4; House and 37, 59, 63, 66–70, 125, 126–9, 134, 145, 150, 171–4; and House's use of his walking stick 66–8; Jung 37, 41, 67; *puer* and 69, 124–9
Tritter, Michael (character in *House*) 39, 53–4, 70–1, 166, 197
Turnbull, Colin 123
Turow, J. 2
TV Guide 11

twin snake emblem 60, 62, 64 (*see also* caduceus)
Tyndareus 62

the unconscious 36; Amber as personification of House's autonomous unconscious 86; the collective knowledge/unconscious of medicine 49–50; denied by House 32; and disease 14–16; energy of 21, 37–8, 61–4, 67–8 (*see also* archetypal energy); and the expression of the *anima* 175; and House's experience 36–7; and incubation periods in thinking 80–6; link with body in individuation 12–13; Mercurius and the collective unconscious 64; mythological gods and the energy of 61–4; the shadow *see* the shadow; as source of archetypes 15–16; unconscious thinking *see* association; incubation periods in thinking; non-directed thinking
undirected thinking *see* non-directed thinking

Vico, Giambattista 152, 154
Vicodin 17, 34, 35, 53, 55, 59, 70–2, 166
the Victim 174
Vogler, Edward (character in *House*) 38, 50, 162, 190, 191
von Franz, M.-L. 118, 185n3, 186n4

Waddell, T. 37
Wakdjunkaga 70
walking stick 59–72; Asclepius, Hermes and the caduceus 60–5, 66–8; House's insignia 65–72; and the status quo 70–2; and the trickster 66–8; Tritter's attack on 70–1; Wilson's revenge through 158
Wallas, G. 82, 83
war 139–40
Ward, Sela 70, 156 (*see also* Stacy)
Weill, Kurt 121
Western medicine, dualistic model 103
Western society, privileging of left-brain functions 101–2
Weston, Michael 173
Whitehead, S. 195
Whitmont, E. 106

wholeness 14 (*see also* individuation)
Wilde, Olivia 22, 60, 182 (*see also*
    Hadley, Remy; Thirteen)
wilful suspension of disbelief 121
Wilson, J. (character in *House*) 31, 46,
    51, 52, 60, 69, 71, 76, 77, 81, 128,
    157, 158, 172, 183, 191, 201; banal
    conversation with 92–4; and
    Holmes's Dr Watson 17, 148–9
Wimsey, Lord Peter (Sayers character)
    138–9, 144
Winters, J. 76, 91
Woman in Black 18
Woodbrooke Quaker Study Centre,
    Birmingham 107–8
Woodman, M. 190, 194, 201
wounded healer: Amfortas wound 169,
    185–6n4; Apollo as 106; aspects and

definitions 105–13; Fisher King 103,
    111, 140, 147, 149, 169; House as 11,
    22, 25, 34, 65, 113–14, 147, 154–5,
    166; House's need of his demons 25;
    ironic double bind of 160; and
    scapegoat, and the archetype of the
    hero 164–7; and the shadow 155;
    who bears a permanent wound
    111–12; who heals and wounds
    106–9; who heals through their
    wounds 112–13; who walked close
    to death and recovered 109–11

Yaniv, I and Meyer, D. E. 81
Young, Robert 1
youth cult 118

Zeus 62, 109